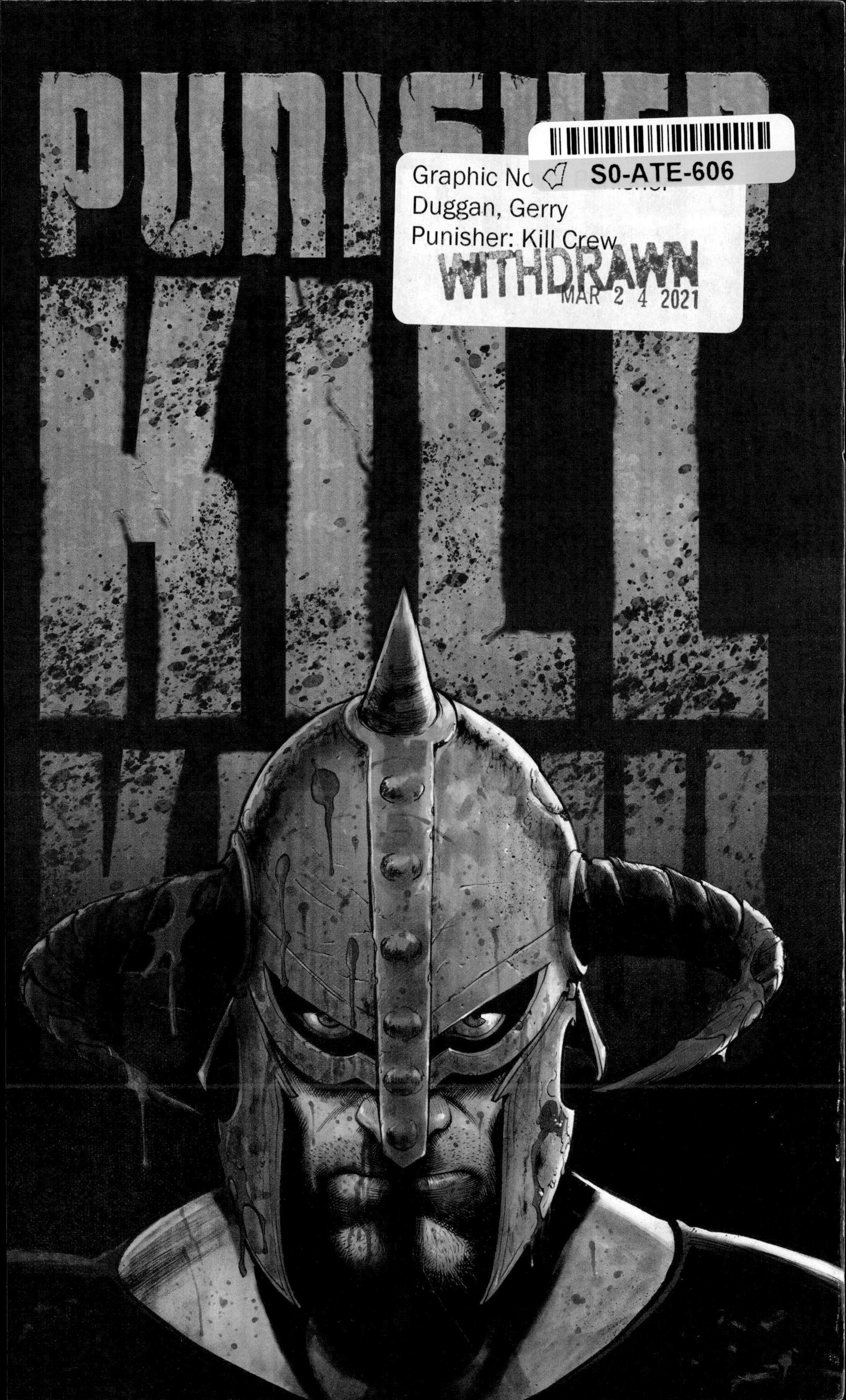
KILL

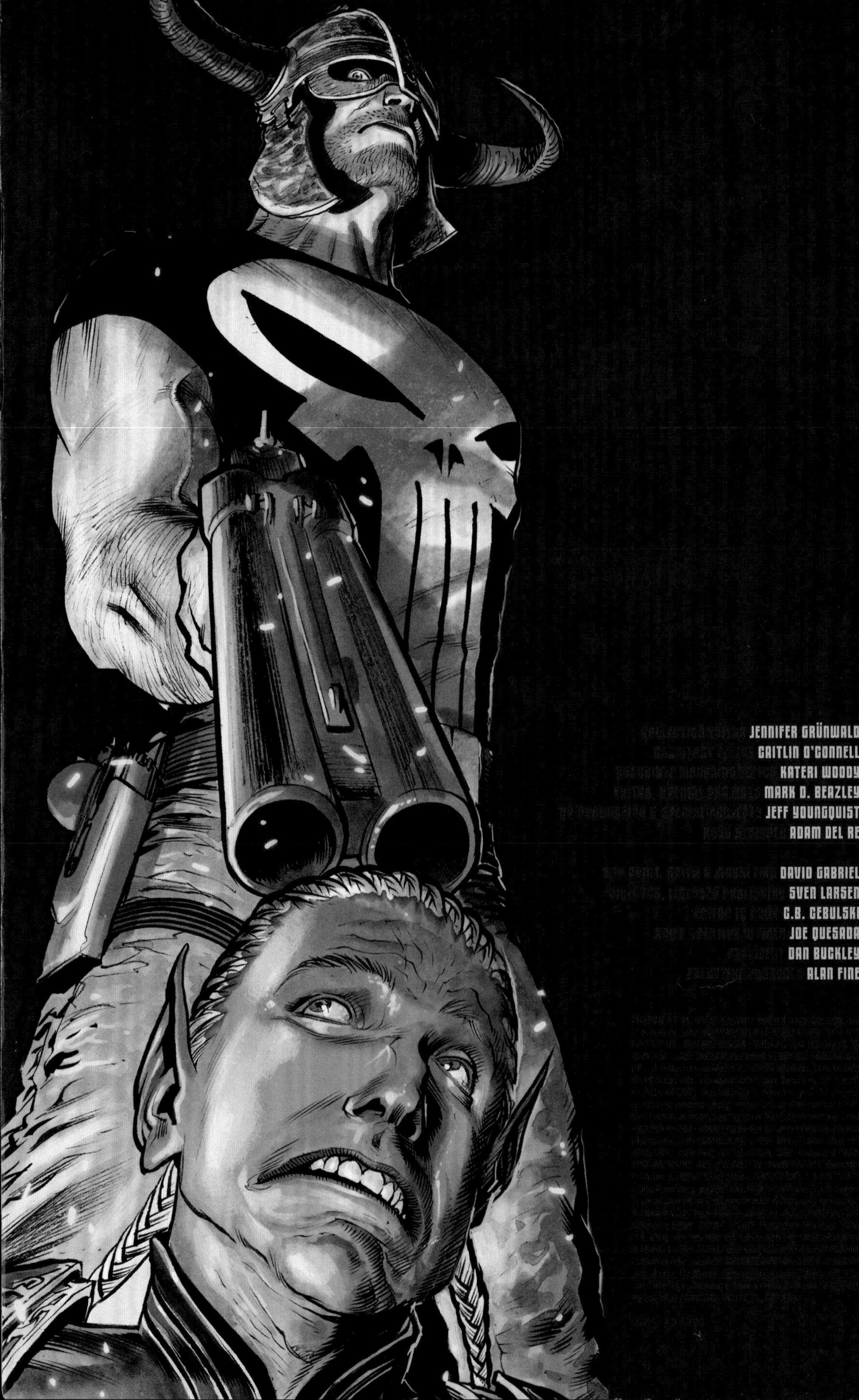

JENNIFER GRÜNWALD
CAITLIN O'CONNELL
KATERI WOODY
MARK D. BEAZLEY
JEFF YOUNGQUIST
ADAM DEL RE

DAVID GABRIEL
SVEN LARSEN
C.B. CEBULSKI
JOE QUESADA
DAN BUCKLEY
ALAN FINE

Malekith the Accursed has been defeated, his armies driven from Midgard and his allies scattered. Thor has been named the new All-Father. The War of the Realms is over. Now its major players must contend with what's left behind.

With Heimdall injured, Daredevil took up his sword during the war to become the God Without Fear. But even for a man with super-senses, the ability to see and hear everything in the Ten Realms has proven overwhelming. Now he has a choice: To find his own god again...or remain one himself.

Jane Foster took up the hammer of the War Thor and helped turn the tide of the war. But after one last mighty blow, the hammer broke apart - and attached itself to Jane. The former Goddess of Thunder...is about to become something else entirely.

Thor's half brother Loki, one of the architects of the war, found his redemption when he intervened to save Lady Freyja and was eaten by his father Laufey, king of the Frost Giants. But the God of Mischief was not done with tricks; at the war's climax, he burst from his father's stomach, killing Laufey and leaving the Frost Giants without a king.

The Punisher took up arms against Malekith's allies and helped drive them from Midgard. But for Frank Castle, there remains some unfinished business...

PUNISHER
KILL KREW

GERRY DUGGAN
WRITER

JUAN FERREYRA
ARTIST

VC'S CORY PETIT
LETTERER

TONY MOORE & DEAN WHITE [#1-5] AND
PHIL NOTO [WAR OF THE REALMS OMEGA]
COVER ART

LINDSEY COHICK
ASSISTANT EDITOR

JAKE THOMAS
EDITOR

SPECIAL THANKS TO DECLAN DUGGAN

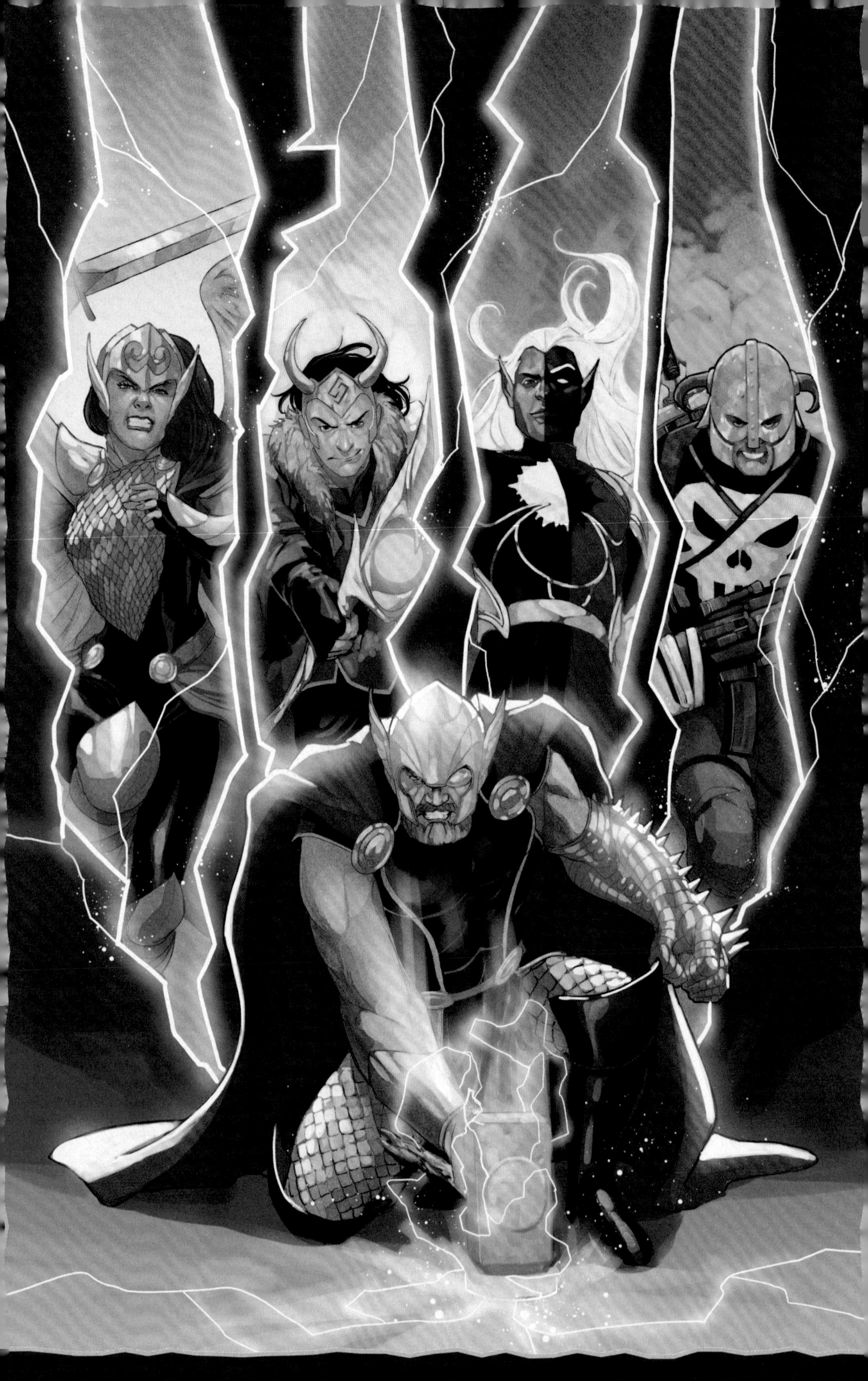

WAR OF THE REALMS OMEGA

NEW YORK CITY.

PUNISHER WAR JOURNAL: THE WAR IS OVER ON EARTH.

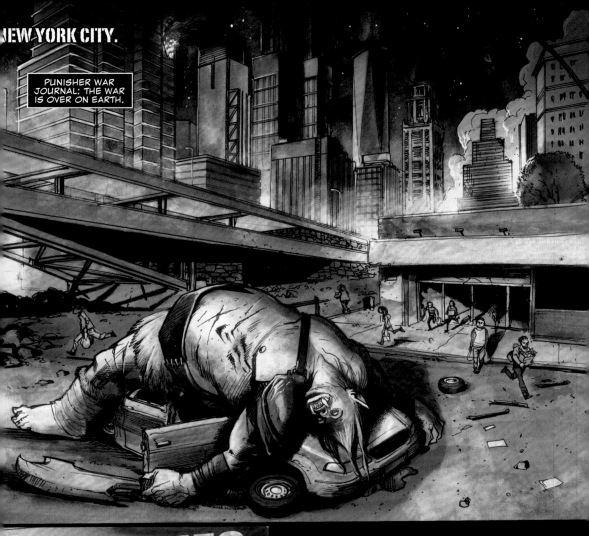

BUT THE FIGHTING ISN'T OVER.

FOR THE LAST FEW WEEKS, EARTH HAS BEEN ON DEFENSE...

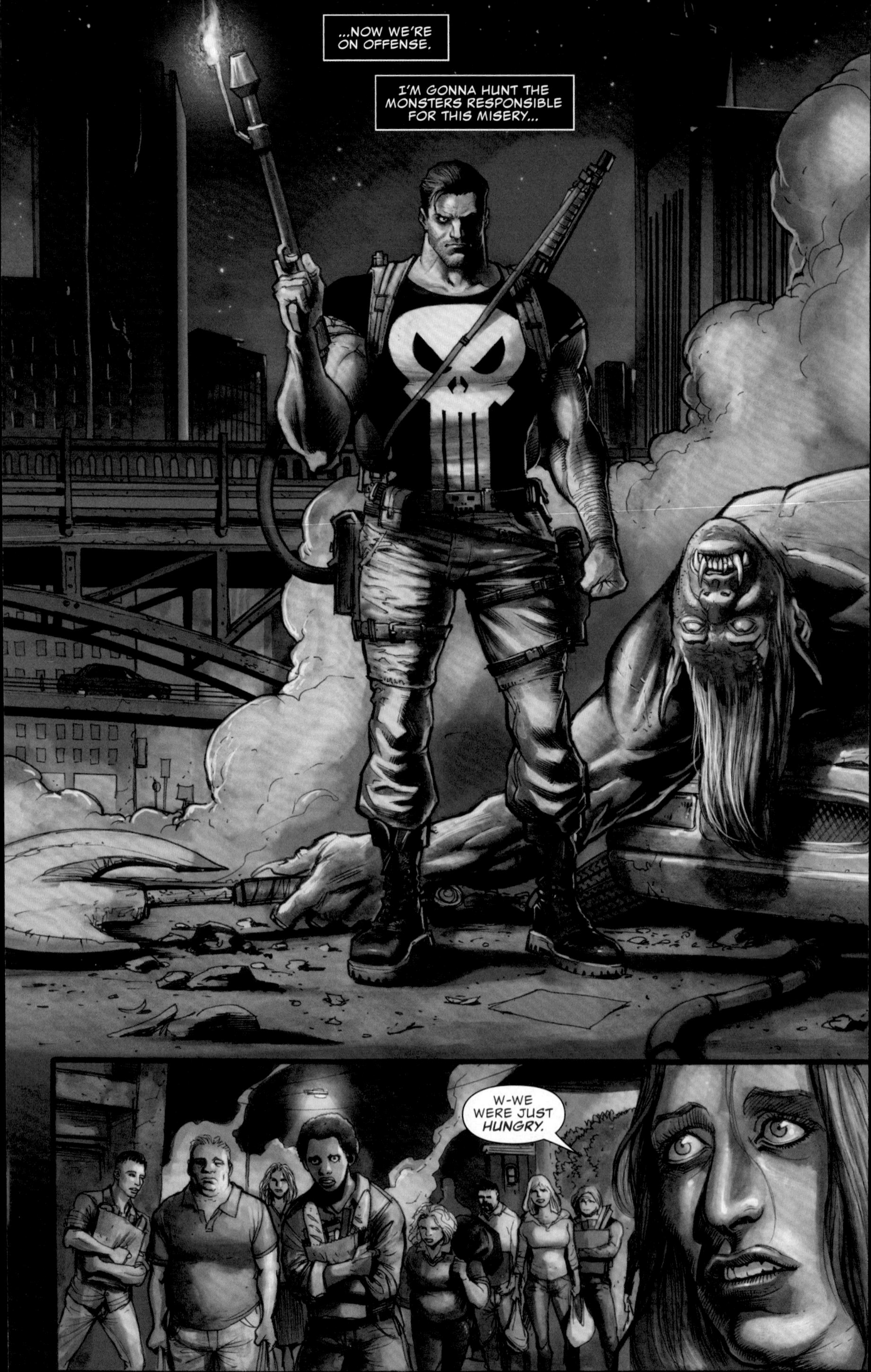
...NOW WE'RE ON OFFENSE.
I'M GONNA HUNT THE MONSTERS RESPONSIBLE FOR THIS MISERY...
W-WE WERE JUST *HUNGRY*.

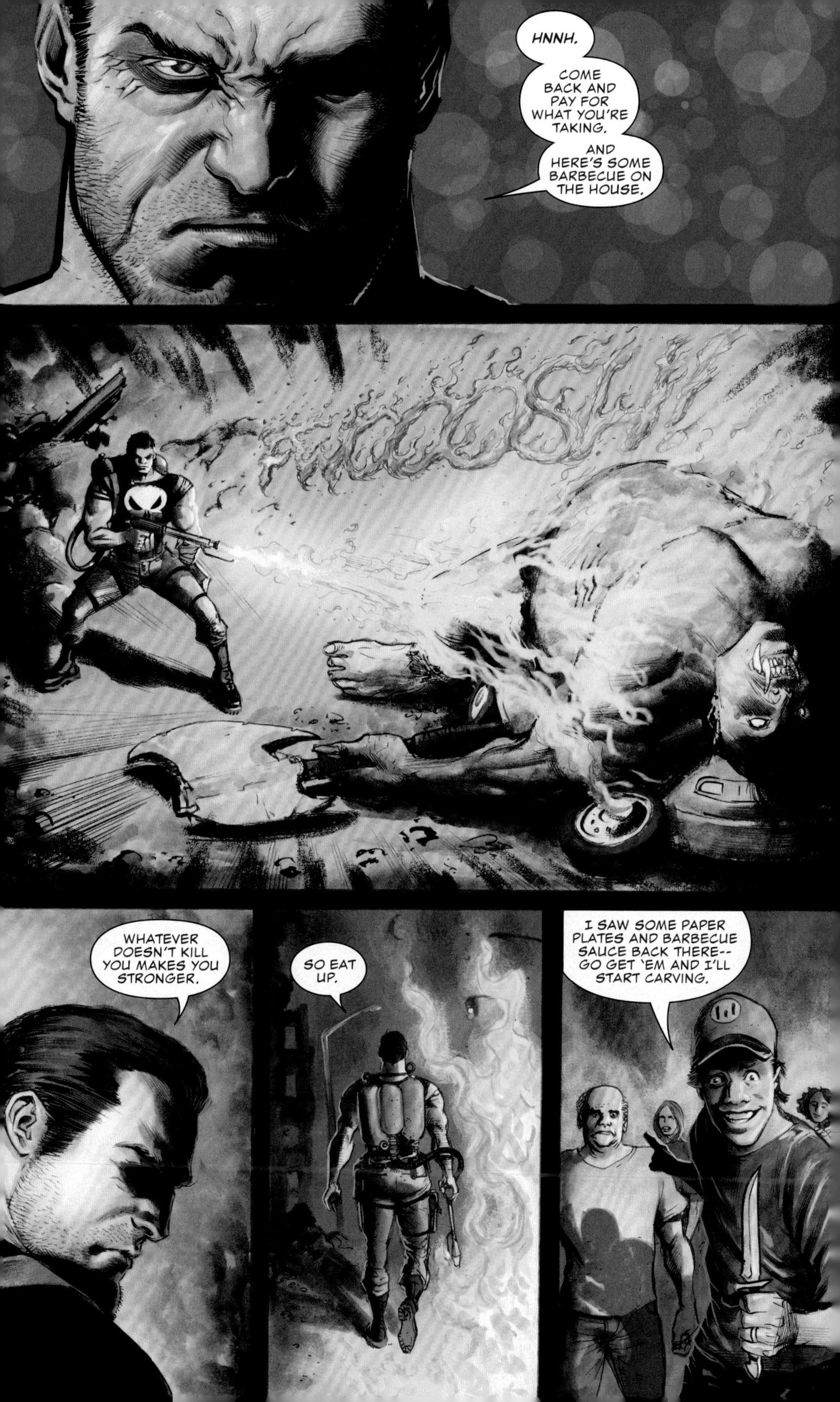
HNNH.
COME BACK AND PAY FOR WHAT YOU'RE TAKING.
AND HERE'S SOME BARBECUE ON THE HOUSE.
FWOOOSHH!
WHATEVER DOESN'T KILL YOU MAKES YOU STRONGER.
SO EAT UP.
I SAW SOME PAPER PLATES AND BARBECUE SAUCE BACK THERE-- GO GET 'EM AND I'LL START CARVING.

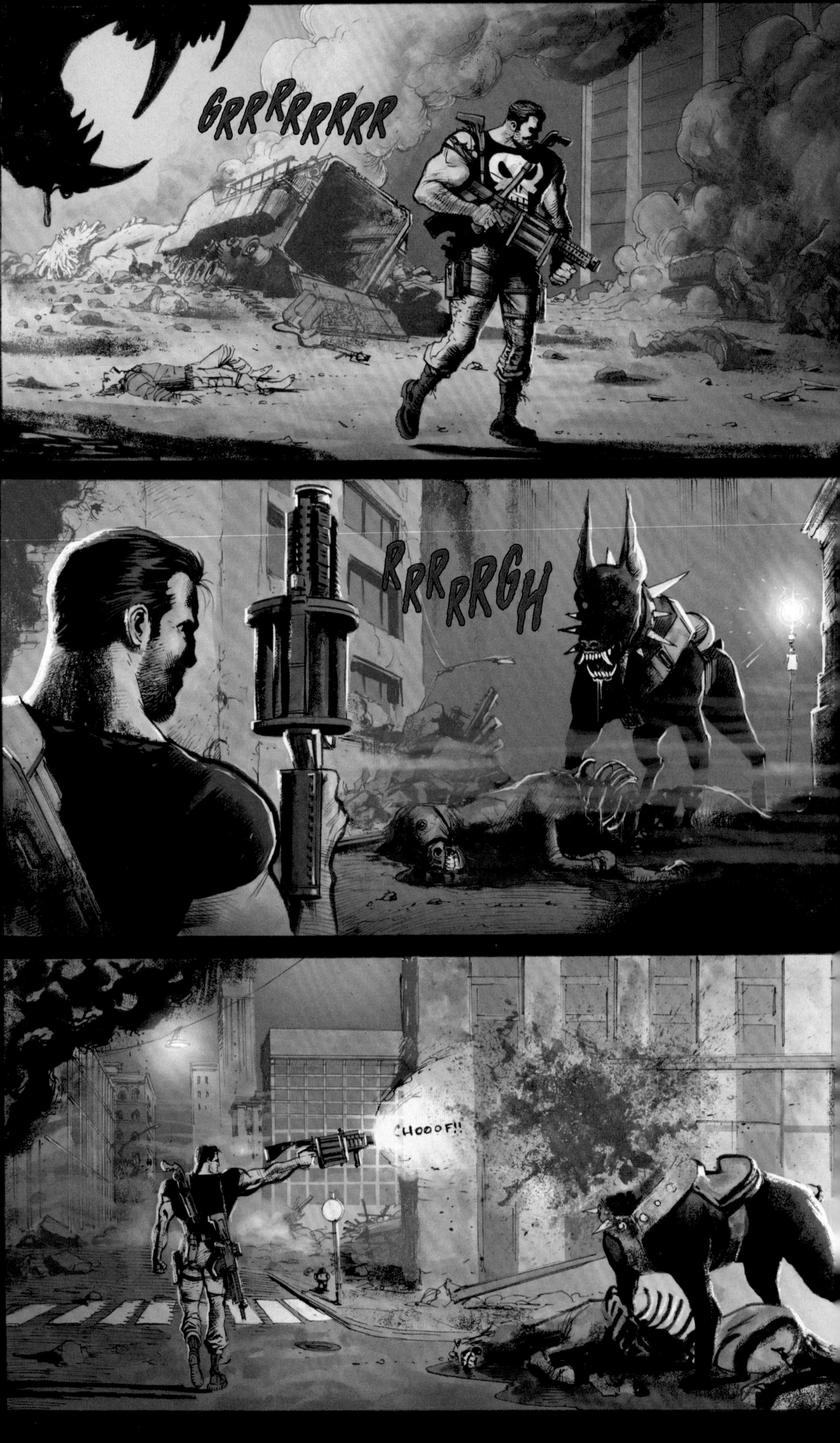
GRRRRRRRR
RRRRRGH
CHOOOF!!

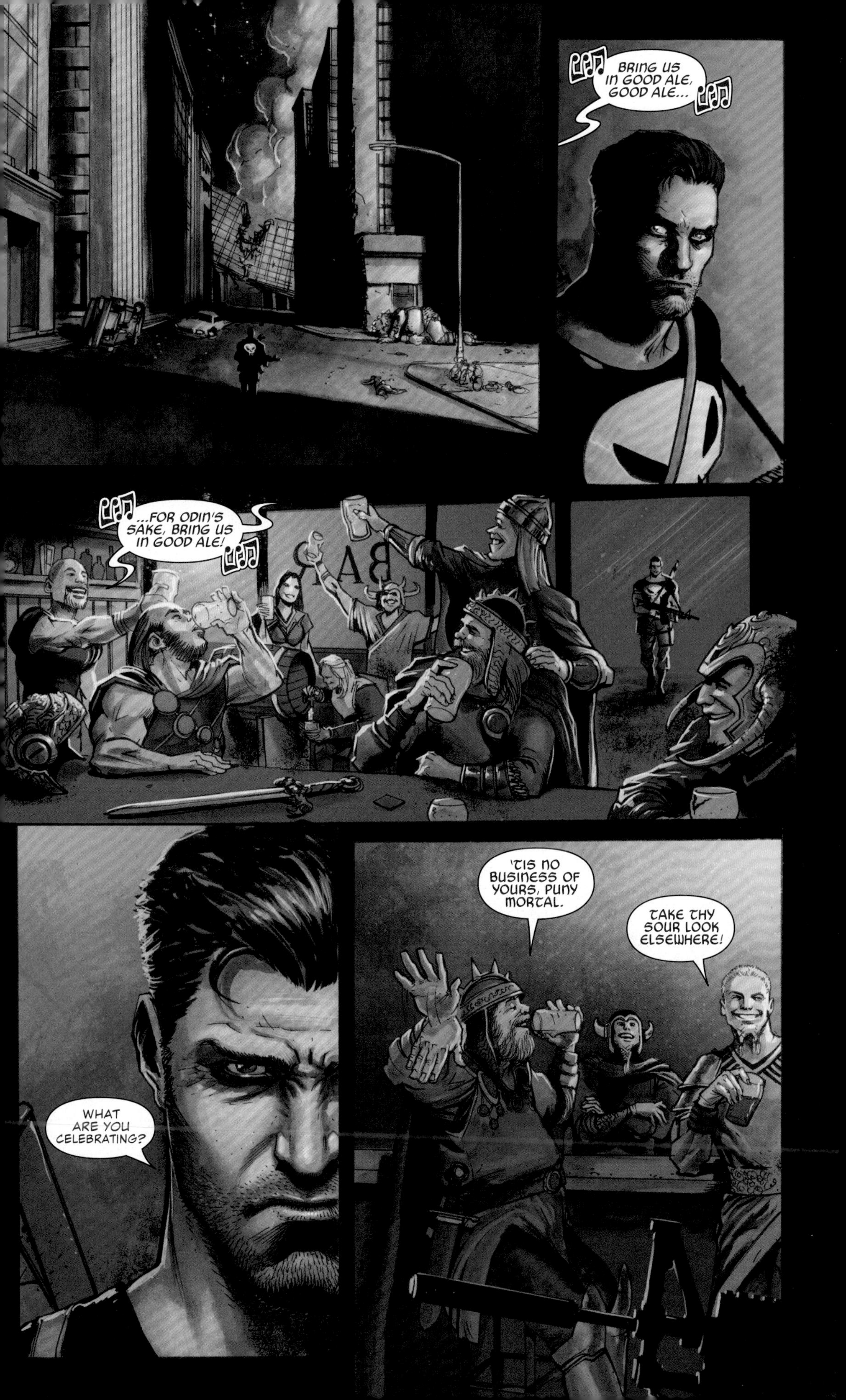
BRING US IN GOOD ALE, GOOD ALE...
...FOR ODIN'S SAKE, BRING US IN GOOD ALE!
WHAT ARE YOU CELEBRATING?
'TIS NO BUSINESS OF YOURS, PUNY MORTAL.
TAKE THY SOUR LOOK ELSEWHERE!

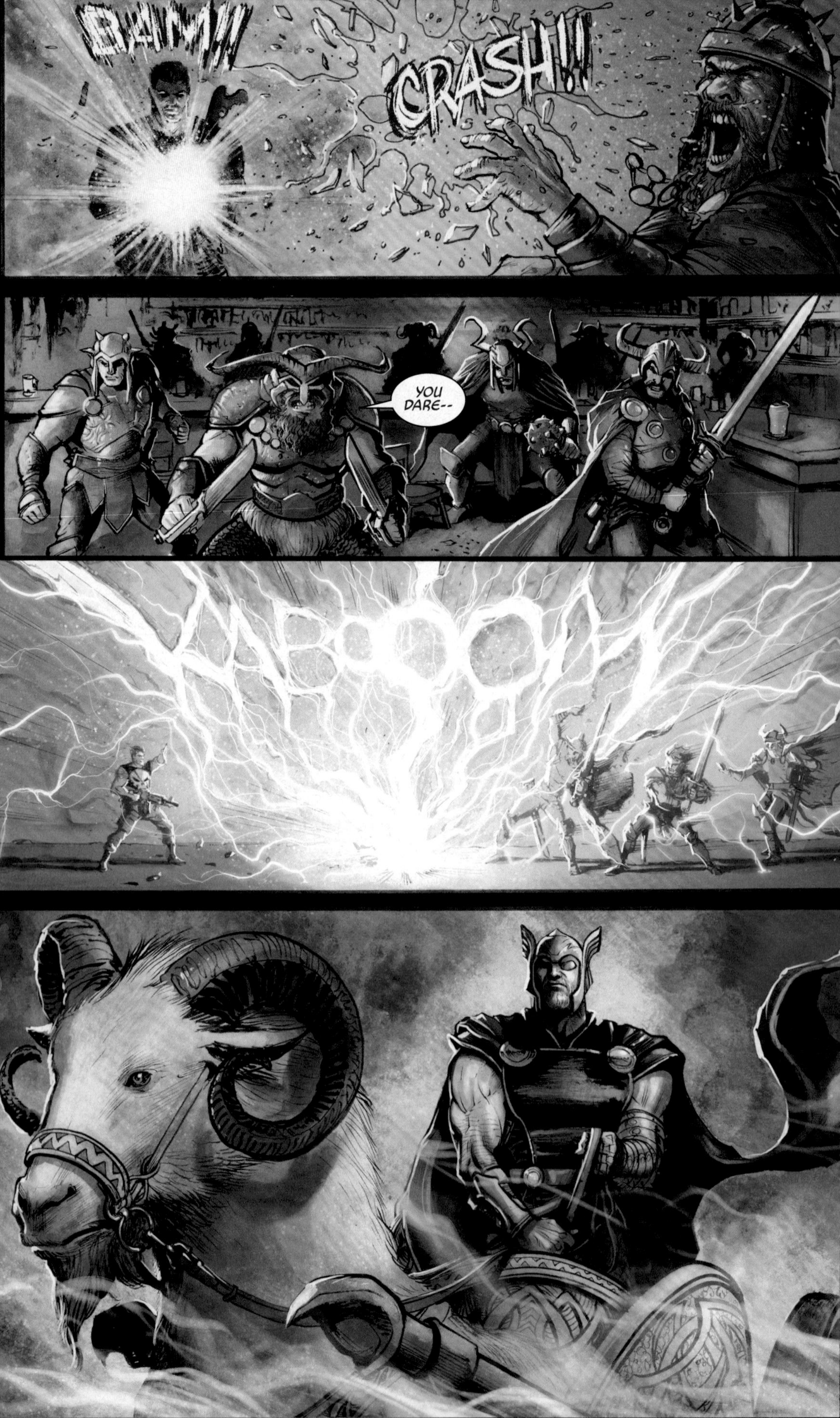
BAM!!
CRASH!!
YOU DARE--
KABOOOOM

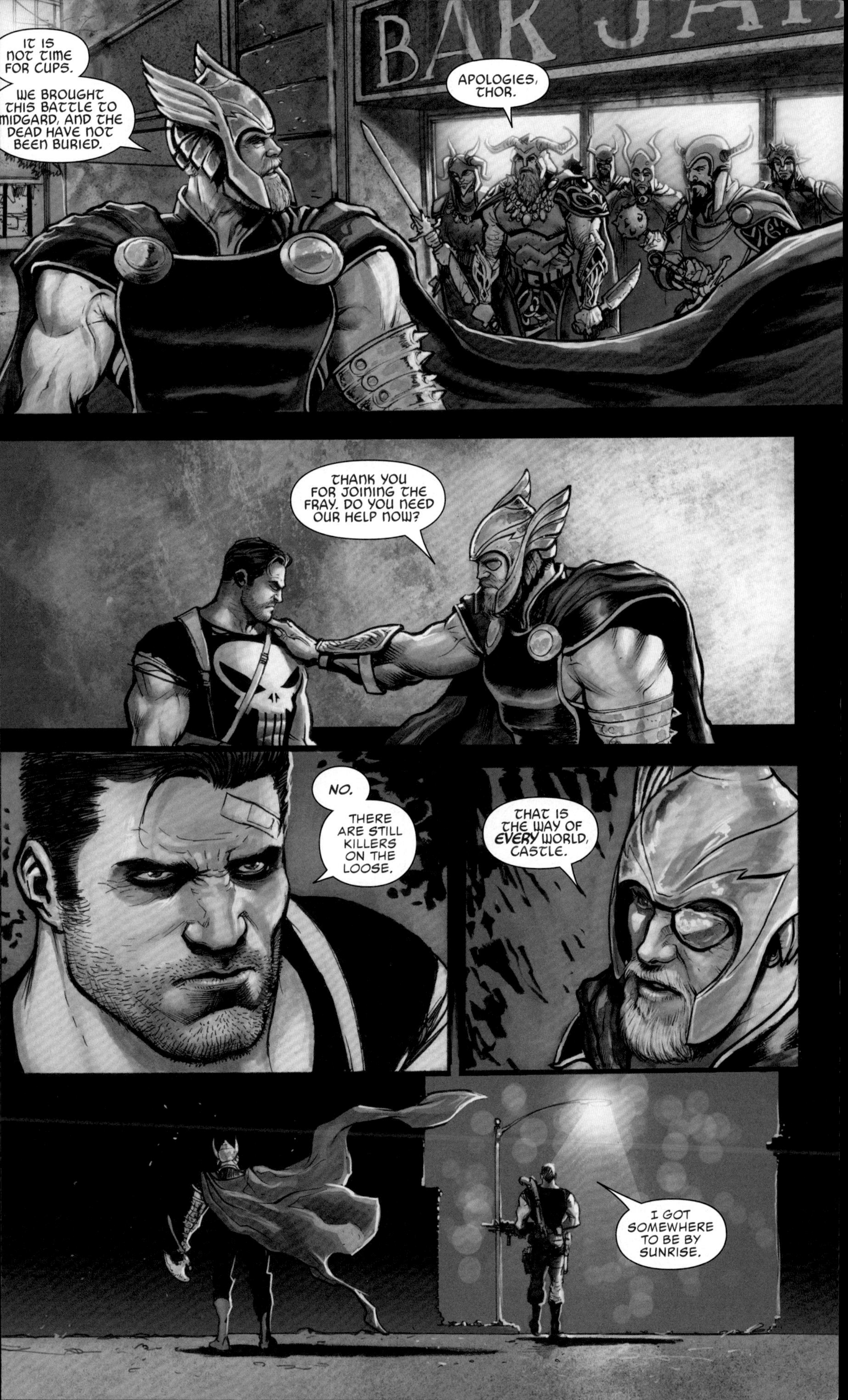
IT IS NOT TIME FOR CUPS.
WE BROUGHT THIS BATTLE TO MIDGARD, AND THE DEAD HAVE NOT BEEN BURIED.
APOLOGIES, THOR.
THANK YOU FOR JOINING THE FRAY. DO YOU NEED OUR HELP NOW?
NO.
THERE ARE STILL KILLERS ON THE LOOSE.
THAT IS THE WAY OF EVERY WORLD, CASTLE.
I GOT SOMEWHERE TO BE BY SUNRISE.

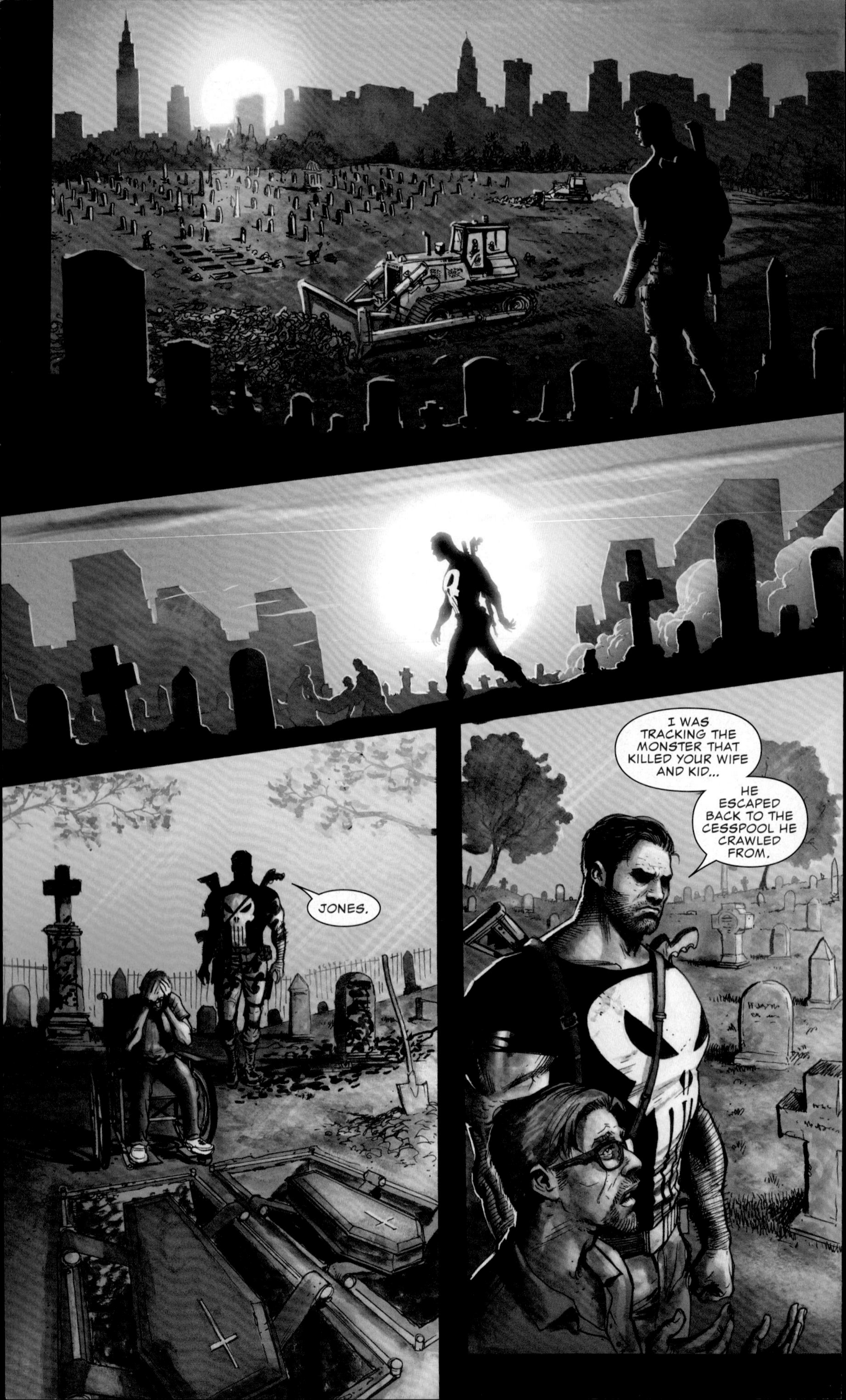
JONES.
I WAS TRACKING THE MONSTER THAT KILLED YOUR WIFE AND KID...
HE ESCAPED BACK TO THE CESSPOOL HE CRAWLED FROM.

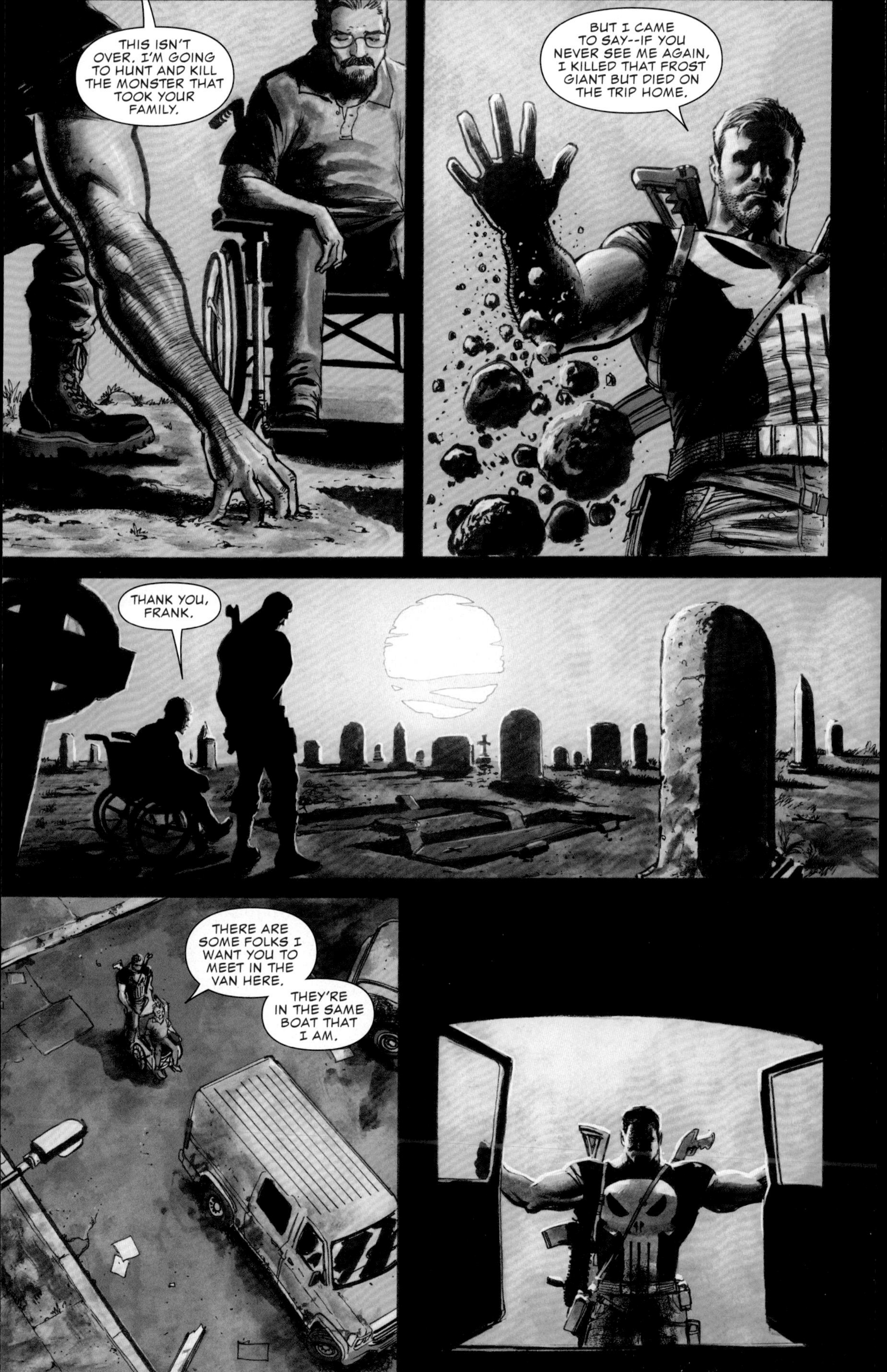
THIS ISN'T OVER. I'M GOING TO HUNT AND KILL THE MONSTER THAT TOOK YOUR FAMILY.
BUT I CAME TO SAY--IF YOU NEVER SEE ME AGAIN, I KILLED THAT FROST GIANT BUT DIED ON THE TRIP HOME.
THANK YOU, FRANK.
THERE ARE SOME FOLKS I WANT YOU TO MEET IN THE VAN HERE.
THEY'RE IN THE SAME BOAT THAT I AM.

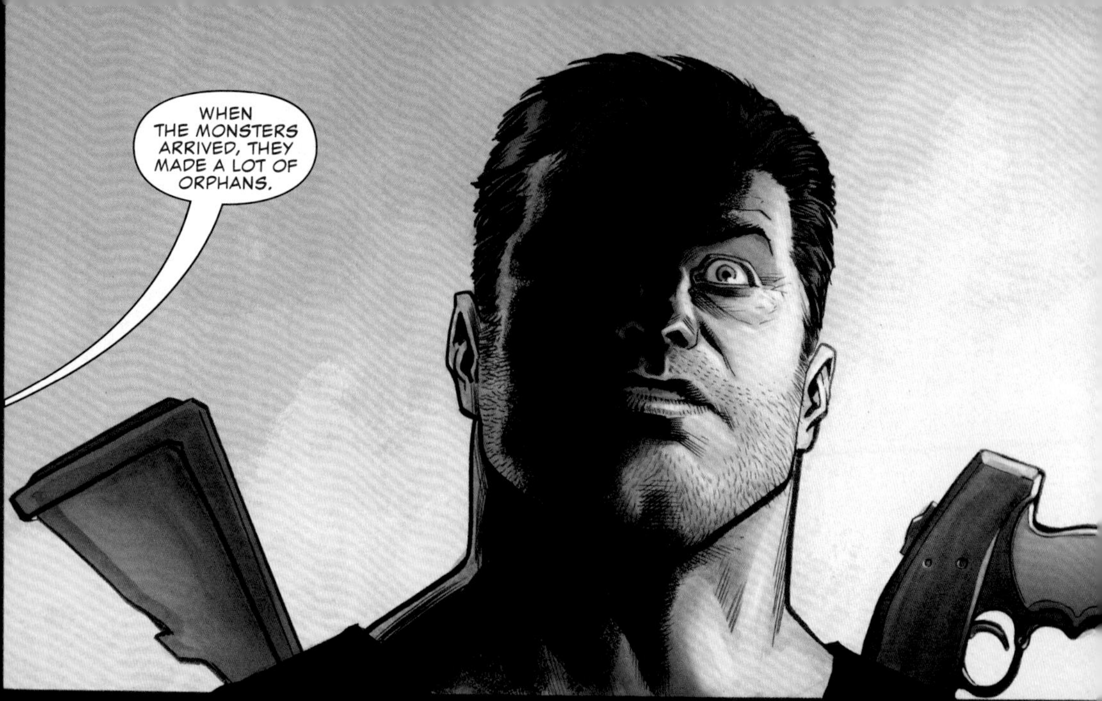
WHEN THE MONSTERS ARRIVED, THEY MADE A LOT OF ORPHANS.

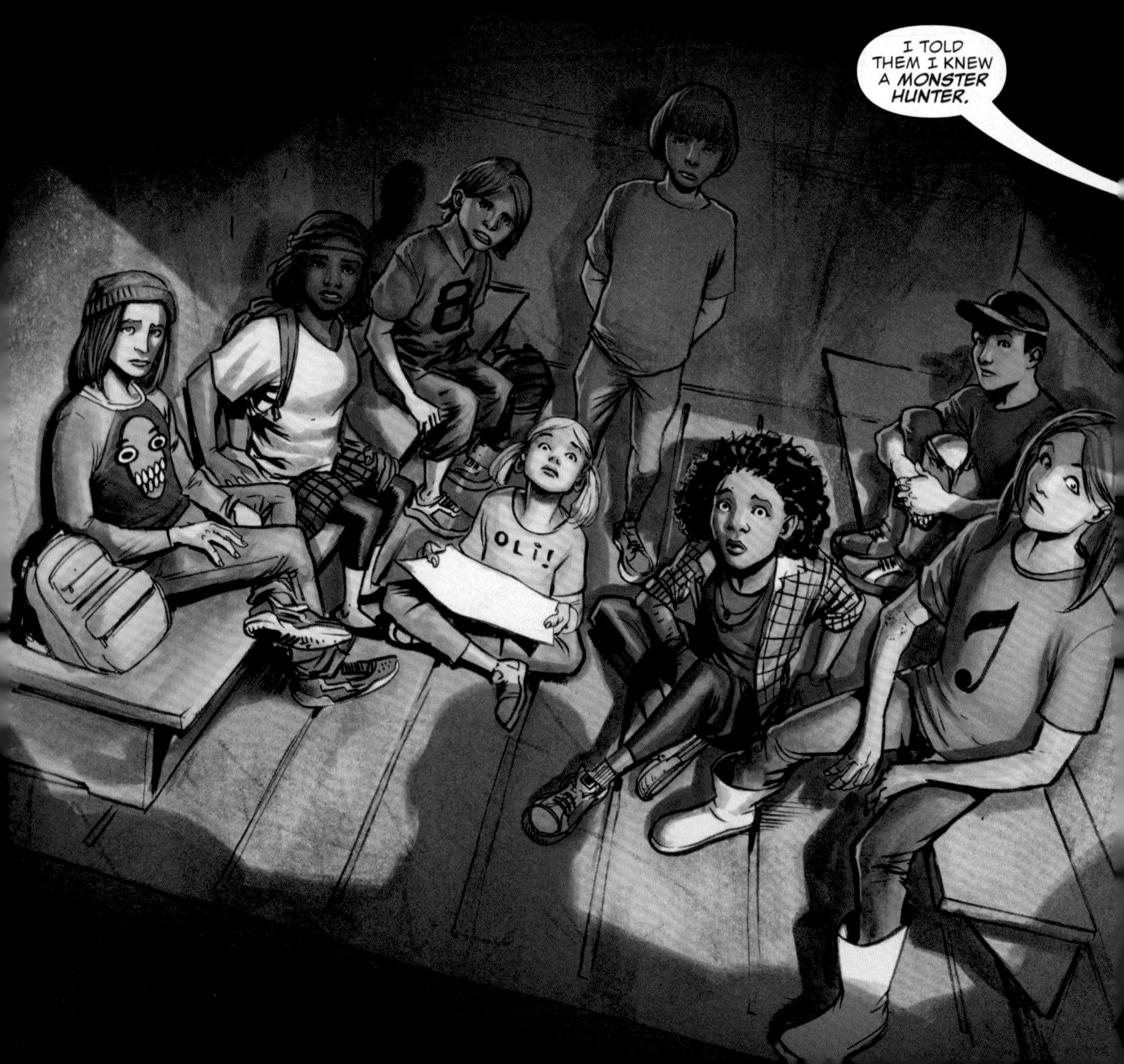
I TOLD THEM I KNEW A *MONSTER HUNTER.*

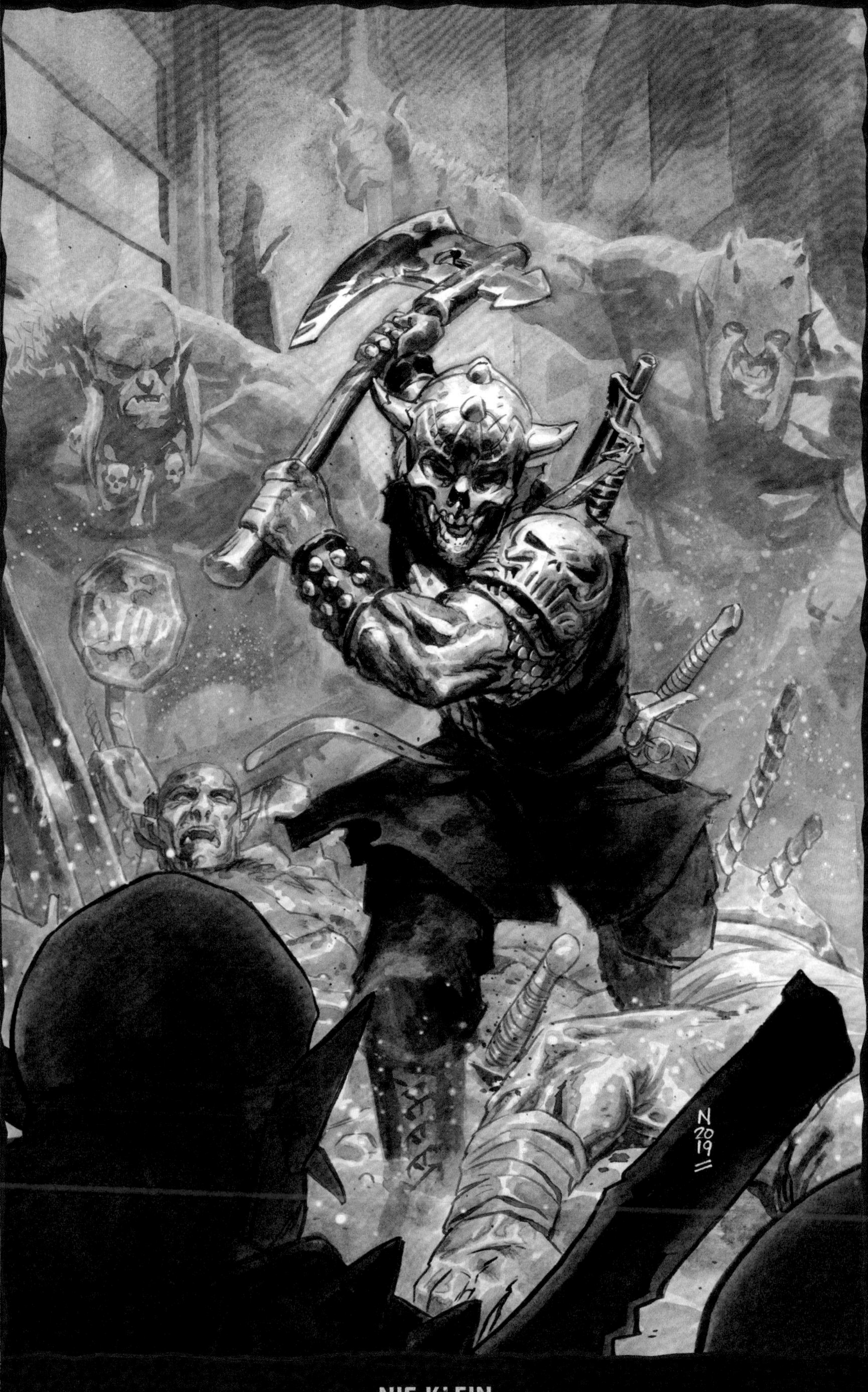
STOP
N
2019

NIC KLEIN

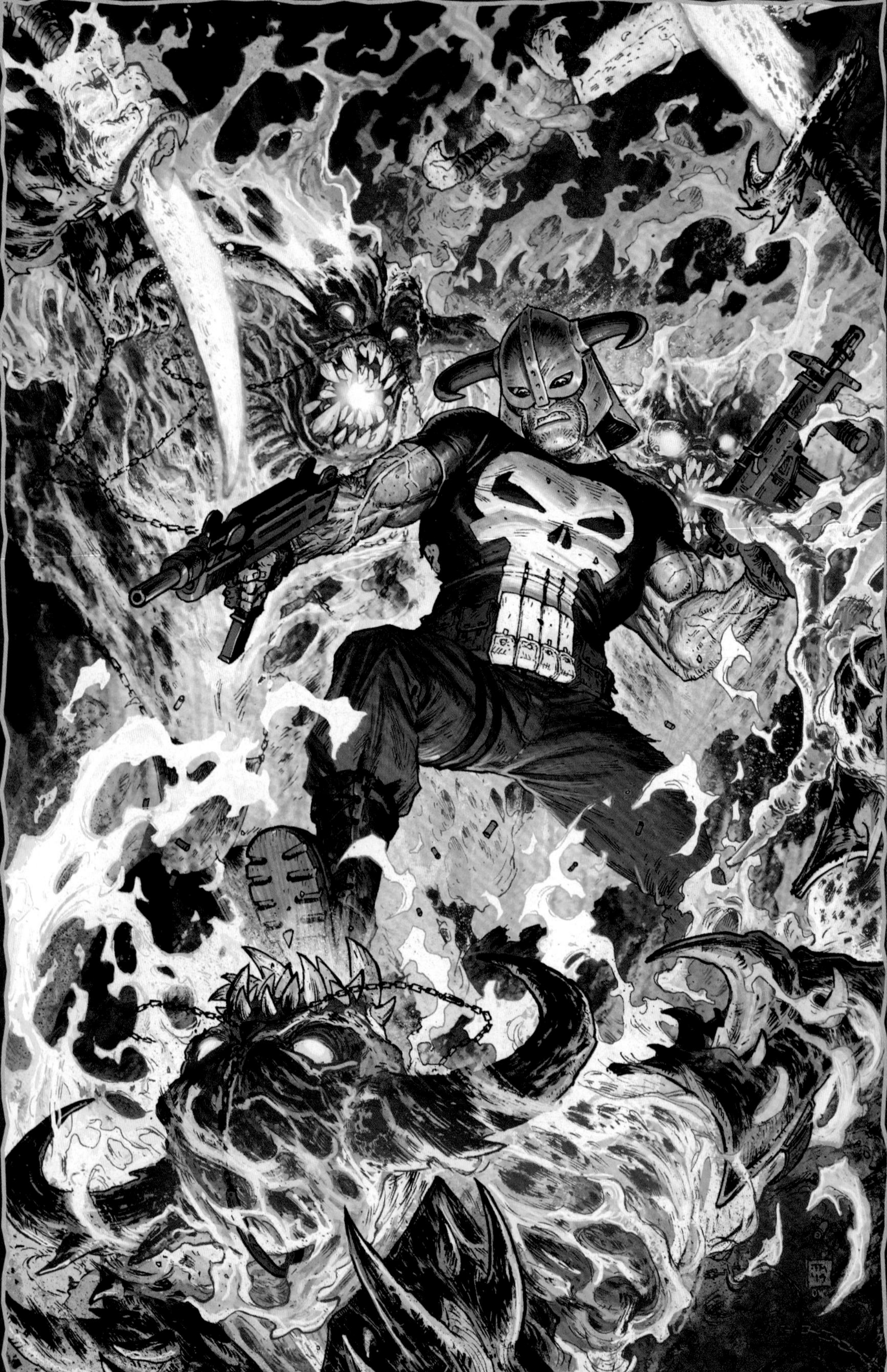

ONE

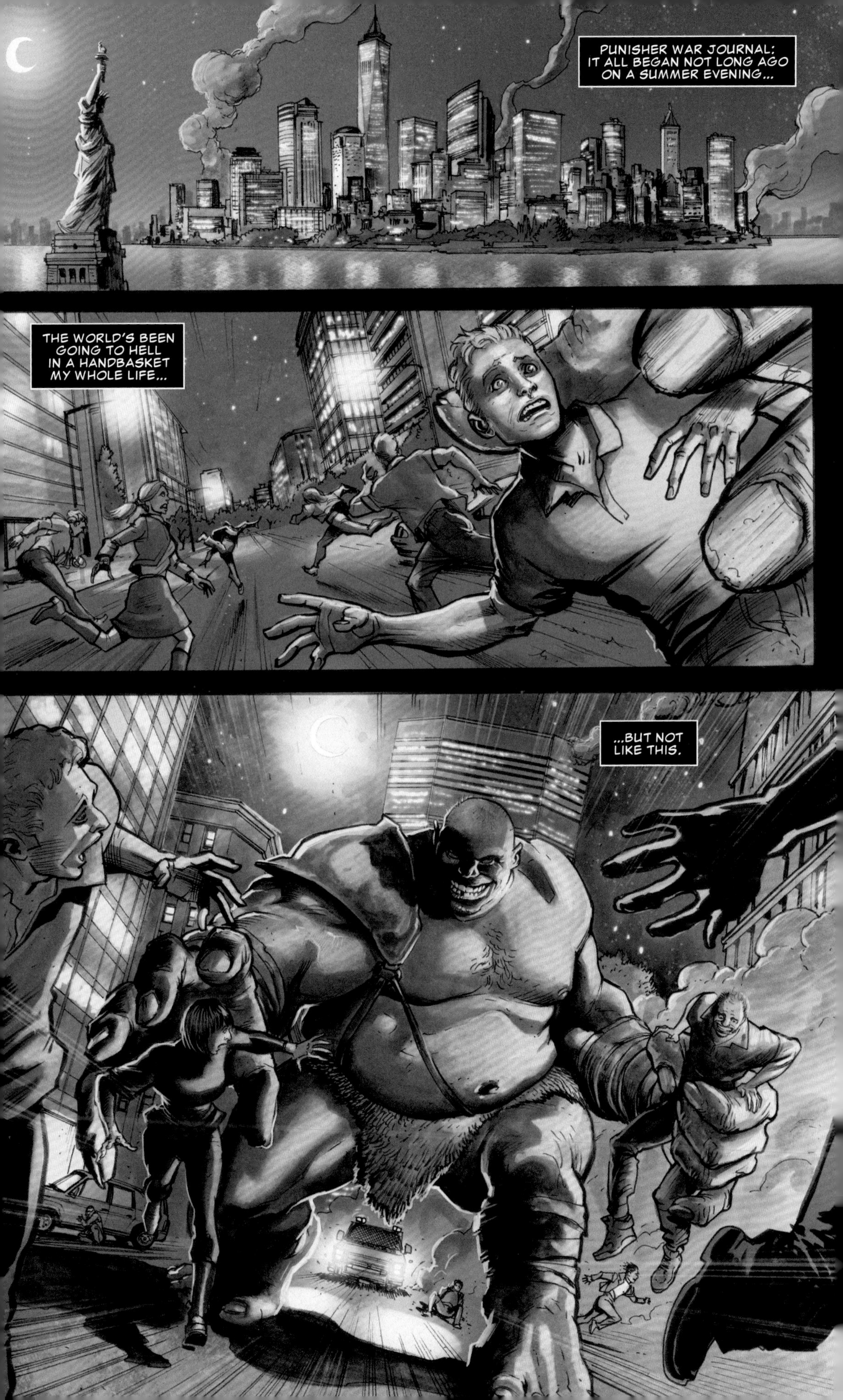
PUNISHER WAR JOURNAL: IT ALL BEGAN NOT LONG AGO ON A SUMMER EVENING...
THE WORLD'S BEEN GOING TO HELL IN A HANDBASKET MY WHOLE LIFE...
...BUT NOT LIKE THIS.

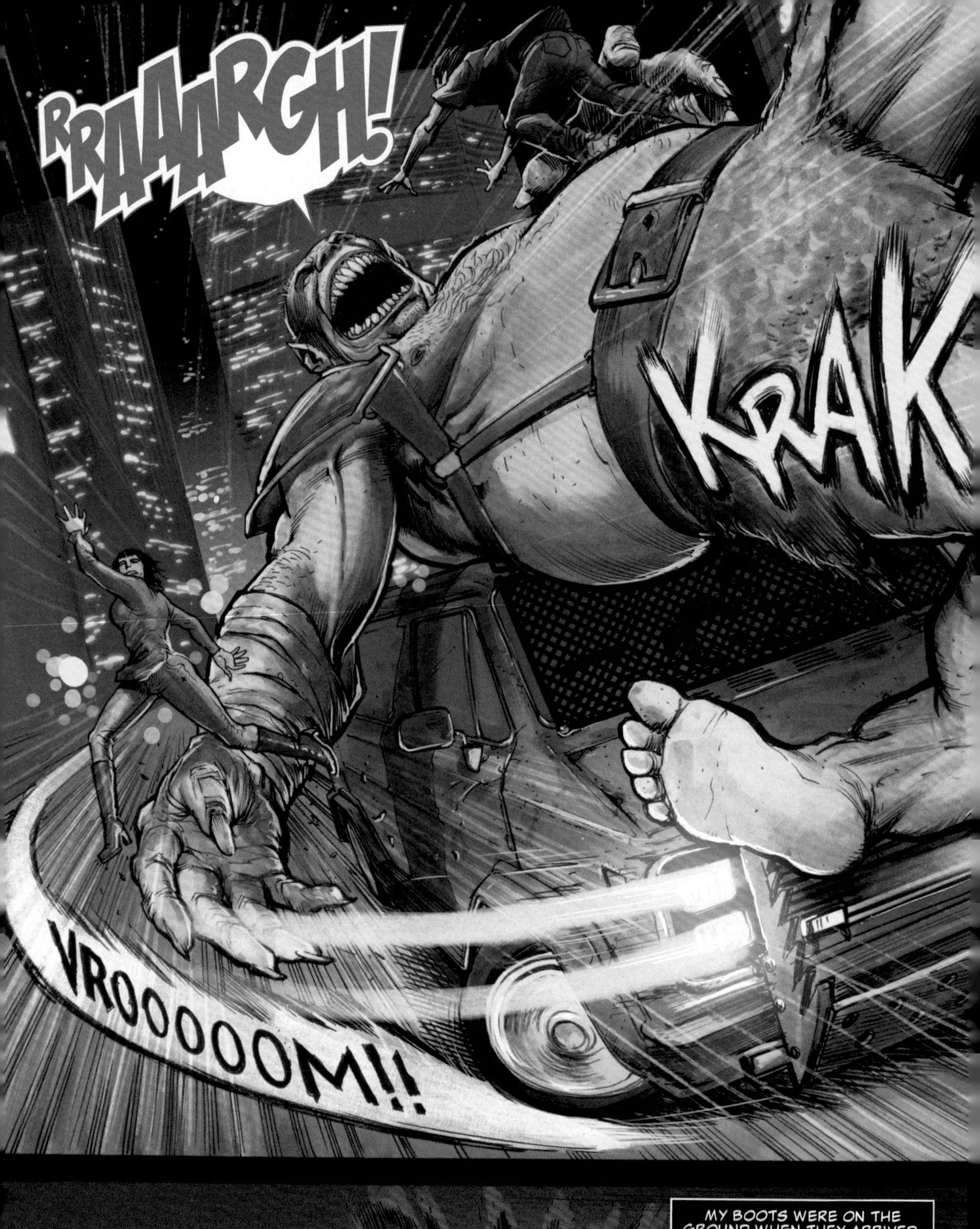
RRAAARGH!
KRAK
VROOOOOM!!
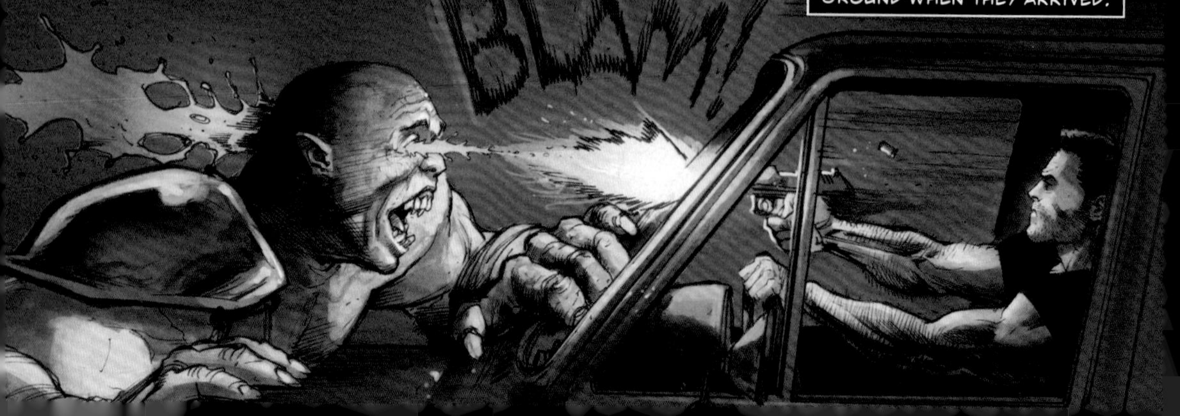
MY BOOTS WERE ON THE GROUND WHEN THEY ARRIVED.
BLAM!

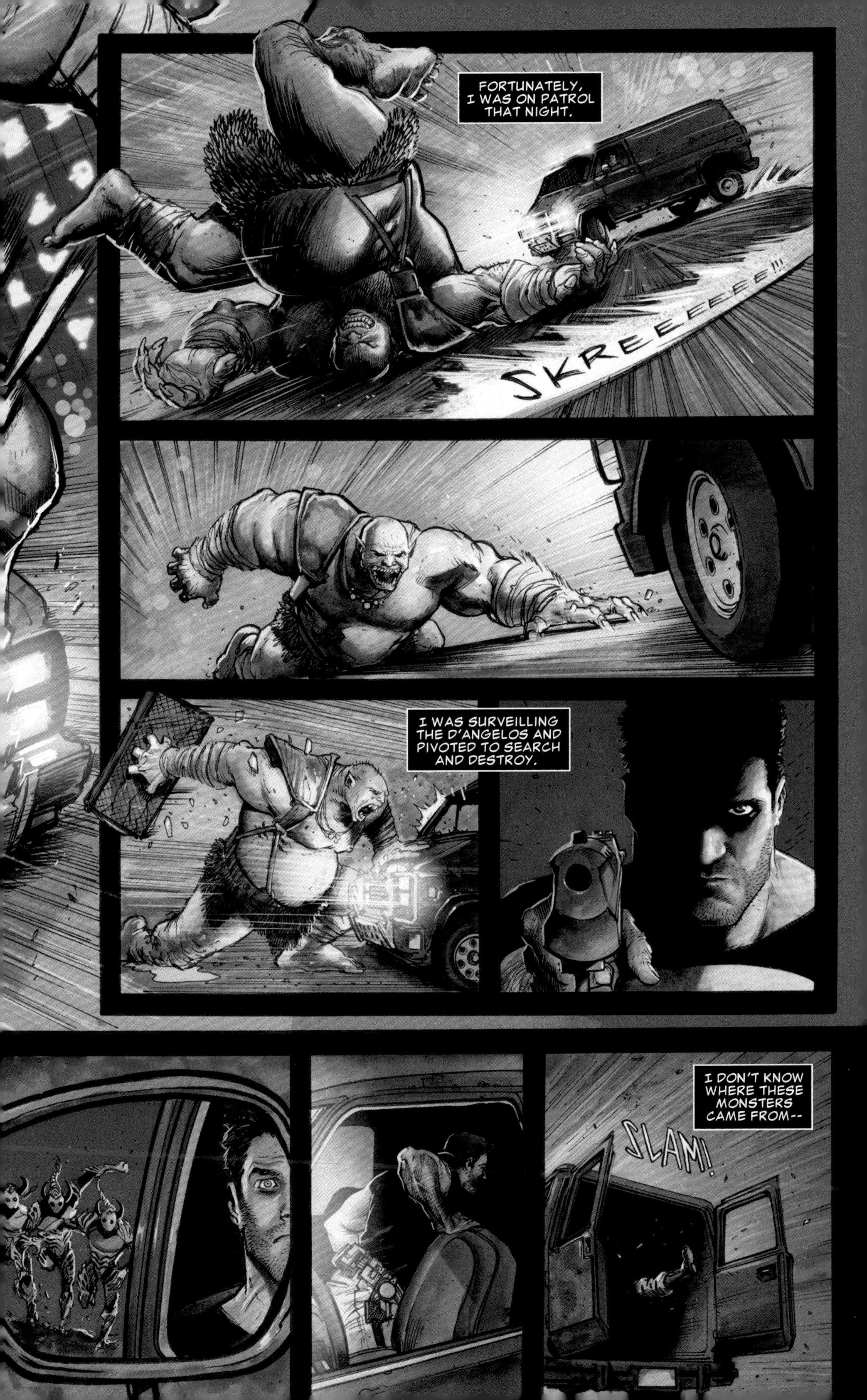
FORTUNATELY, I WAS ON PATROL THAT NIGHT.
SKREEEEEEE!!!
I WAS SURVEILLING THE D'ANGELOS AND PIVOTED TO SEARCH AND DESTROY.
I DON'T KNOW WHERE THESE MONSTERS CAME FROM--
SLAM!

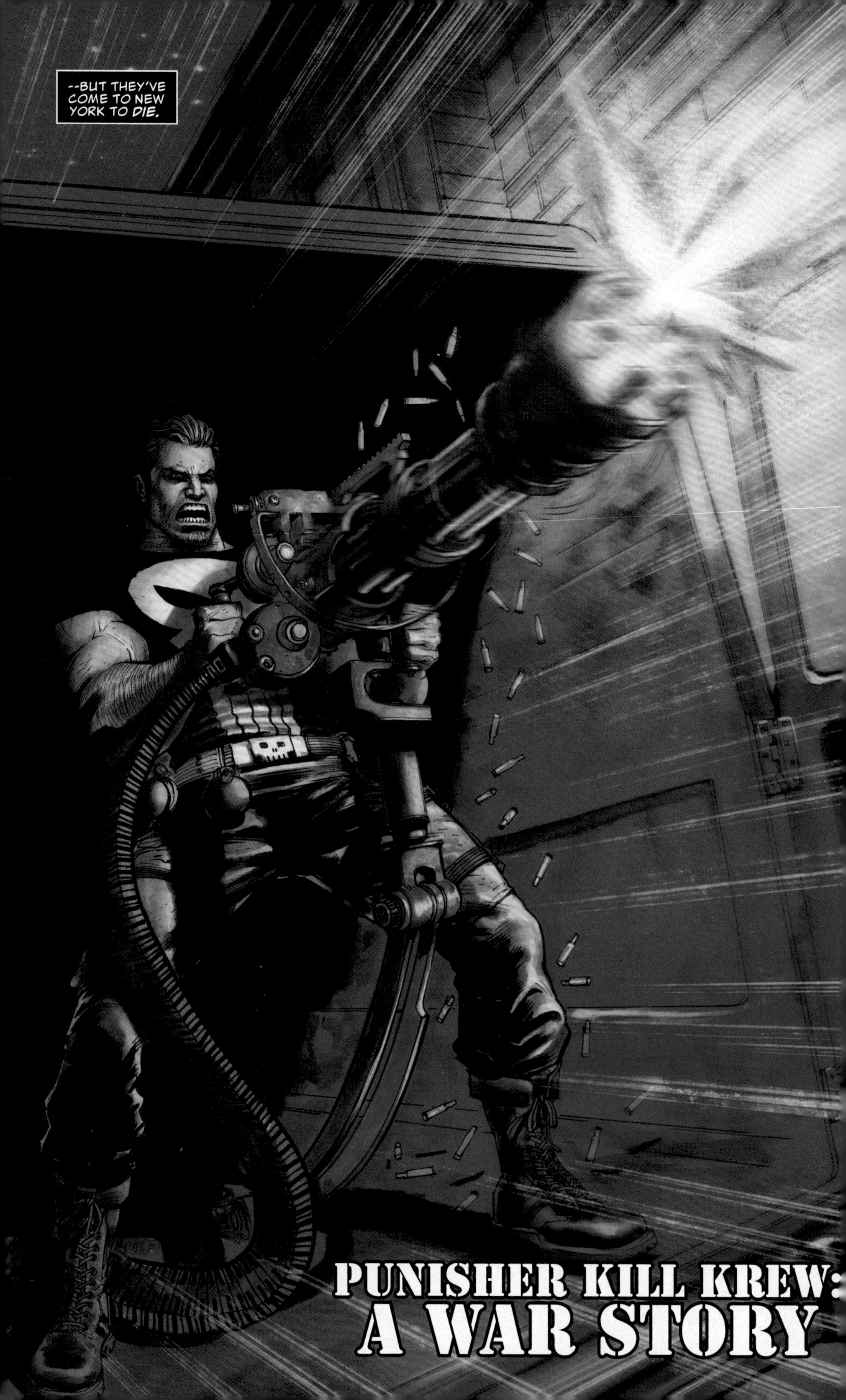
--BUT THEY'VE COME TO NEW YORK TO DIE.
PUNISHER KILL KREW:
A WAR STORY

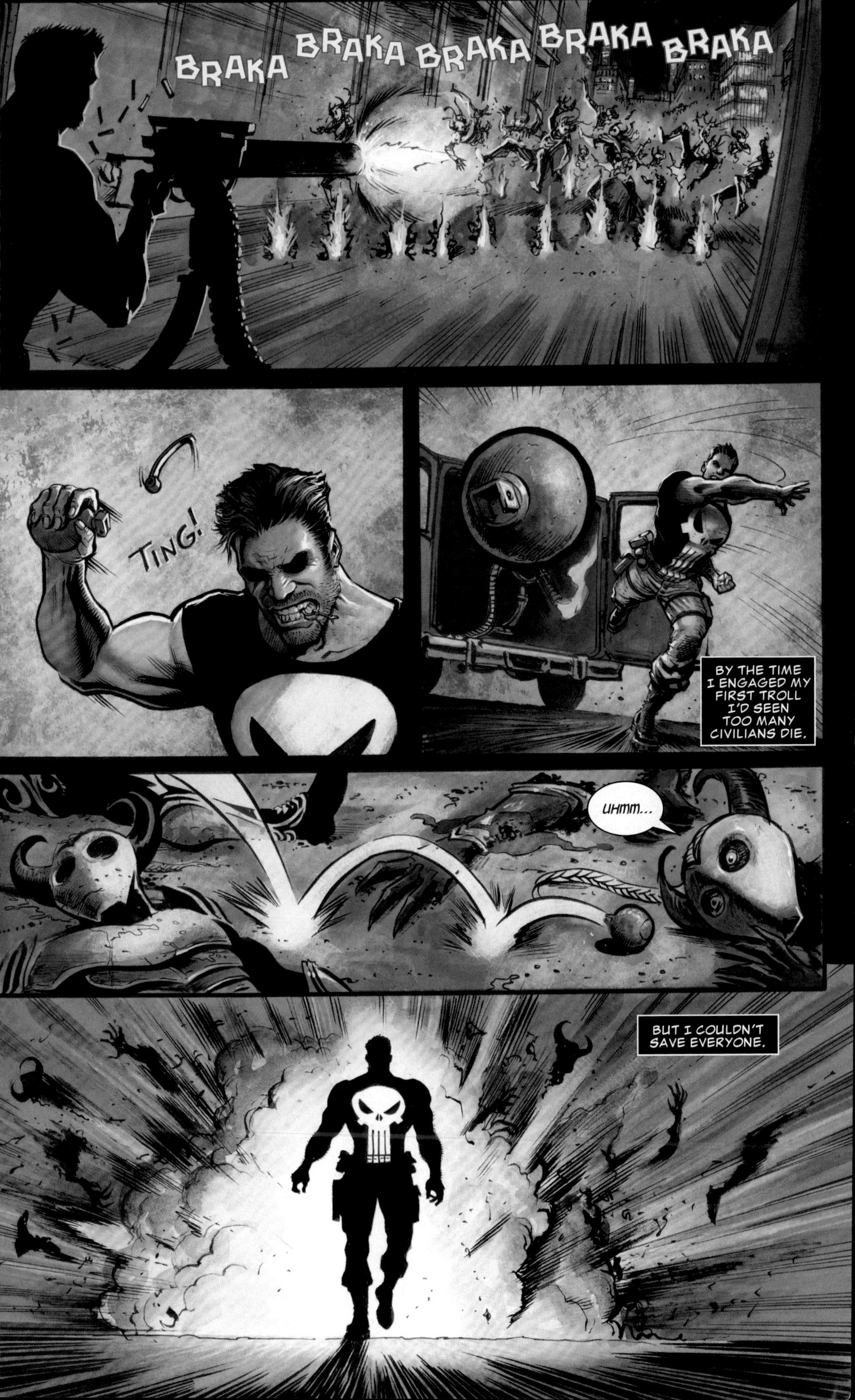
BRAKA BRAKA BRAKA BRAKA BRAKA
TING!
BY THE TIME I ENGAGED MY FIRST TROLL I'D SEEN TOO MANY CIVILIANS DIE.
UHMM...
BUT I COULDN'T SAVE EVERYONE.

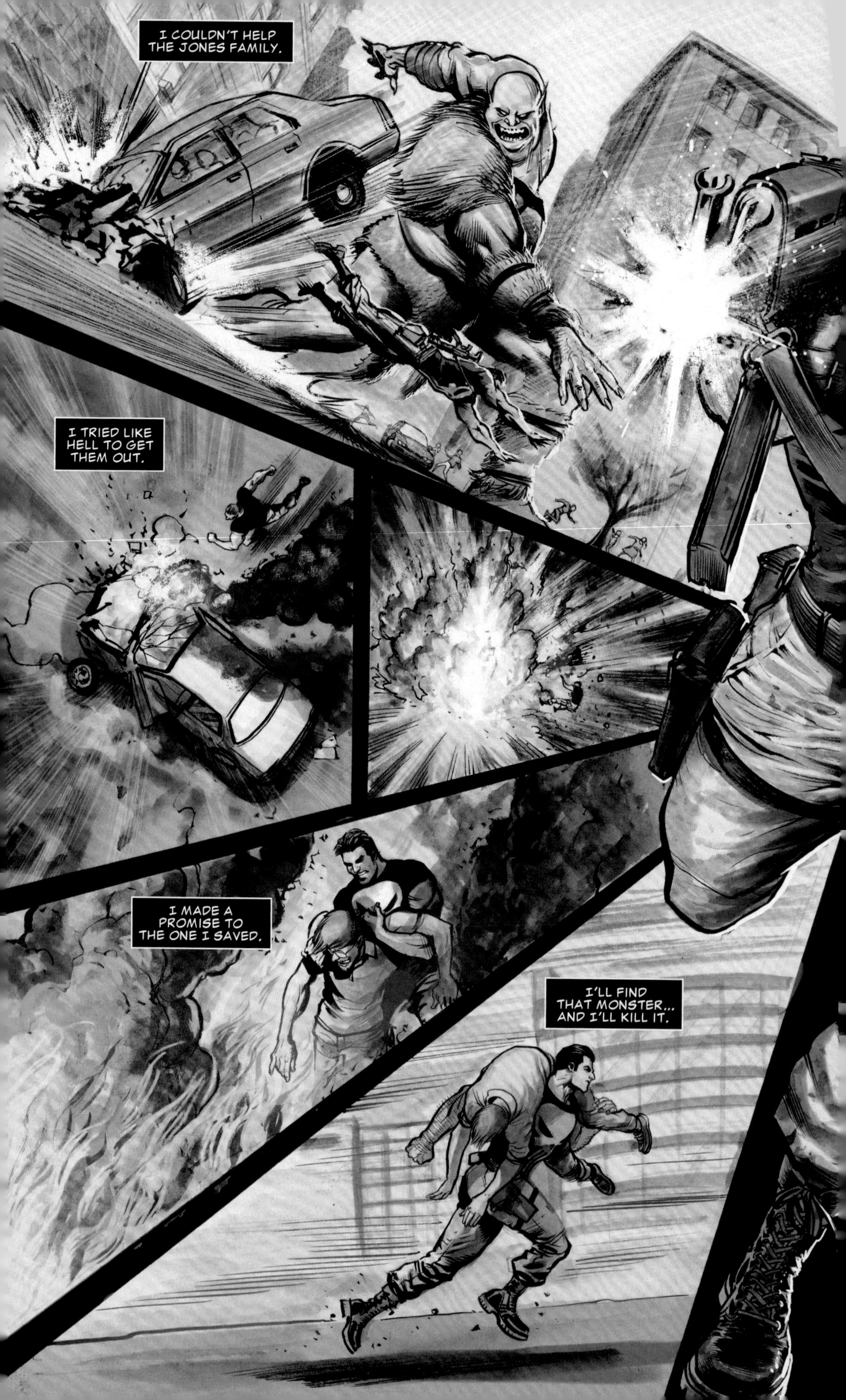
I COULDN'T HELP THE JONES FAMILY.
I TRIED LIKE HELL TO GET THEM OUT.
I MADE A PROMISE TO THE ONE I SAVED.
I'LL FIND THAT MONSTER... AND I'LL KILL IT.

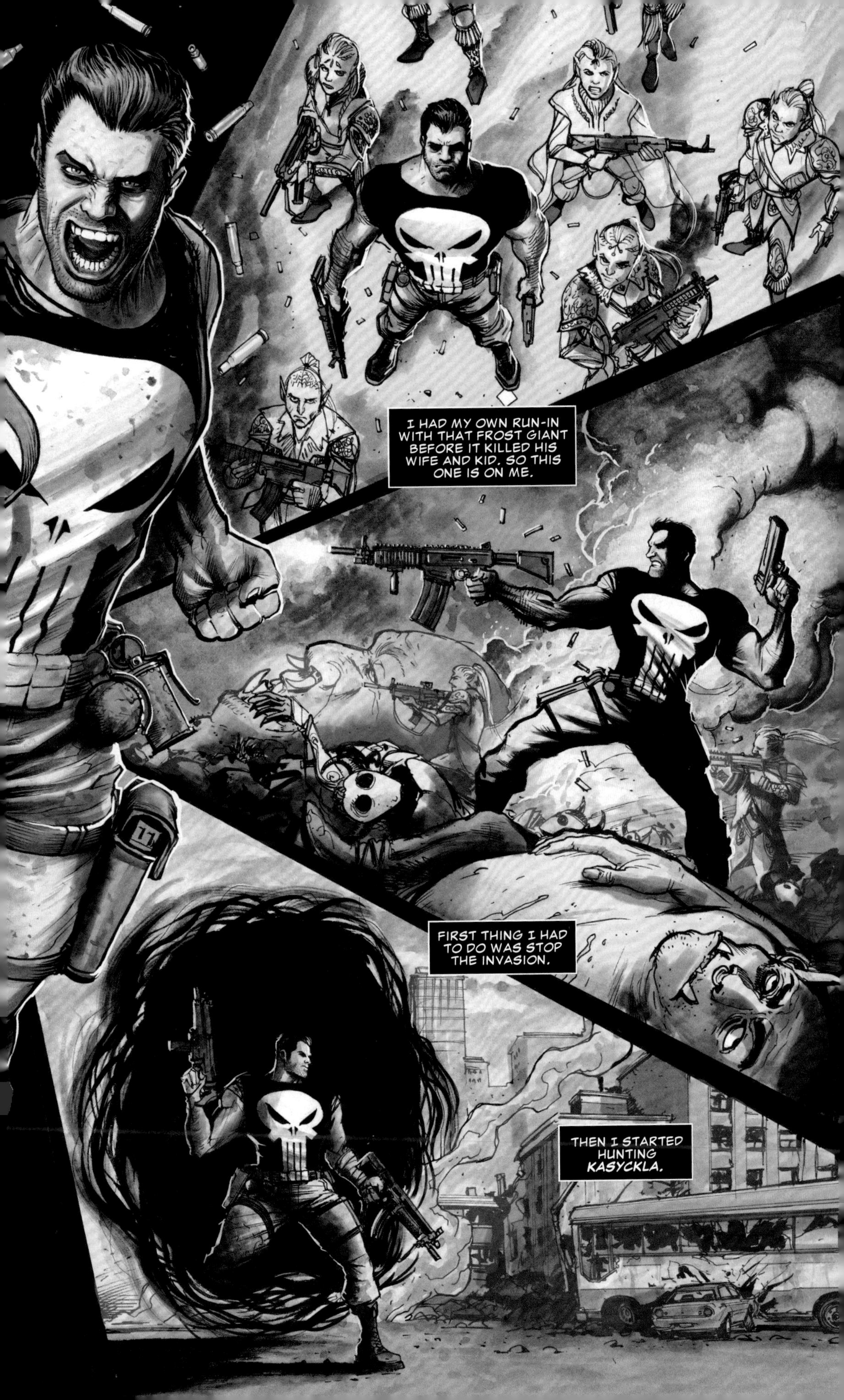
I HAD MY OWN RUN-IN WITH THAT FROST GIANT BEFORE IT KILLED HIS WIFE AND KID. SO THIS ONE IS ON ME.
FIRST THING I HAD TO DO WAS STOP THE INVASION.
THEN I STARTED HUNTING *KASYCKLA*.

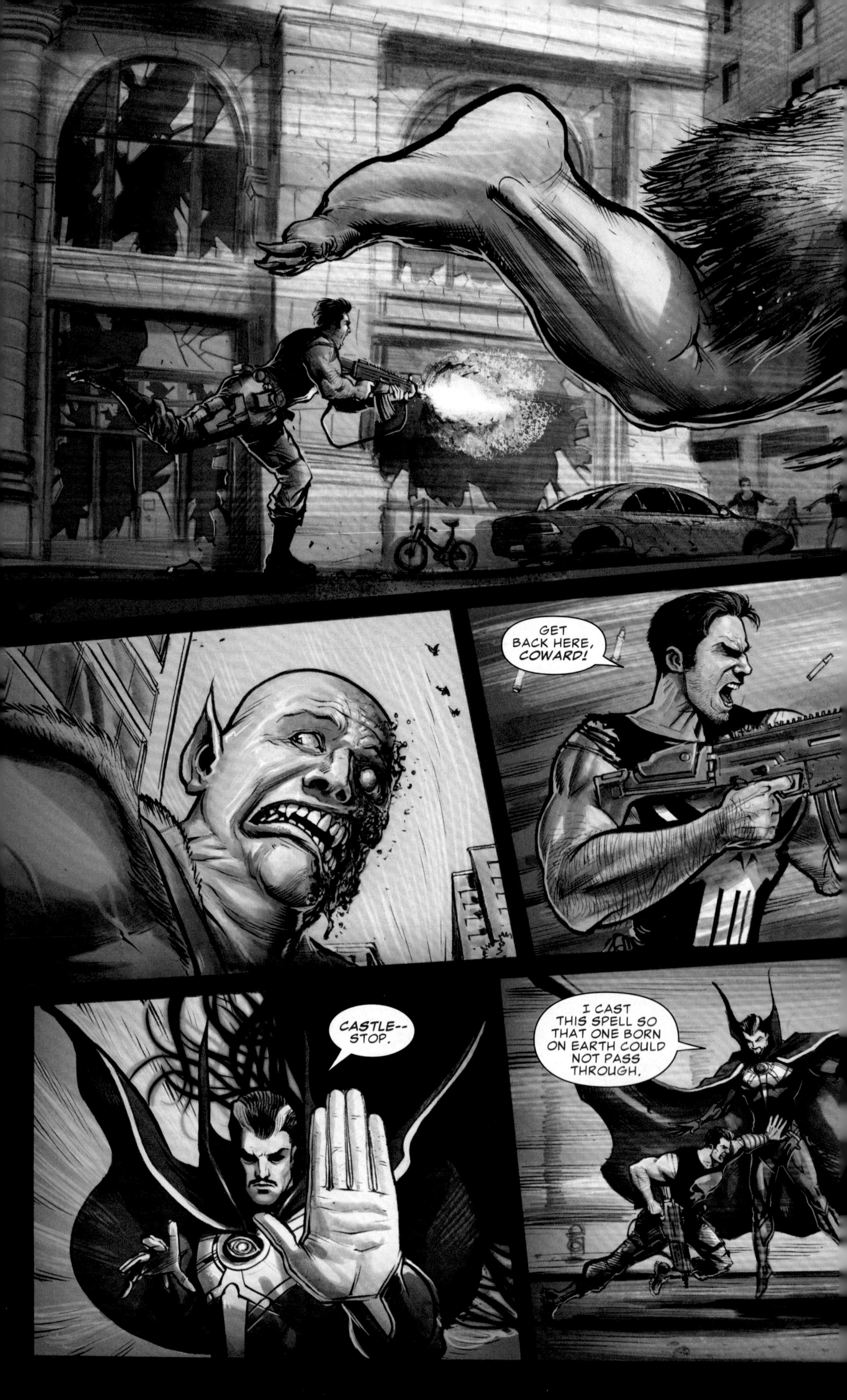
GET BACK HERE, COWARD!
CASTLE-- STOP.
I CAST THIS SPELL SO THAT ONE BORN ON EARTH COULD NOT PASS THROUGH.

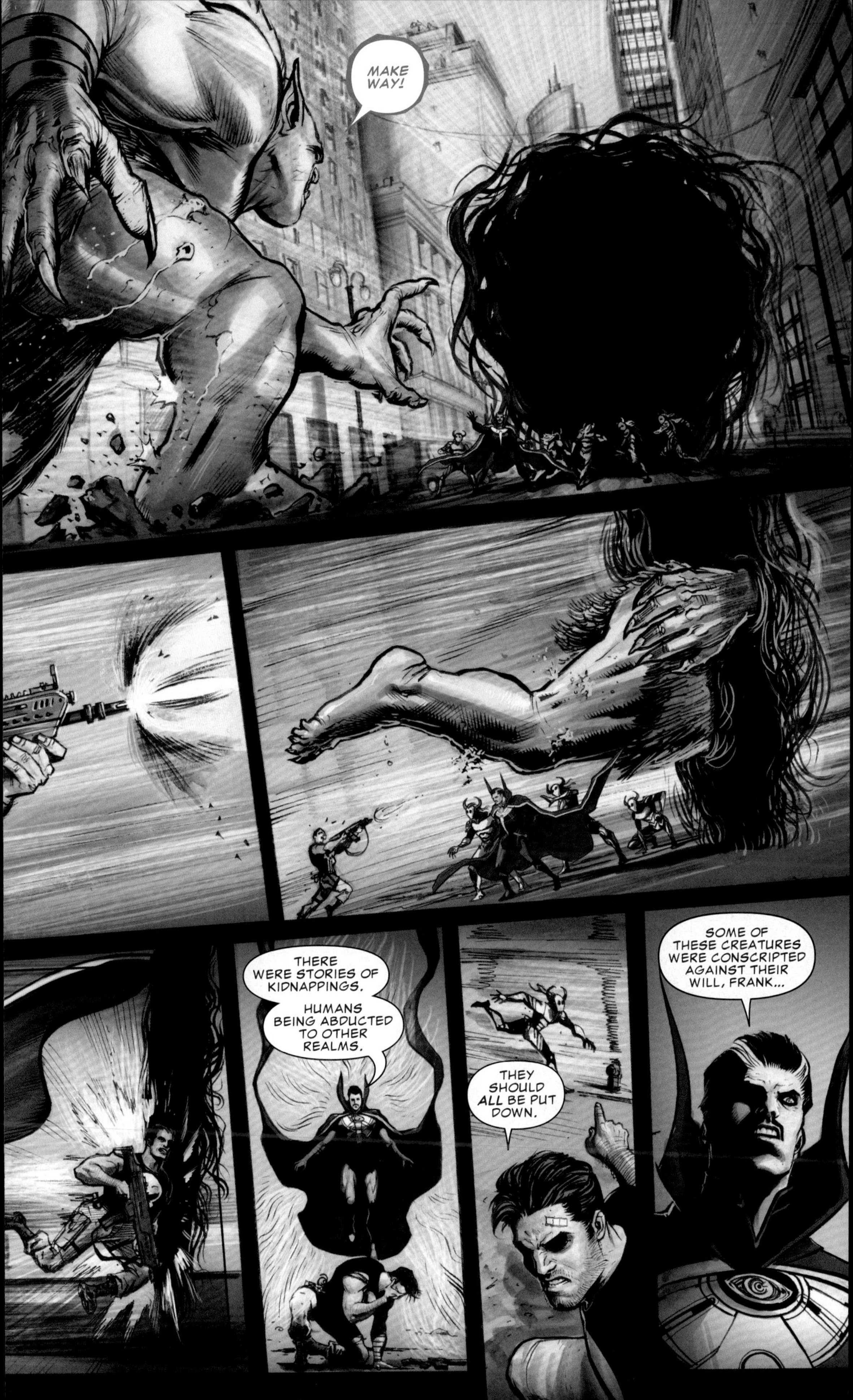
MAKE WAY!
THERE WERE STORIES OF KIDNAPPINGS.
HUMANS BEING ABDUCTED TO OTHER REALMS.
THEY SHOULD ALL BE PUT DOWN.
SOME OF THESE CREATURES WERE CONSCRIPTED AGAINST THEIR WILL, FRANK...

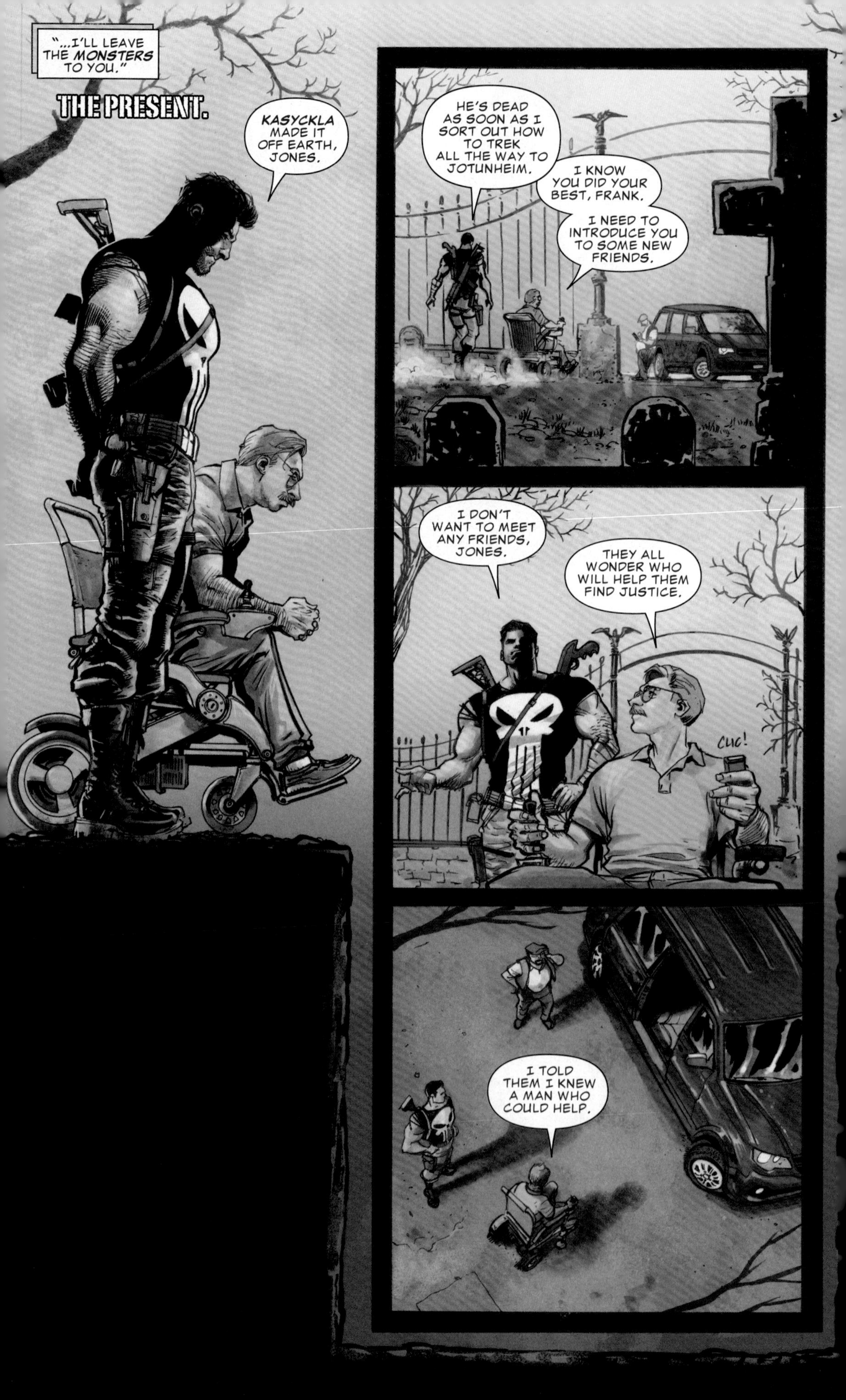
"...I'LL LEAVE THE MONSTERS TO YOU."
THE PRESENT.
KASYCKLA MADE IT OFF EARTH, JONES.
HE'S DEAD AS SOON AS I SORT OUT HOW TO TREK ALL THE WAY TO JOTUNHEIM.
I KNOW YOU DID YOUR BEST, FRANK.
I NEED TO INTRODUCE YOU TO SOME NEW FRIENDS.
I DON'T WANT TO MEET ANY FRIENDS, JONES.
THEY ALL WONDER WHO WILL HELP THEM FIND JUSTICE.
CLIC!
I TOLD THEM I KNEW A MAN WHO COULD HELP.

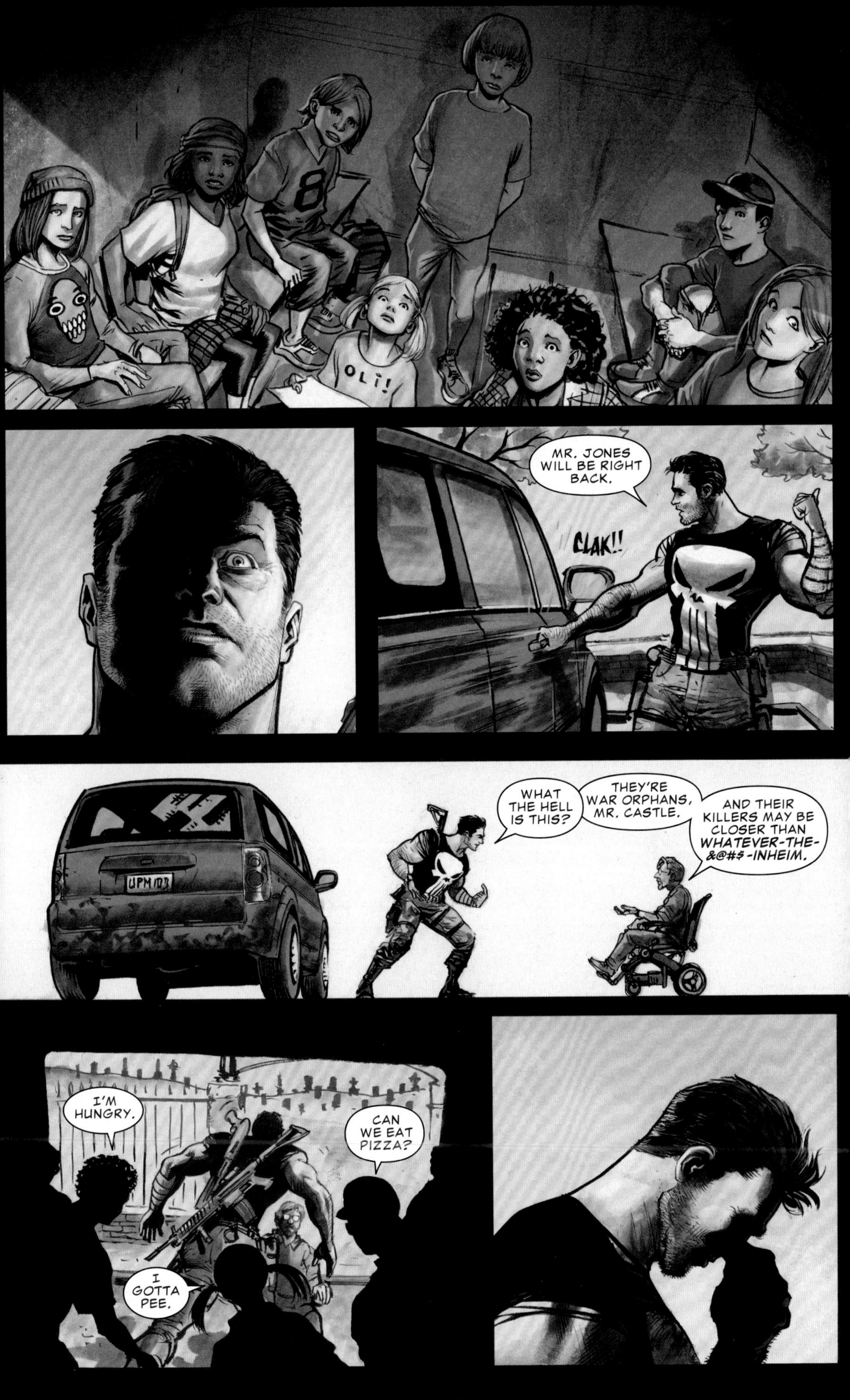
OLI!
MR. JONES WILL BE RIGHT BACK.
CLAK!!
WHAT THE HELL IS THIS?
THEY'RE WAR ORPHANS, MR. CASTLE.
AND THEIR KILLERS MAY BE CLOSER THAN WHATEVER-THE-&@#$-INHEIM.
I'M HUNGRY.
CAN WE EAT PIZZA?
I GOTTA PEE.

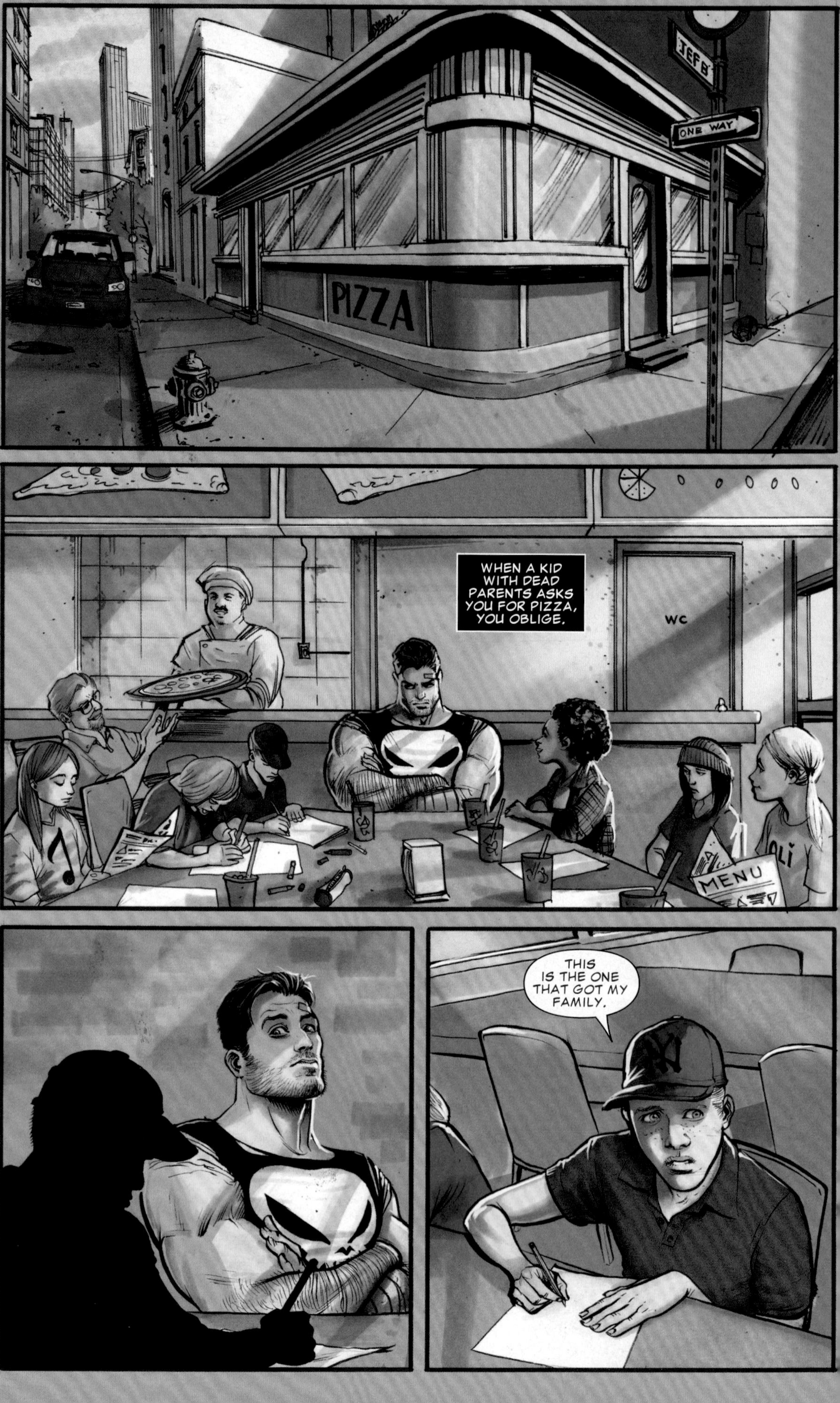
ONE WAY
PIZZA
WHEN A KID WITH DEAD PARENTS ASKS YOU FOR PIZZA, YOU OBLIGE.
WC
MENU
THIS IS THE ONE THAT GOT MY FAMILY.

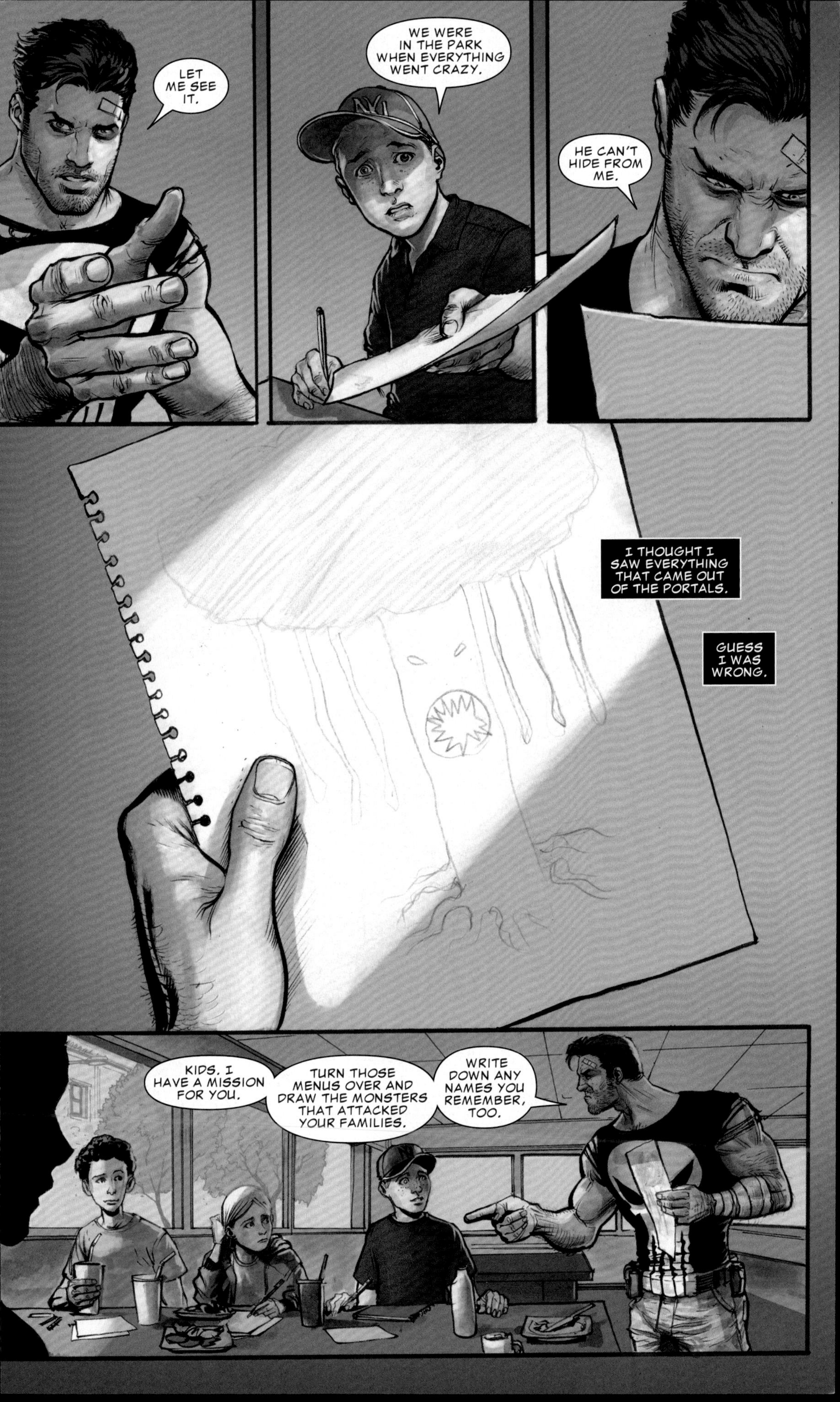
LET ME SEE IT.
WE WERE IN THE PARK WHEN EVERYTHING WENT CRAZY.
HE CAN'T HIDE FROM ME.
I THOUGHT I SAW EVERYTHING THAT CAME OUT OF THE PORTALS.
GUESS I WAS WRONG.
KIDS. I HAVE A MISSION FOR YOU.
TURN THOSE MENUS OVER AND DRAW THE MONSTERS THAT ATTACKED YOUR FAMILIES.
WRITE DOWN ANY NAMES YOU REMEMBER, TOO.

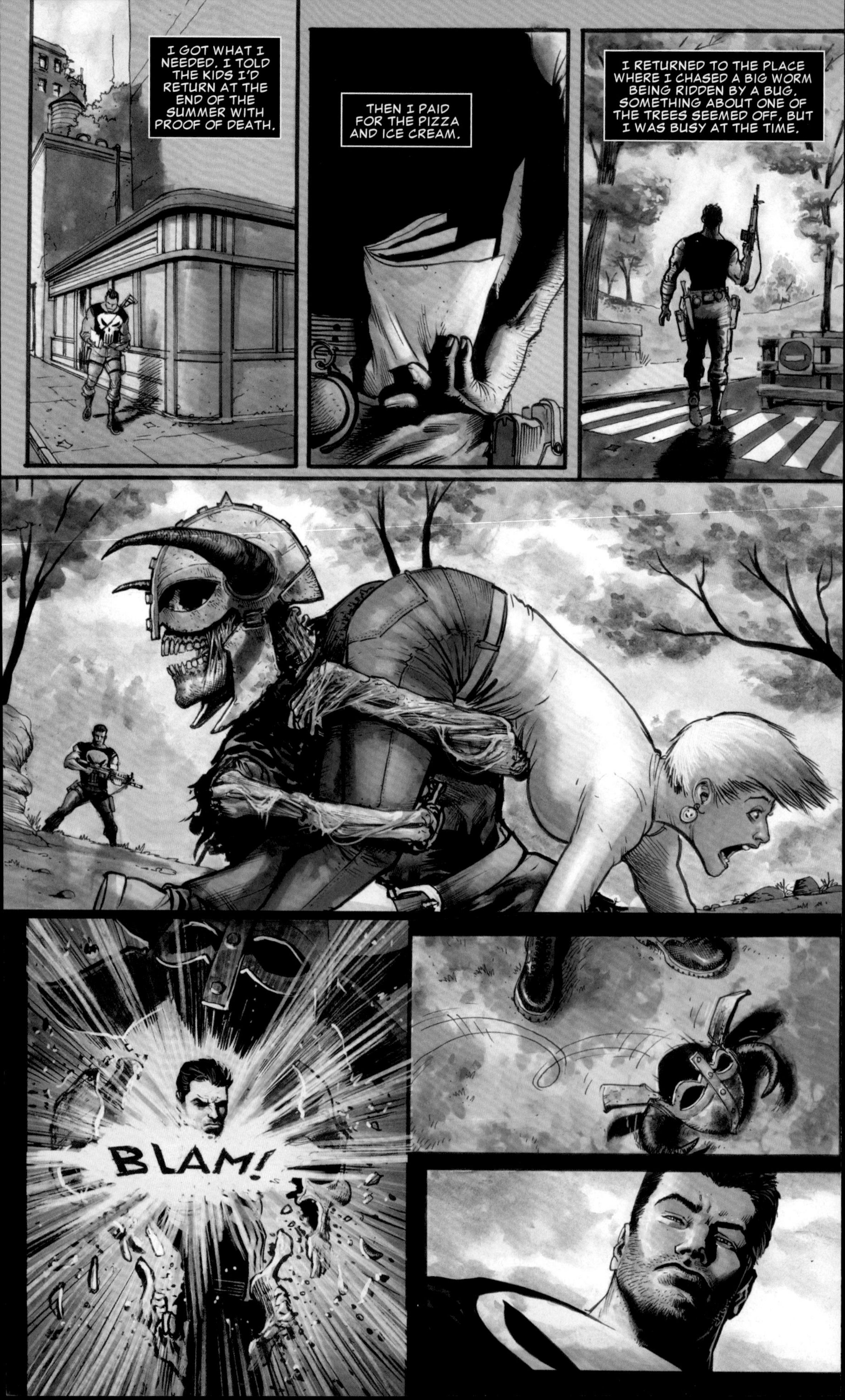
I GOT WHAT I NEEDED. I TOLD THE KIDS I'D RETURN AT THE END OF THE SUMMER WITH PROOF OF DEATH.
THEN I PAID FOR THE PIZZA AND ICE CREAM.
I RETURNED TO THE PLACE WHERE I CHASED A BIG WORM BEING RIDDEN BY A BUG. SOMETHING ABOUT ONE OF THE TREES SEEMED OFF, BUT I WAS BUSY AT THE TIME.
BLAM!

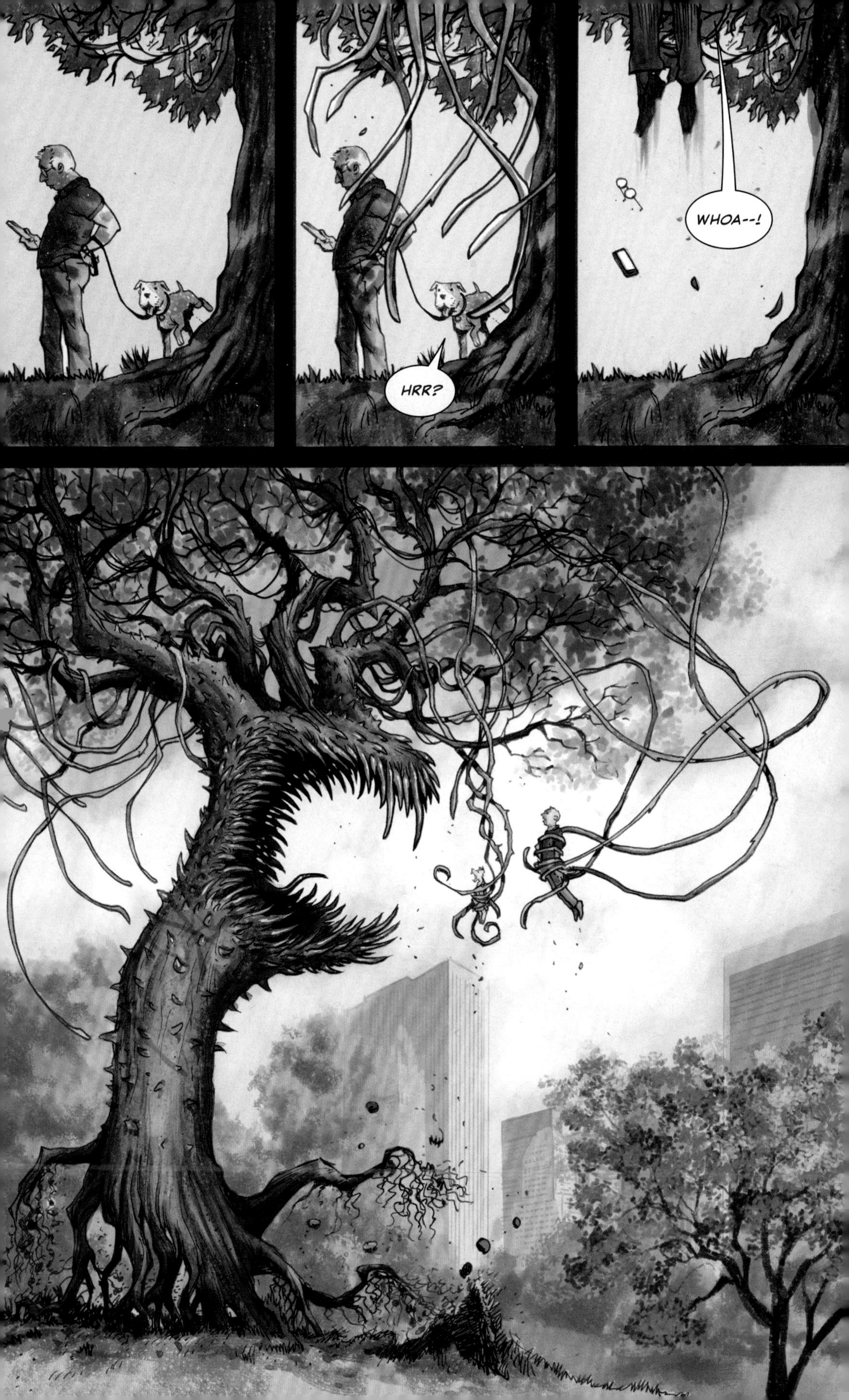
HRR?
WHOA--!

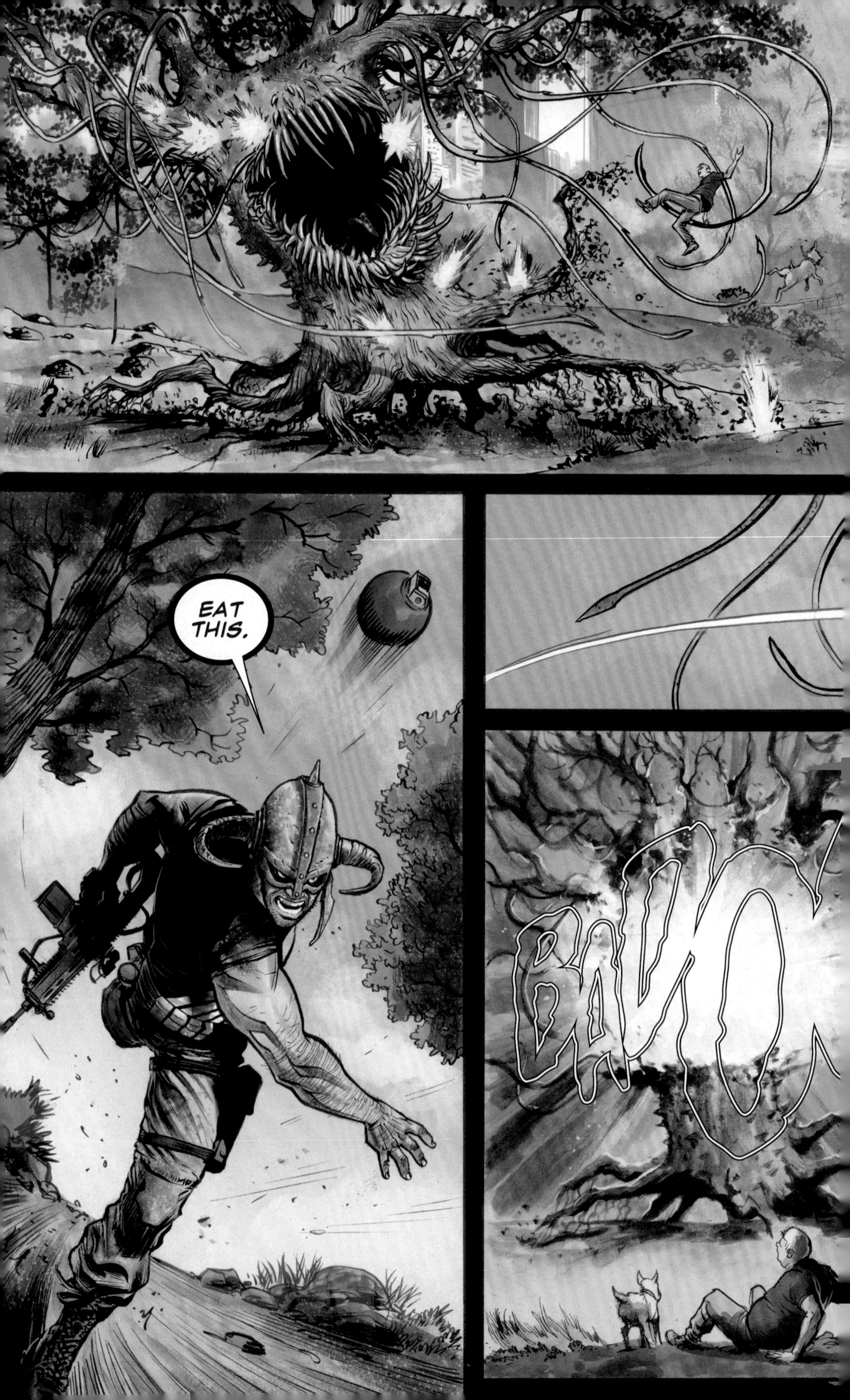
EAT THIS.
BOOM

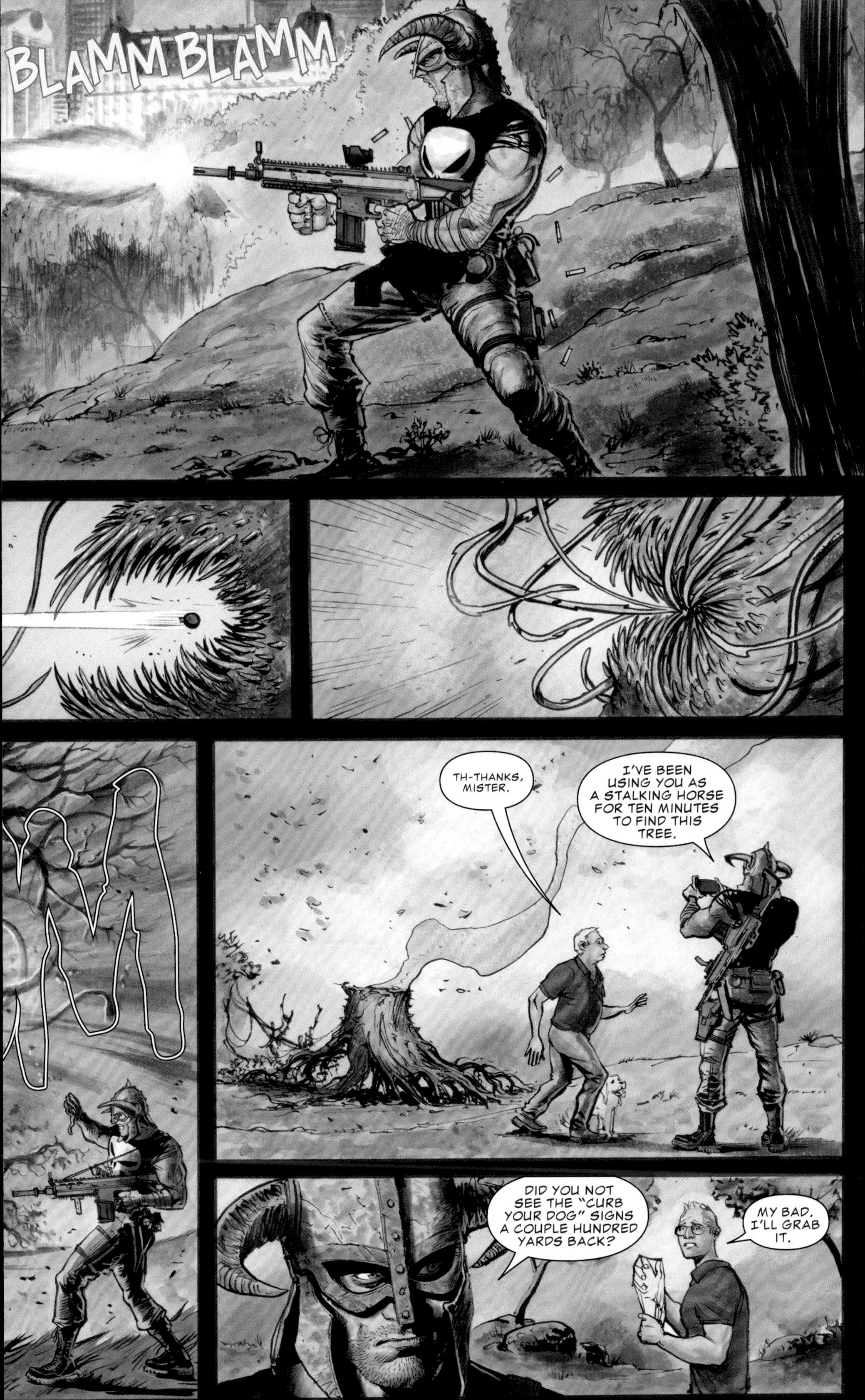
BLAMM BLAMM
M
TH-THANKS, MISTER.
I'VE BEEN USING YOU AS A STALKING HORSE FOR TEN MINUTES TO FIND THIS TREE.
DID YOU NOT SEE THE "CURB YOUR DOG" SIGNS A COUPLE HUNDRED YARDS BACK?
MY BAD. I'LL GRAB IT.

SANCTUM SANCTORUM.
GREENWICH VILLAGE.

SORRY, BUT THIS IS A RED ZONE AND THERE'S A HYDRANT, SO...

I NEED YOUR HELP.

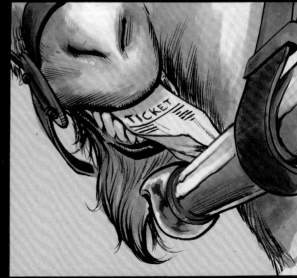

TICKET

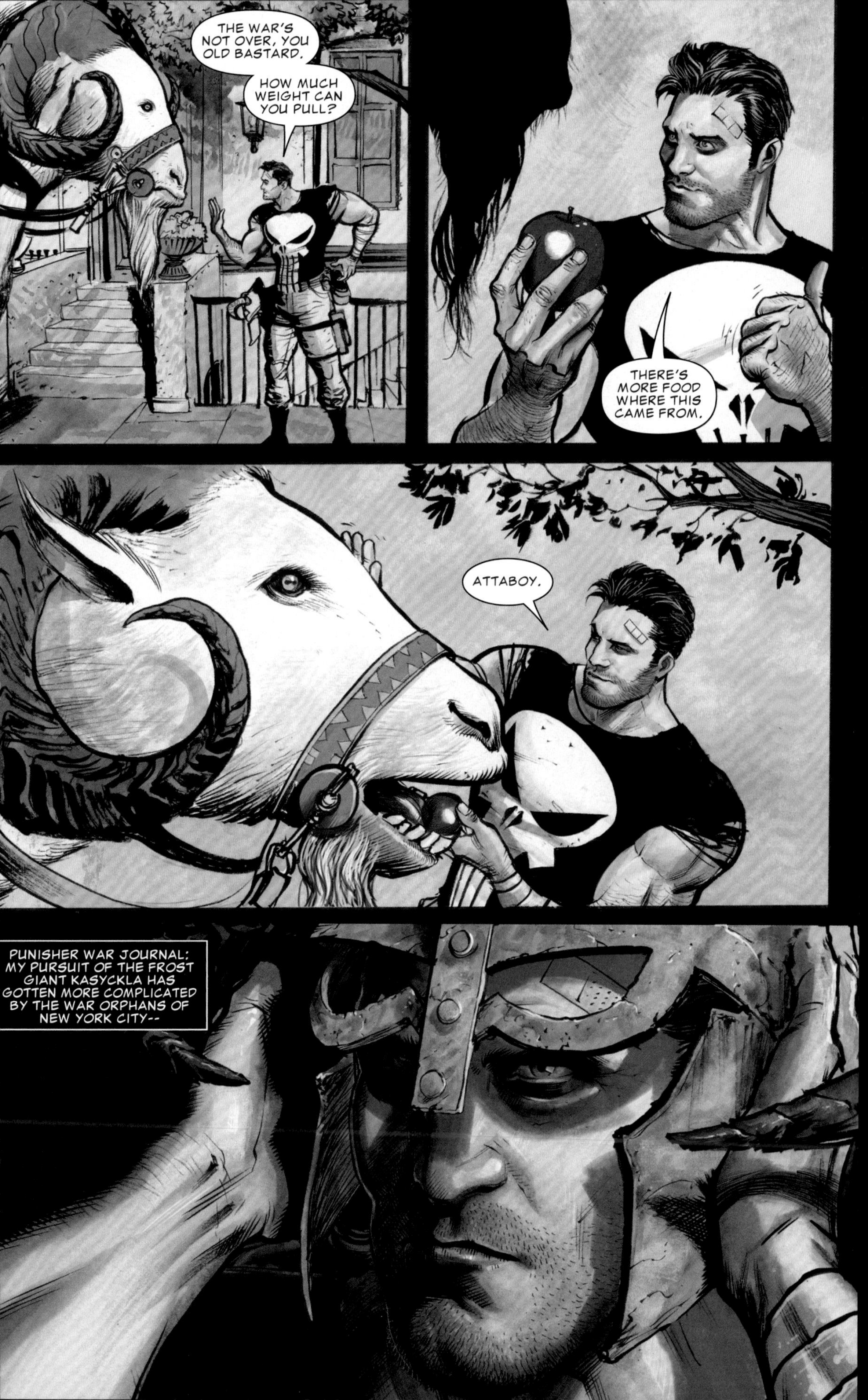
THE WAR'S NOT OVER, YOU OLD BASTARD.
HOW MUCH WEIGHT CAN YOU PULL?
THERE'S MORE FOOD WHERE THIS CAME FROM.
ATTABOY.
PUNISHER WAR JOURNAL: MY PURSUIT OF THE FROST GIANT KASYCKLA HAS GOTTEN MORE COMPLICATED BY THE WAR ORPHANS OF NEW YORK CITY--

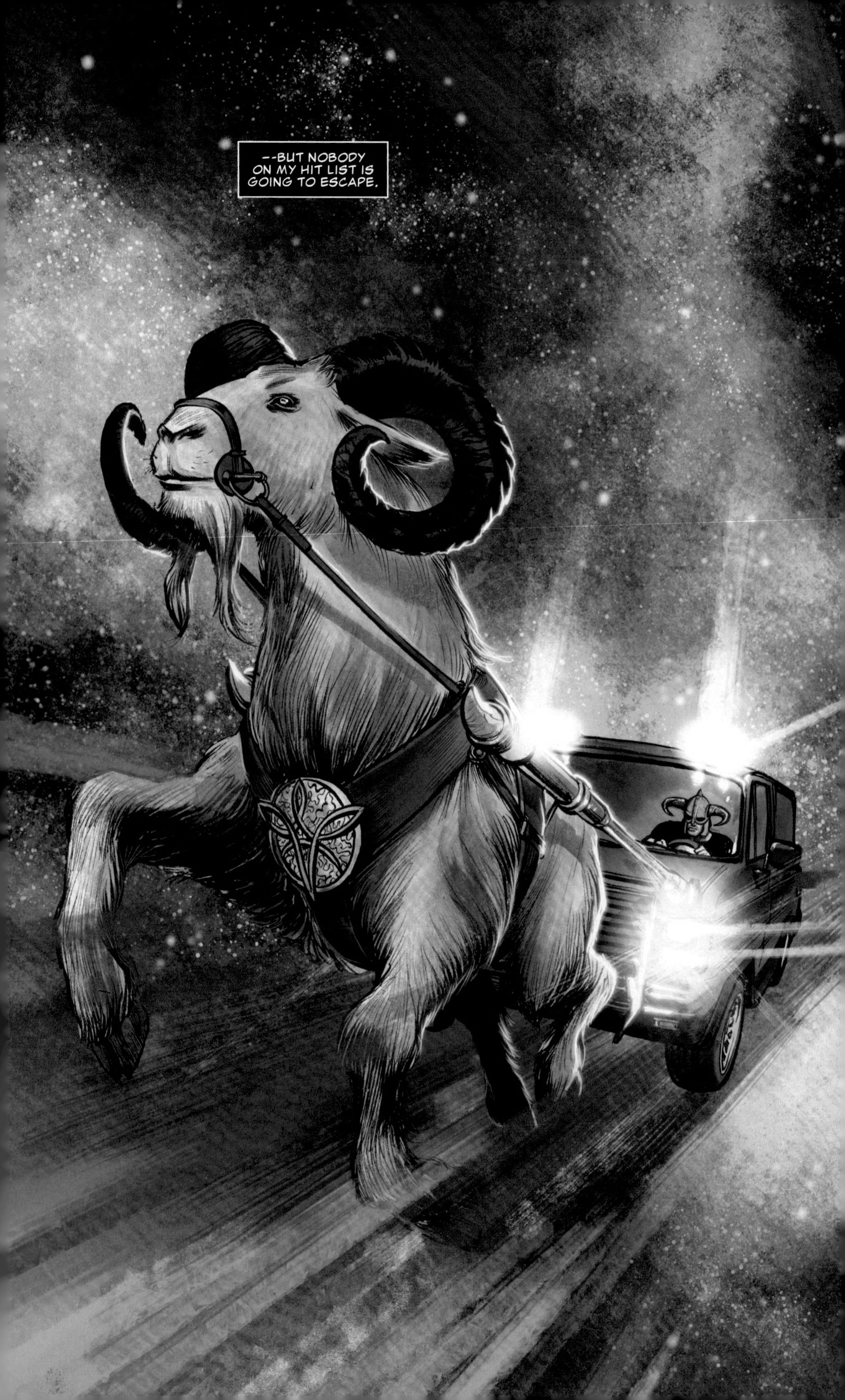
--BUT NOBODY ON MY HIT LIST IS GOING TO ESCAPE.

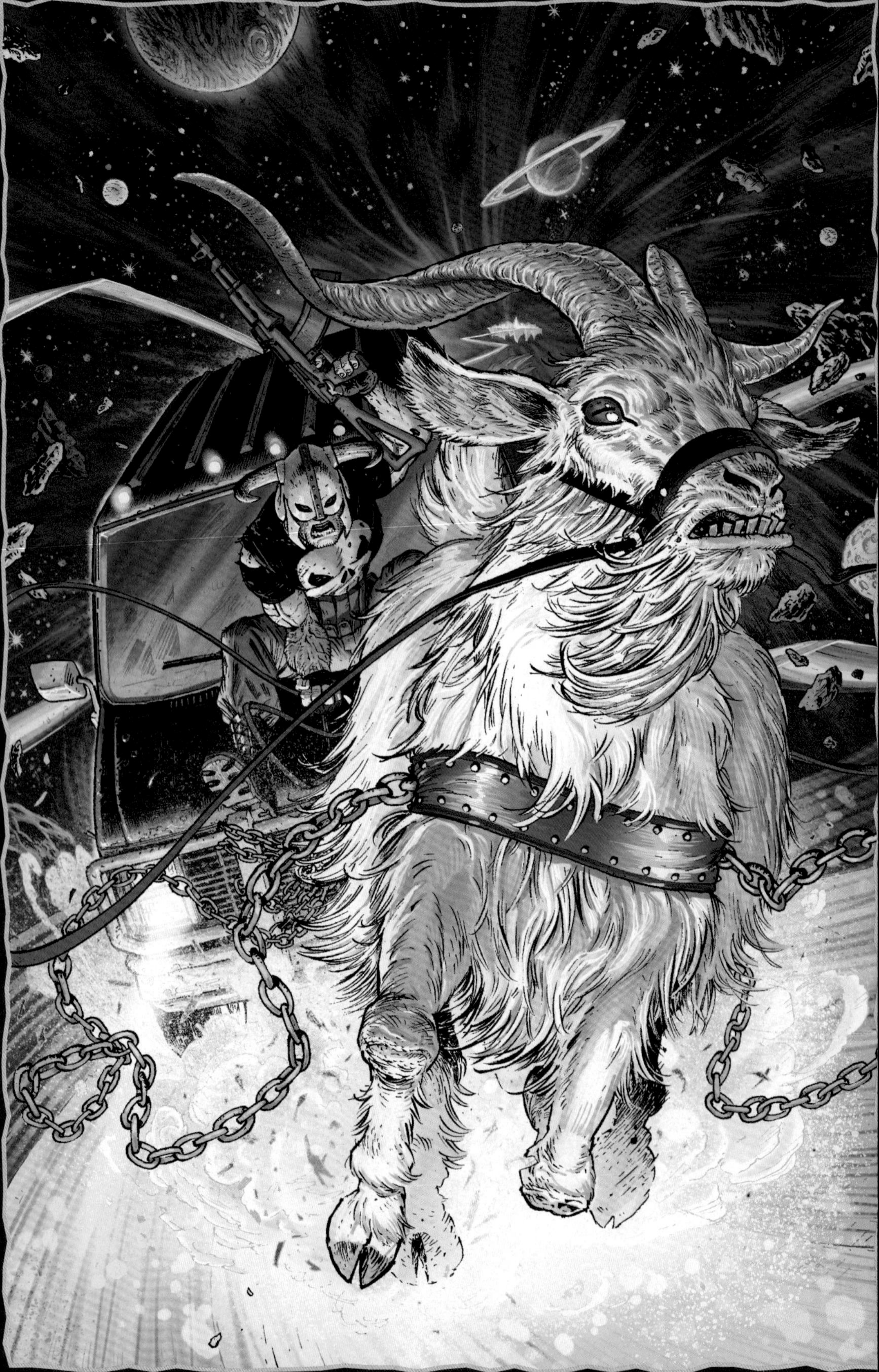

TWO

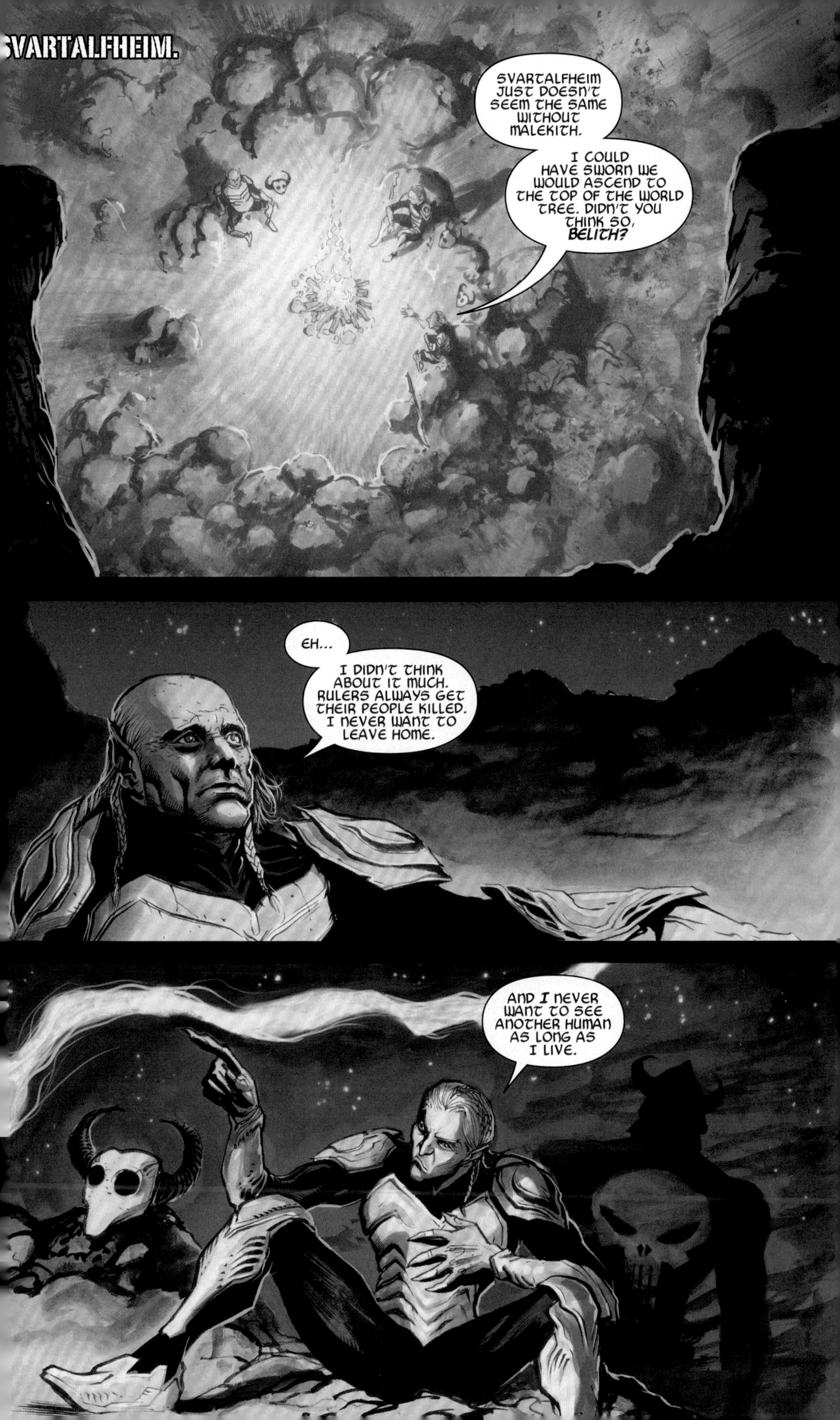
SVARTALFHEIM.
SVARTALFHEIM JUST DOESN'T SEEM THE SAME WITHOUT MALEKITH.
I COULD HAVE SWORN WE WOULD ASCEND TO THE TOP OF THE WORLD TREE. DIDN'T YOU THINK SO, BELITH?
EH...
I DIDN'T THINK ABOUT IT MUCH. RULERS ALWAYS GET THEIR PEOPLE KILLED. I NEVER WANT TO LEAVE HOME.
AND I NEVER WANT TO SEE ANOTHER HUMAN AS LONG AS I LIVE.

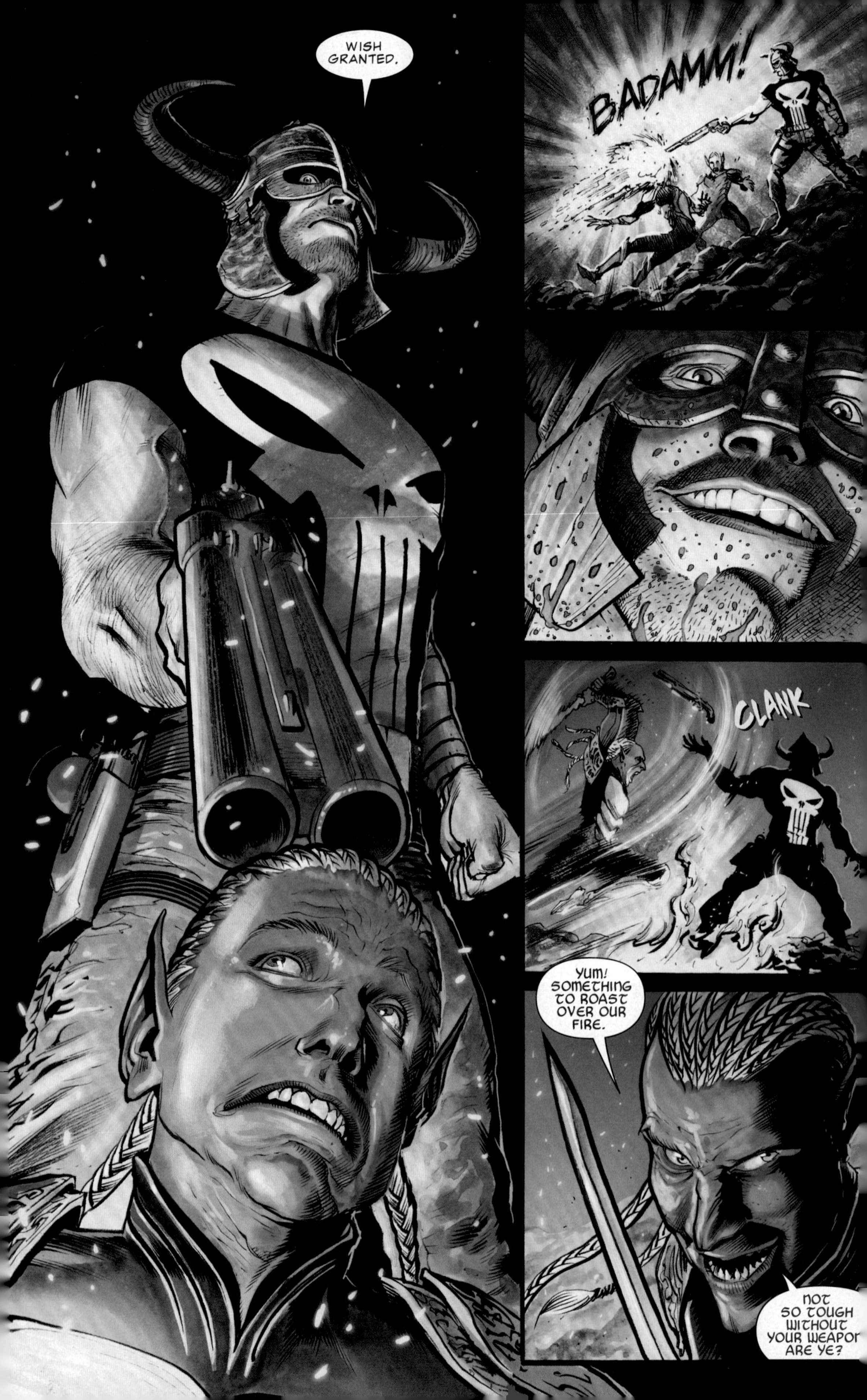
WISH GRANTED.
BADAMM!
CLANK
YUM! SOMETHING TO ROAST OVER OUR FIRE.
NOT SO TOUGH WITHOUT YOUR WEAPON ARE YE?

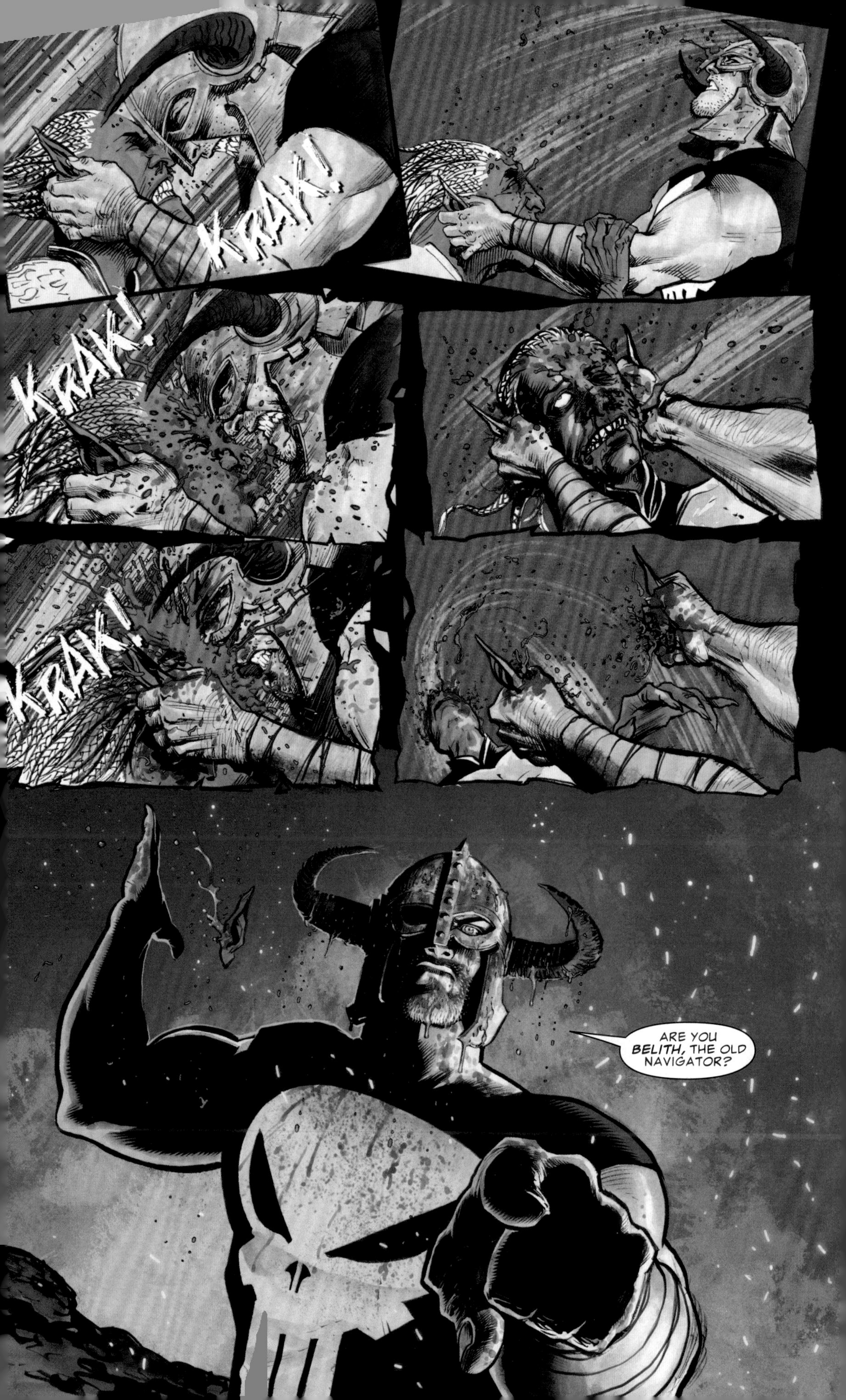
KRAK!
KRAK!
KRAK!
ARE YOU BELITH, THE OLD NAVIGATOR?

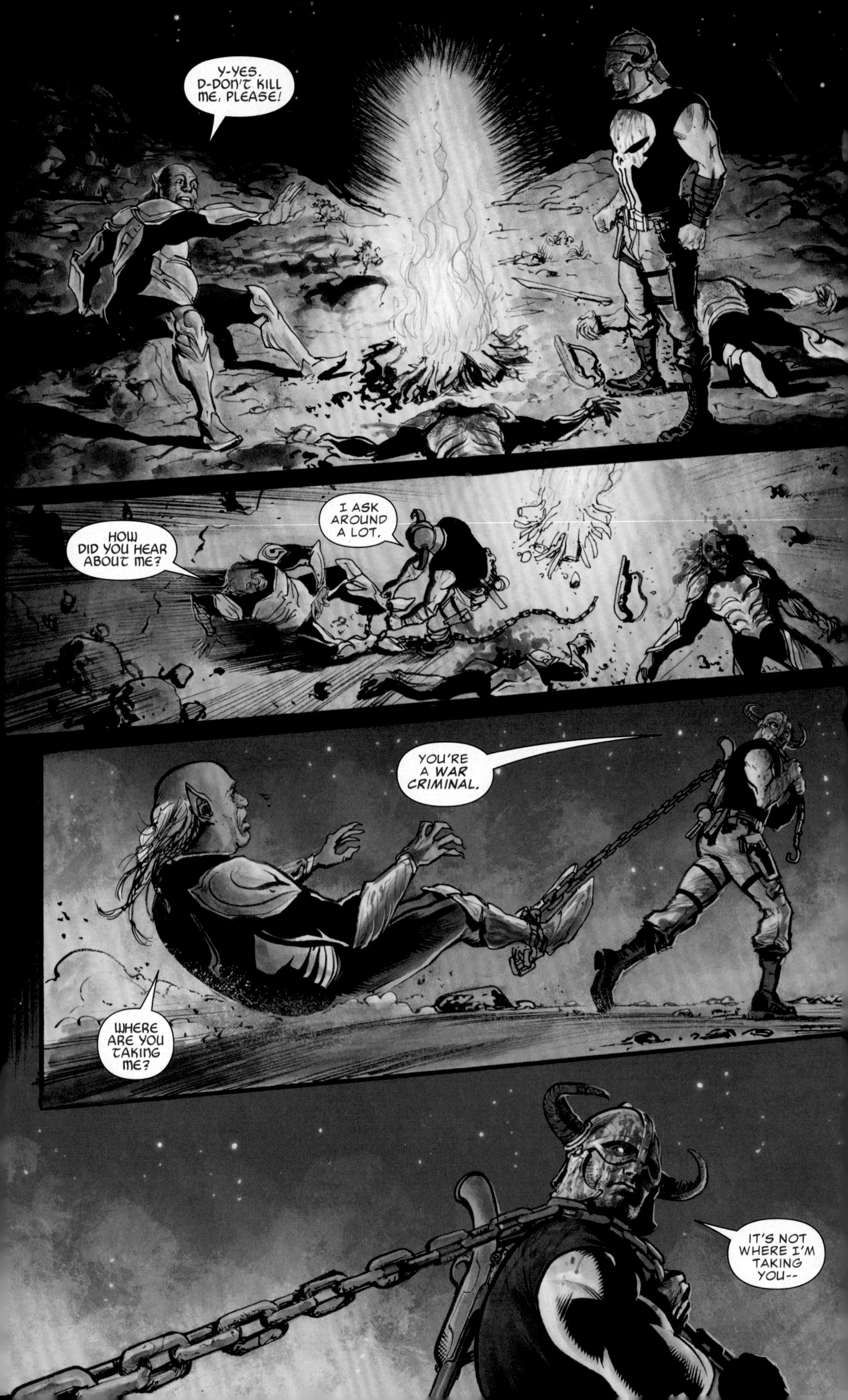
Y-YES. D-DON'T KILL ME, PLEASE!
HOW DID YOU HEAR ABOUT ME?
I ASK AROUND A LOT.
YOU'RE A WAR CRIMINAL.
WHERE ARE YOU TAKING ME?
IT'S NOT WHERE I'M TAKING YOU--

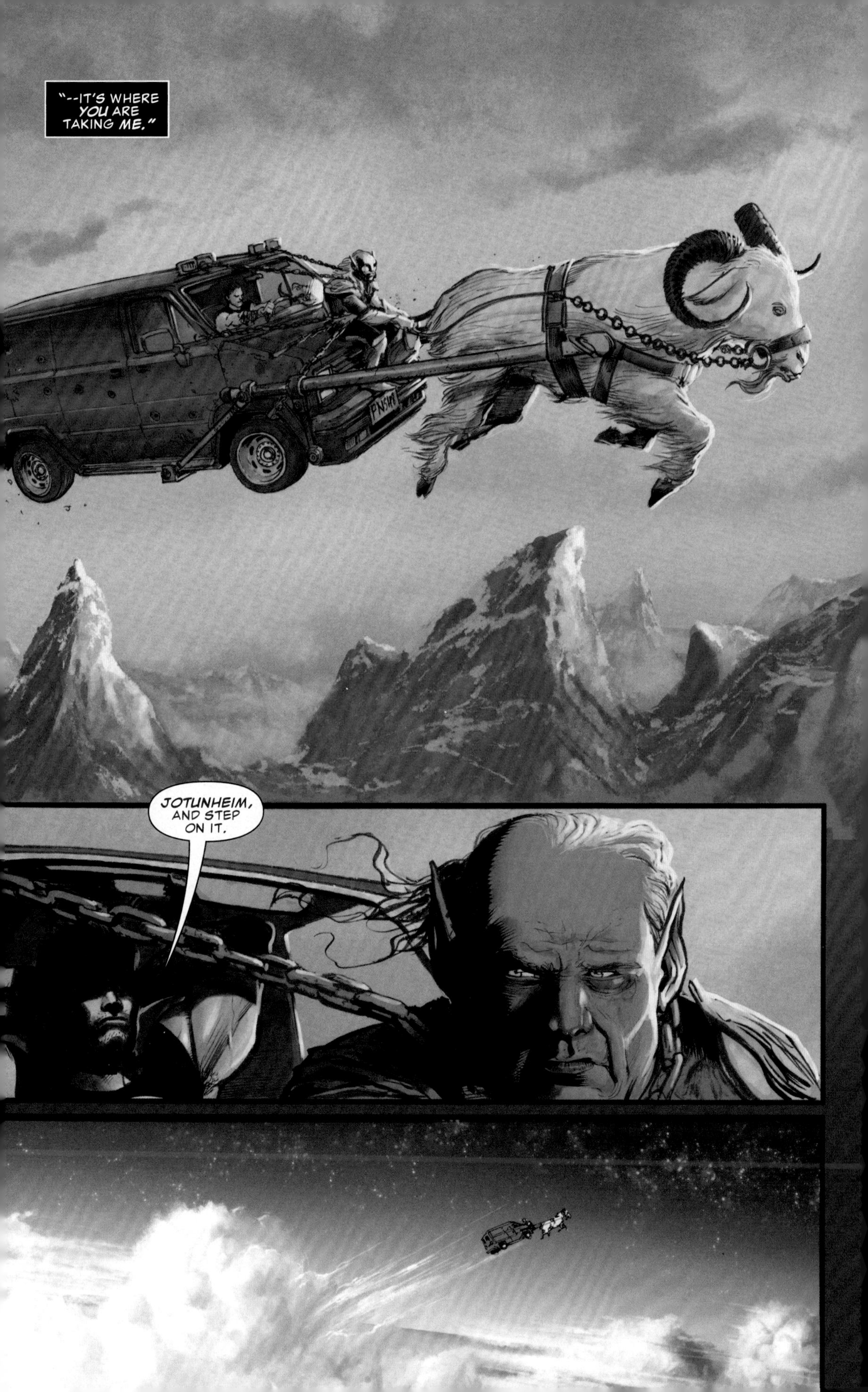
"--IT'S WHERE YOU ARE TAKING ME."
JOTUNHEIM, AND STEP ON IT.

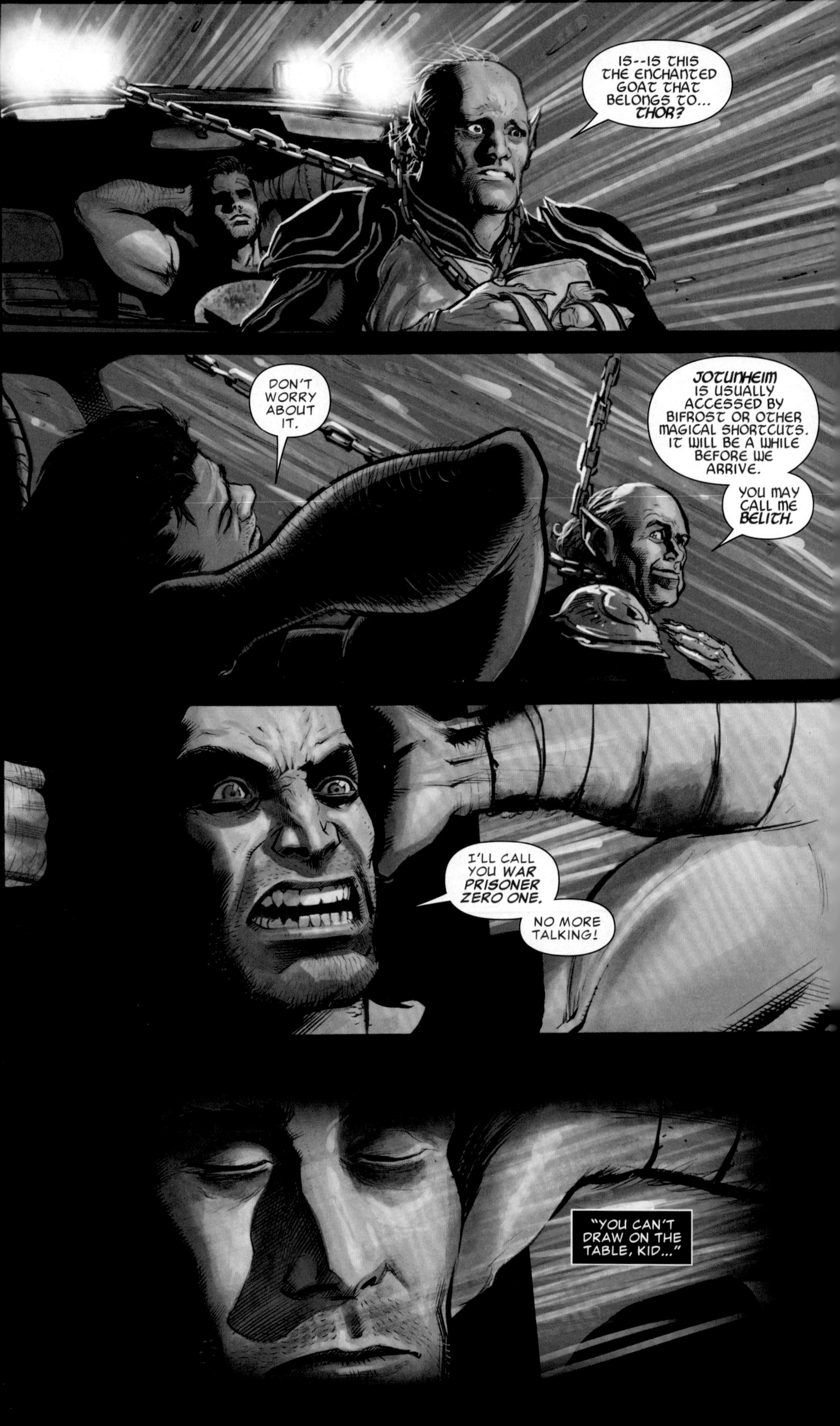
IS--IS THIS THE ENCHANTED GOAT THAT BELONGS TO... THOR?
DON'T WORRY ABOUT IT.
JOTUNHEIM IS USUALLY ACCESSED BY BIFROST OR OTHER MAGICAL SHORTCUTS. IT WILL BE A WHILE BEFORE WE ARRIVE.
YOU MAY CALL ME BELITH.
I'LL CALL YOU WAR PRISONER ZERO ONE.
NO MORE TALKING!
"YOU CAN'T DRAW ON THE TABLE, KID..."

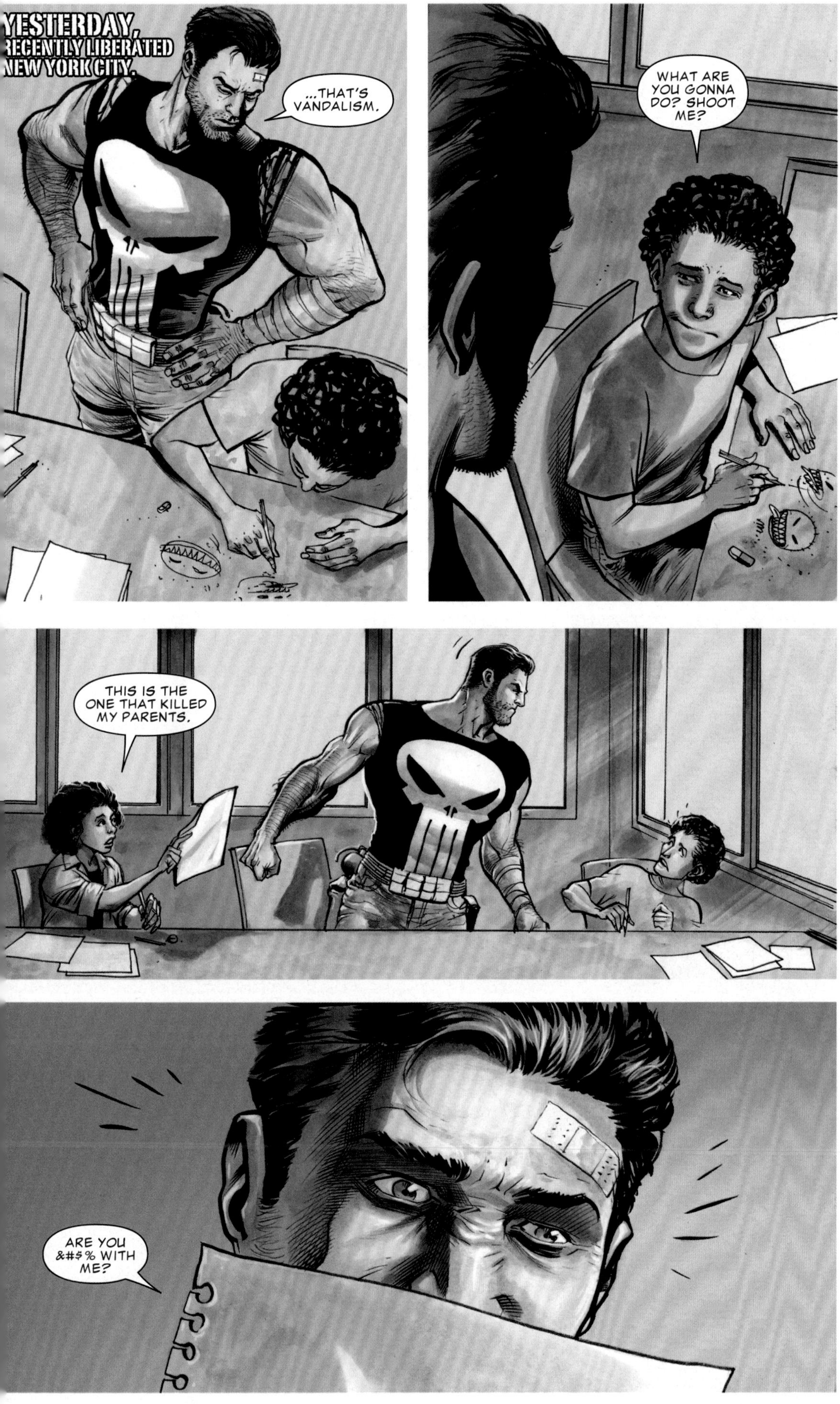
YESTERDAY,
RECENTLY LIBERATED
NEW YORK CITY.
...THAT'S VANDALISM.
WHAT ARE YOU GONNA DO? SHOOT ME?
THIS IS THE ONE THAT KILLED MY PARENTS.
ARE YOU &#$% WITH ME?

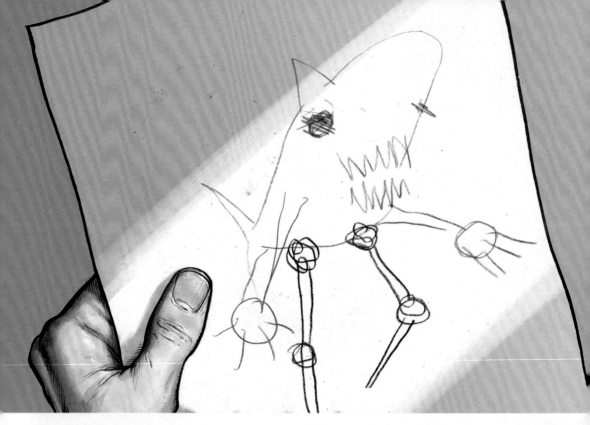

NO. IT SAID IT WAS MADE BY SCIENCE FOR WAR.

FINE. I'LL COME BACK TO EARTH WITH PROOF OF DEATH.

IN THE MEANTIME, I PAID FOR EVERYONE TO HAVE ICE CREAM.

MAKE SURE THAT EVERYONE WHO WANTS ICE CREAM GETS SOME.

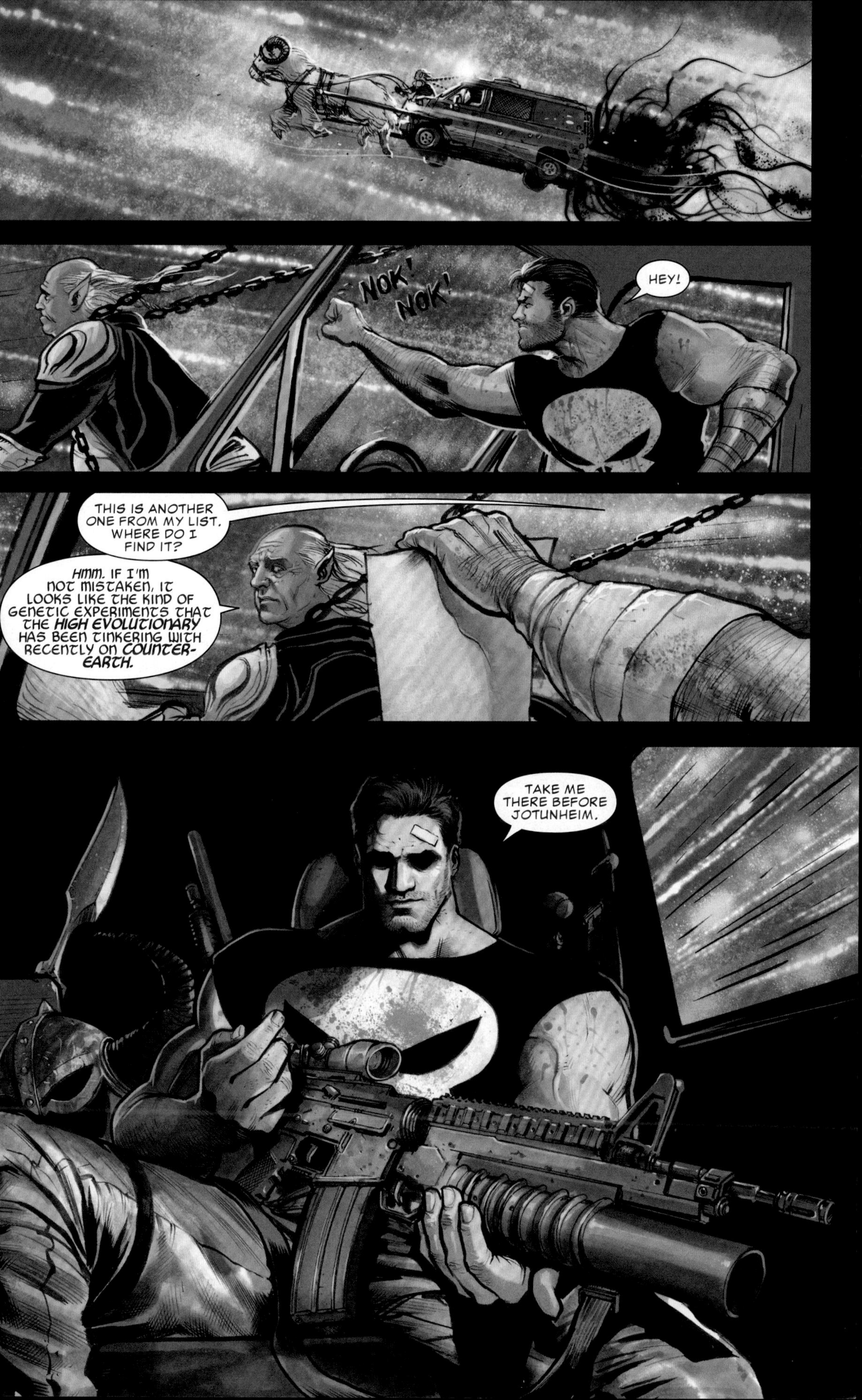
NOK! NOK!
HEY!
THIS IS ANOTHER ONE FROM MY LIST. WHERE DO I FIND IT?
HMM. IF I'M NOT MISTAKEN, IT LOOKS LIKE THE KIND OF GENETIC EXPERIMENTS THAT THE HIGH EVOLUTIONARY HAS BEEN TINKERING WITH RECENTLY ON COUNTER-EARTH.
TAKE ME THERE BEFORE JOTUNHEIM.

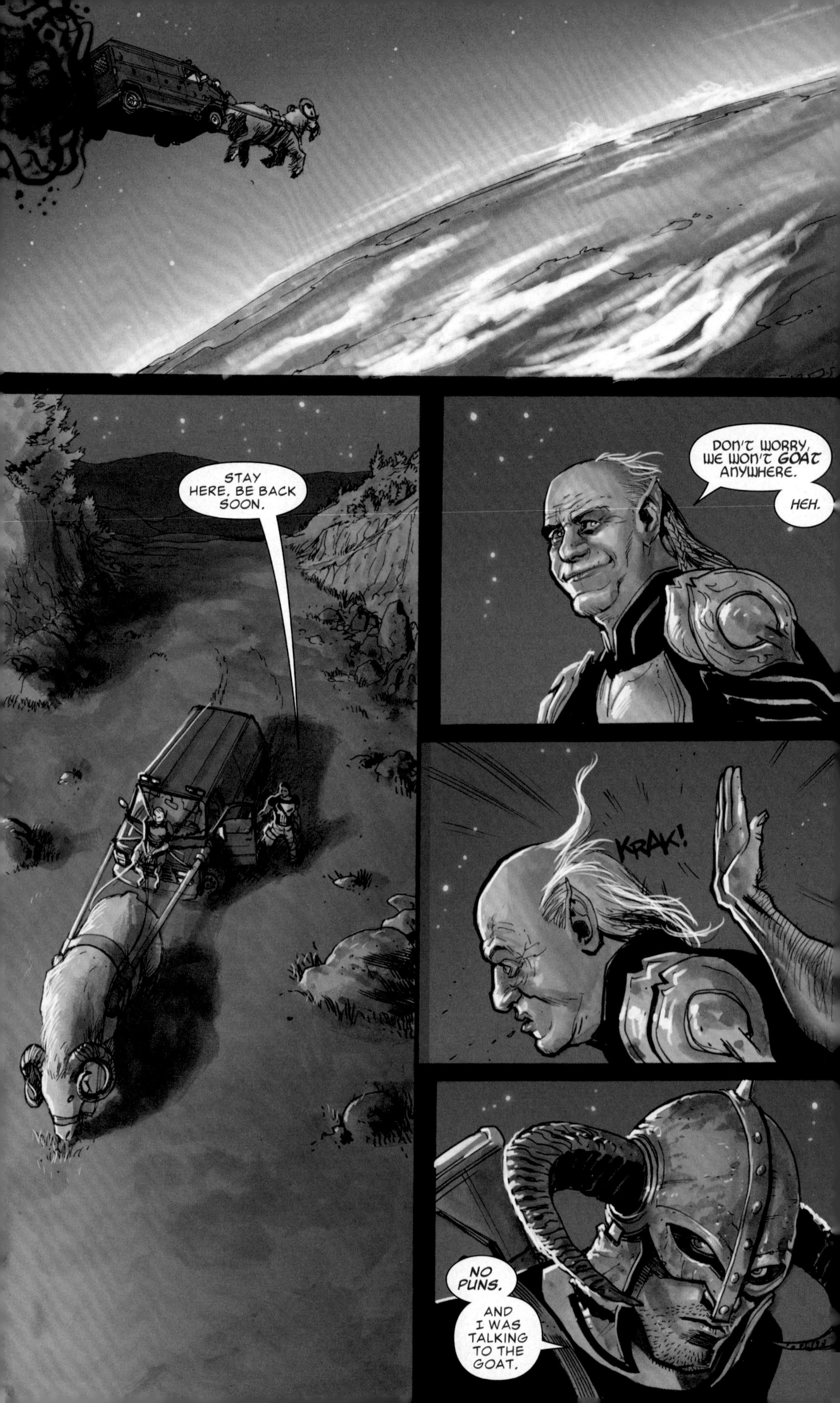
STAY HERE. BE BACK SOON.
DON'T WORRY, WE WON'T GOAT ANYWHERE.
HEH.
KRAK!
NO PUNS.
AND I WAS TALKING TO THE GOAT.

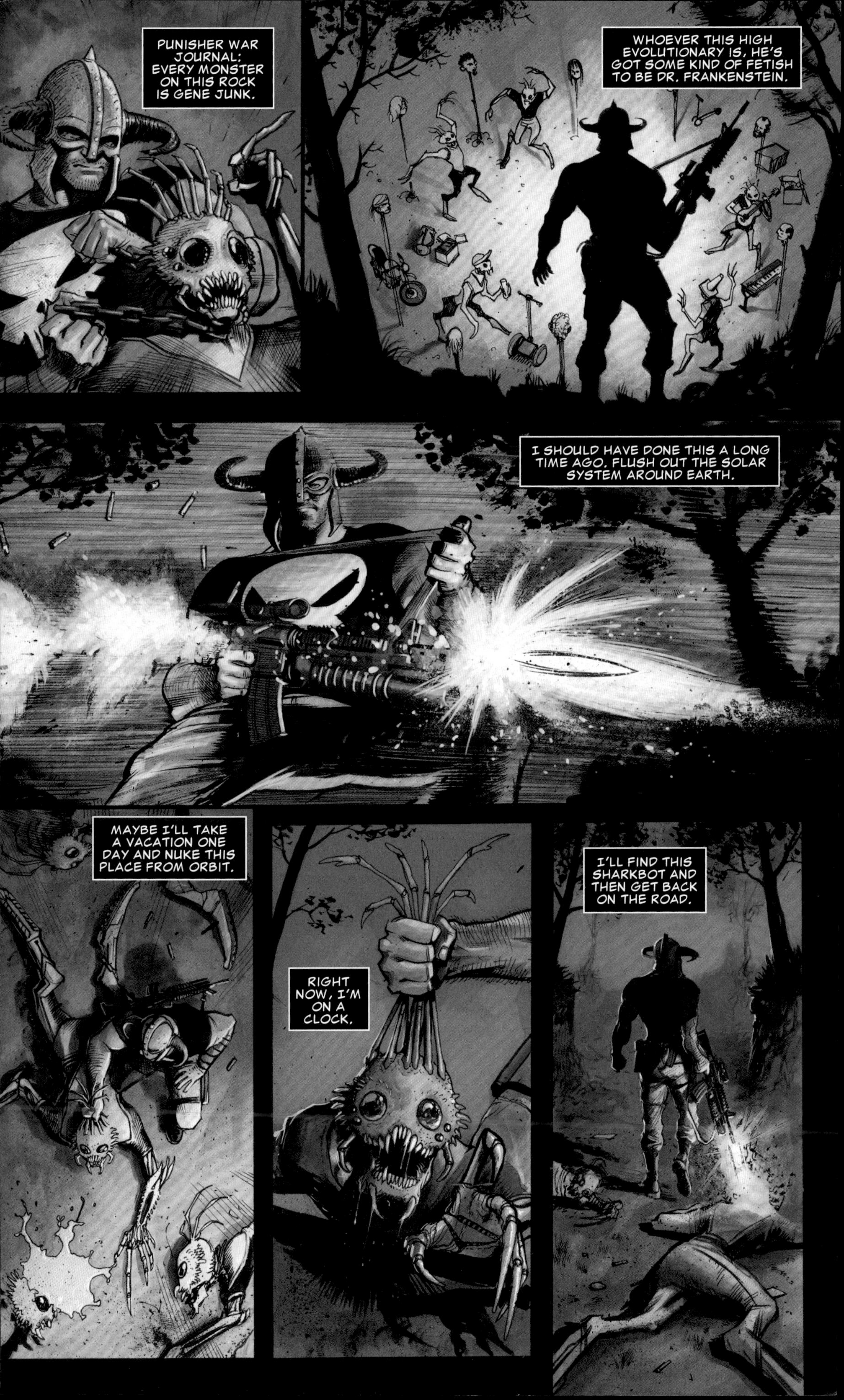
PUNISHER WAR JOURNAL: EVERY MONSTER ON THIS ROCK IS GENE JUNK.
WHOEVER THIS HIGH EVOLUTIONARY IS, HE'S GOT SOME KIND OF FETISH TO BE DR. FRANKENSTEIN.
I SHOULD HAVE DONE THIS A LONG TIME AGO. FLUSH OUT THE SOLAR SYSTEM AROUND EARTH.
MAYBE I'LL TAKE A VACATION ONE DAY AND NUKE THIS PLACE FROM ORBIT.
RIGHT NOW, I'M ON A CLOCK.
I'LL FIND THIS SHARKBOT AND THEN GET BACK ON THE ROAD.

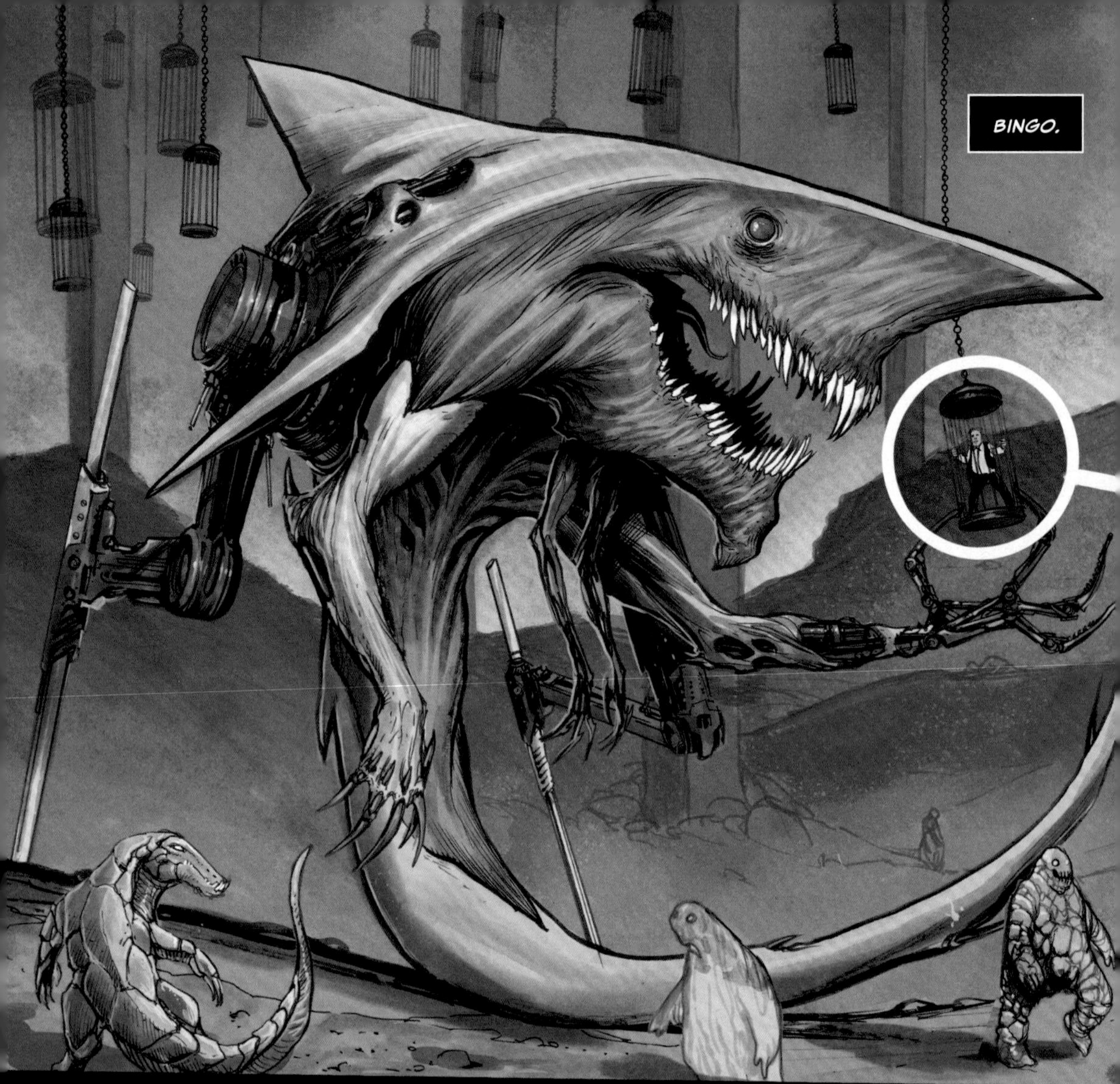
BINGO.
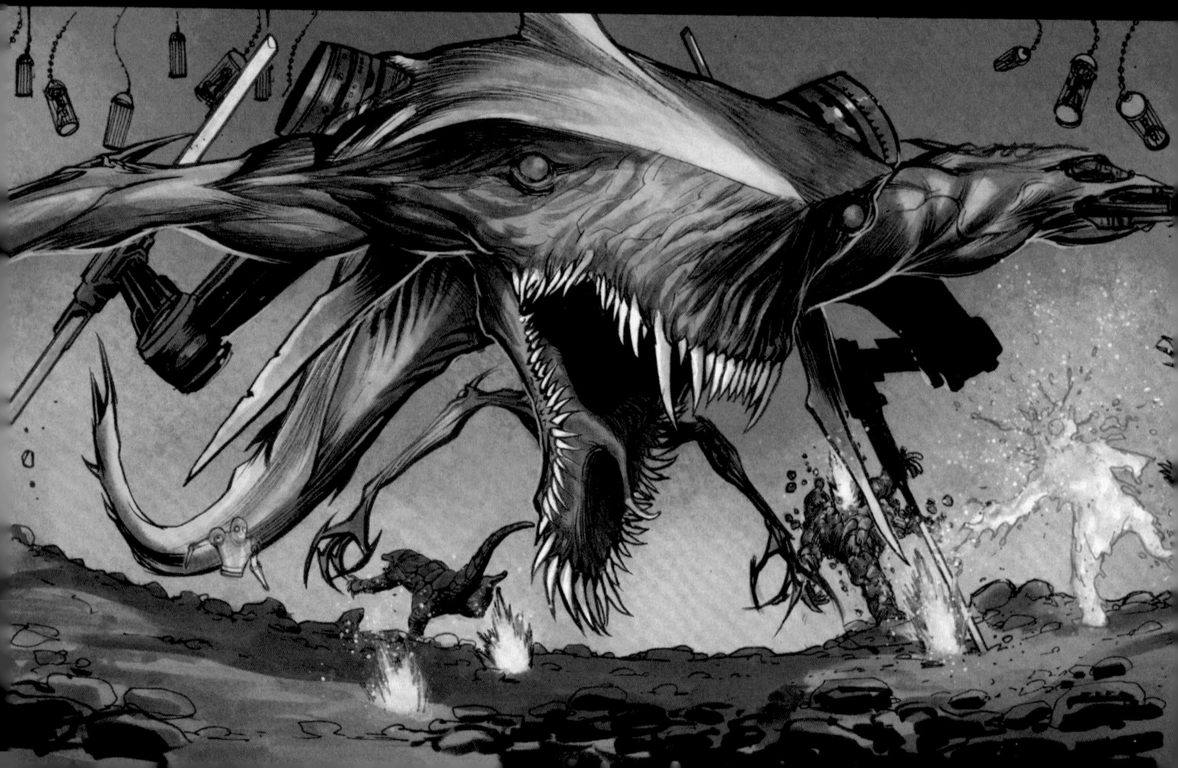

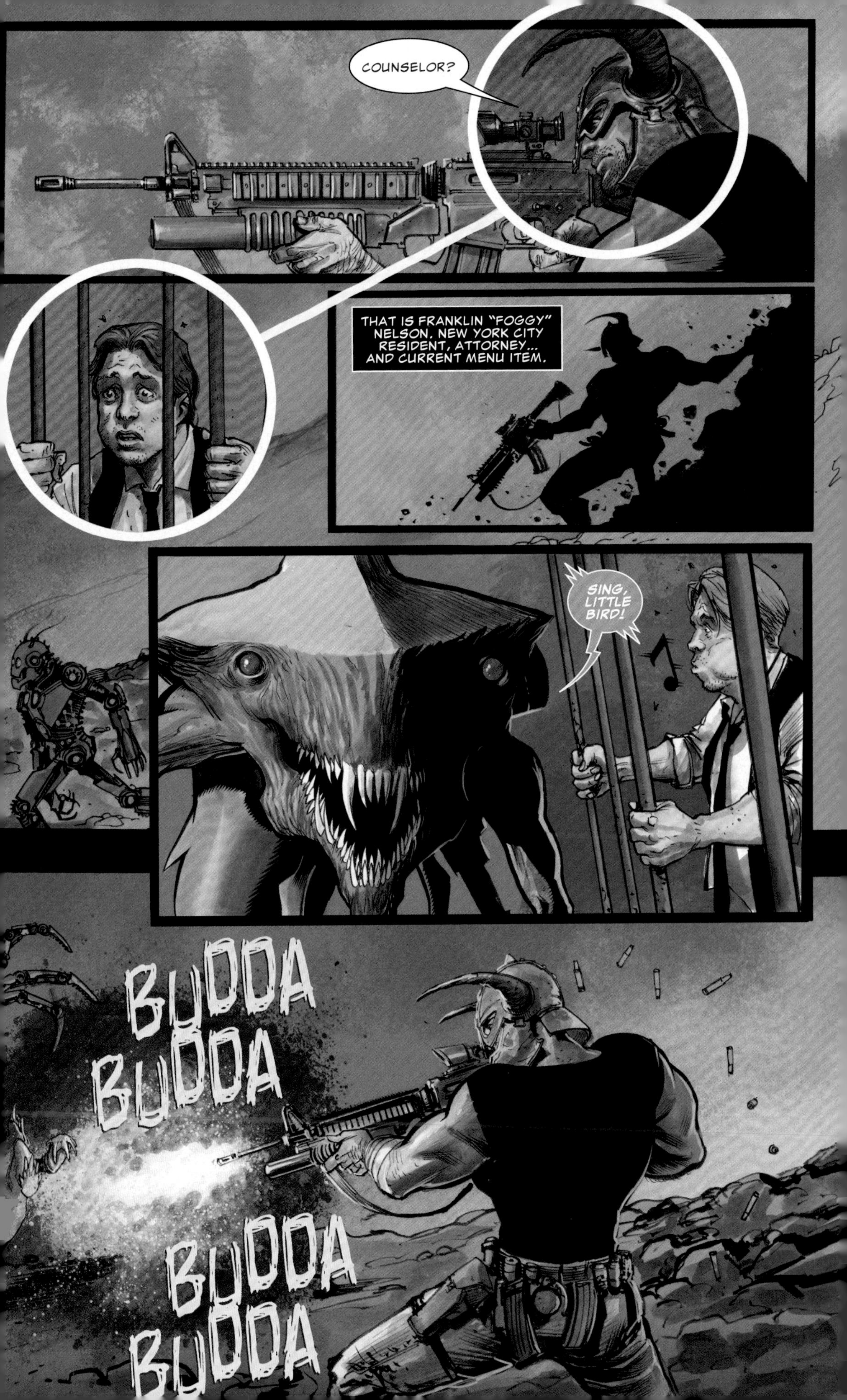
COUNSELOR?
THAT IS FRANKLIN "FOGGY" NELSON. NEW YORK CITY RESIDENT, ATTORNEY... AND CURRENT MENU ITEM.
SING, LITTLE BIRD!
BUDDA BUDDA
BUDDA BUDDA

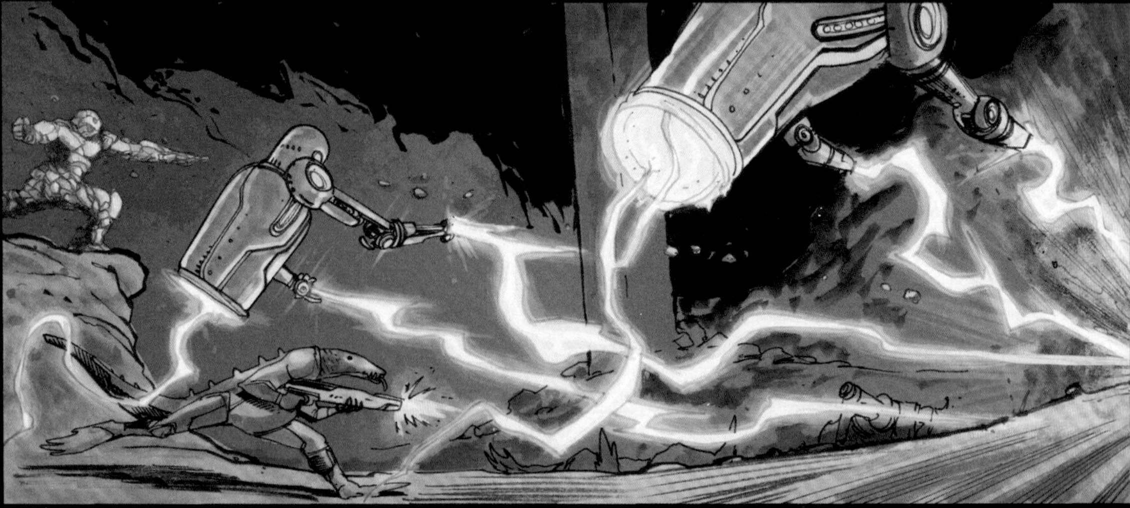

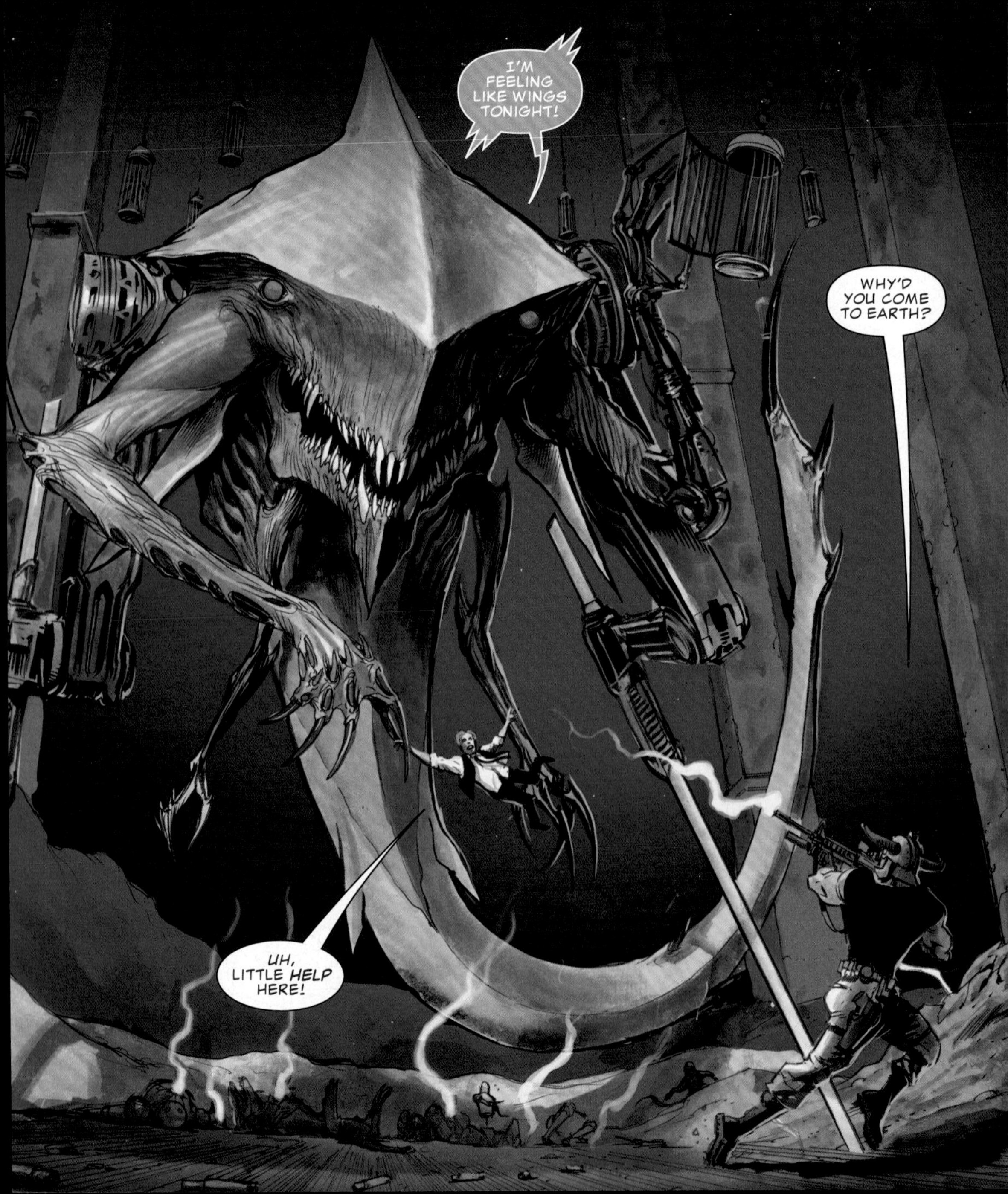
I'M FEELING LIKE WINGS TONIGHT!
WHY'D YOU COME TO EARTH?
UH, LITTLE HELP HERE!

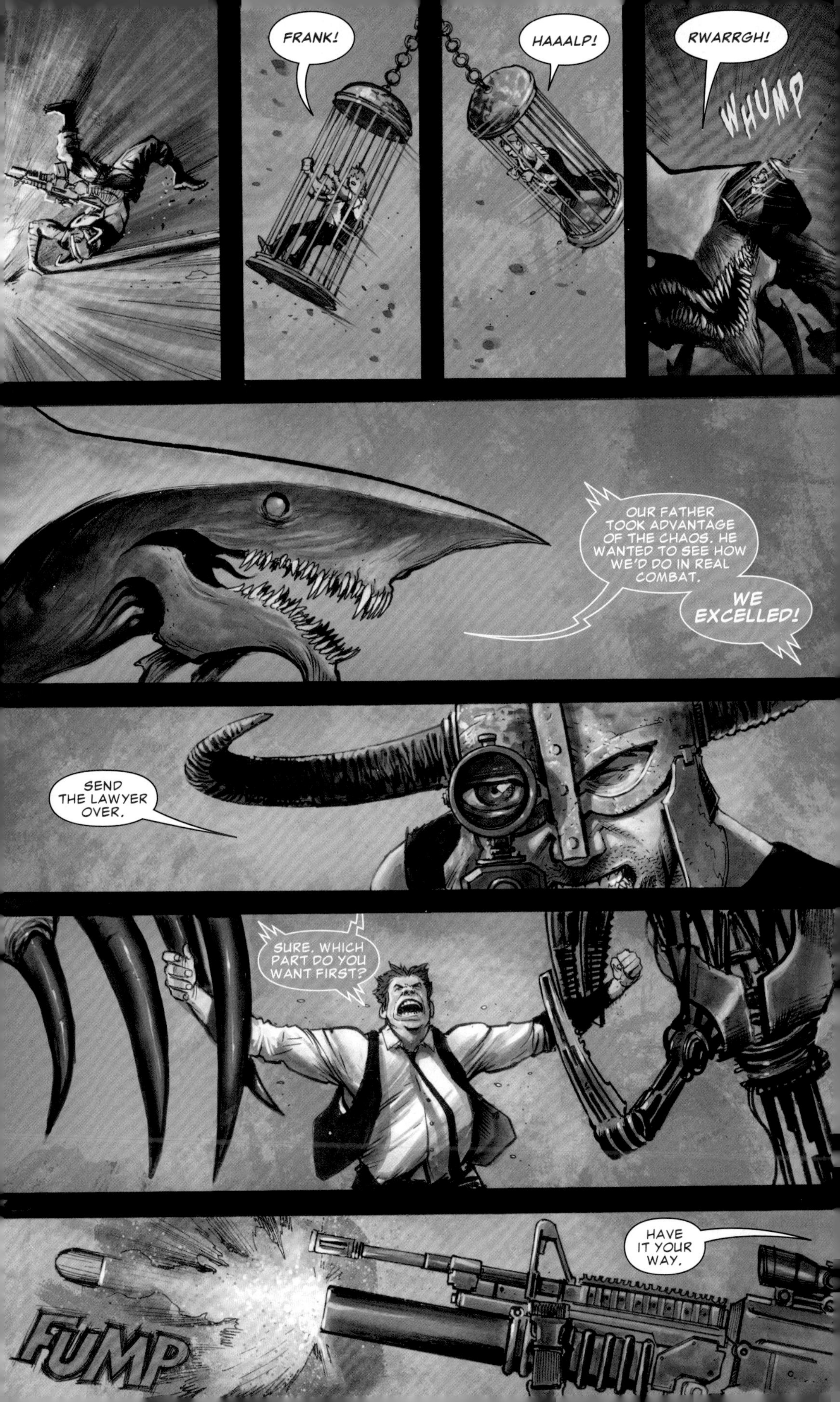
FRANK!
HAAALP!
RWARRGH!
WHUMP
OUR FATHER TOOK ADVANTAGE OF THE CHAOS. HE WANTED TO SEE HOW WE'D DO IN REAL COMBAT.
WE EXCELLED!
SEND THE LAWYER OVER.
SURE. WHICH PART DO YOU WANT FIRST?
HAVE IT YOUR WAY.
FUMP

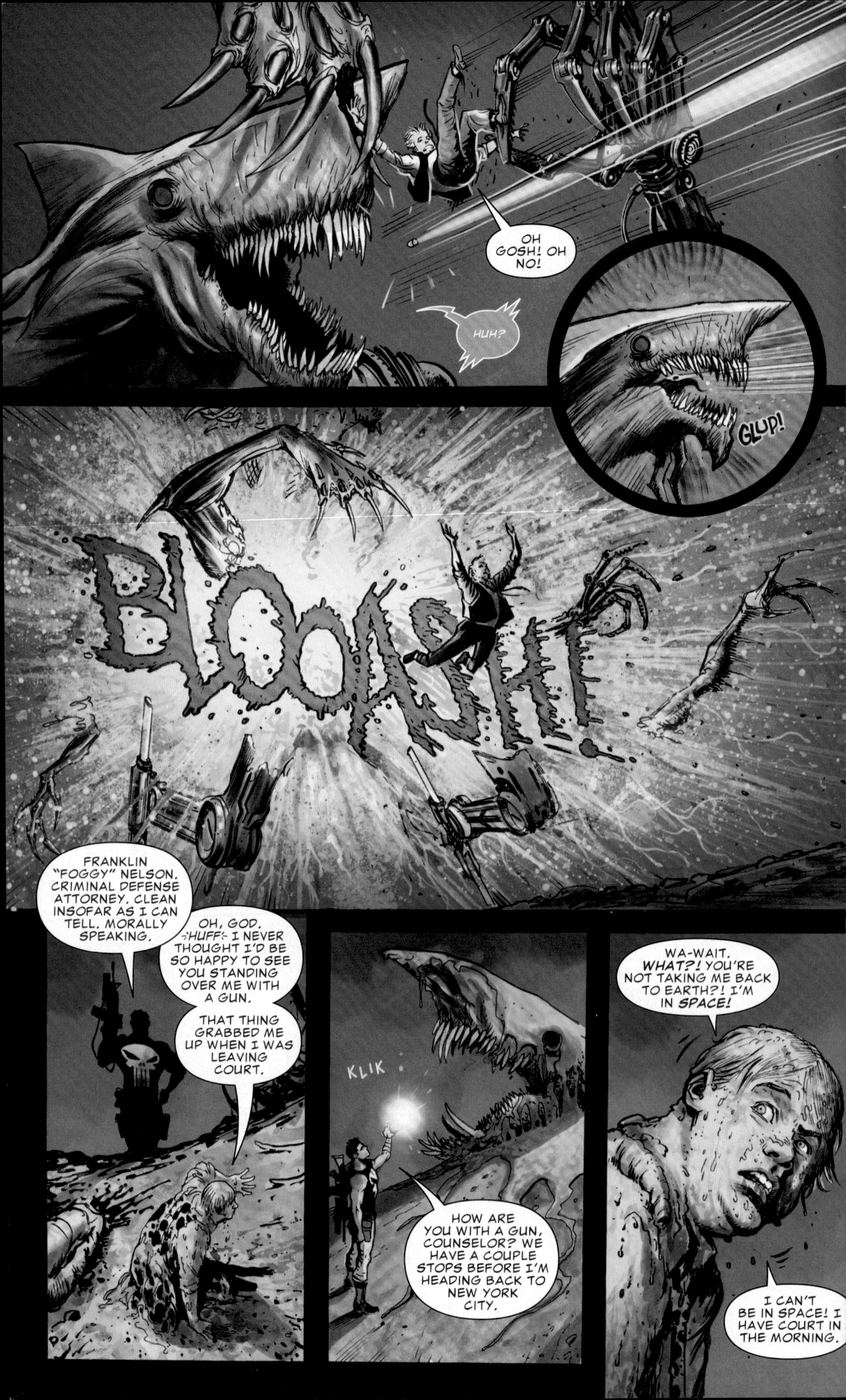
OH GOSH! OH NO!
HUH?
GLUP!
BLOOOSHT!
FRANKLIN "FOGGY" NELSON. CRIMINAL DEFENSE ATTORNEY. CLEAN INSOFAR AS I CAN TELL. MORALLY SPEAKING.
OH, GOD. -HUFF- I NEVER THOUGHT I'D BE SO HAPPY TO SEE YOU STANDING OVER ME WITH A GUN.
THAT THING GRABBED ME UP WHEN I WAS LEAVING COURT.
KLIK
HOW ARE YOU WITH A GUN, COUNSELOR? WE HAVE A COUPLE STOPS BEFORE I'M HEADING BACK TO NEW YORK CITY.
WA-WAIT. WHAT?! YOU'RE NOT TAKING ME BACK TO EARTH?! I'M IN SPACE!
I CAN'T BE IN SPACE! I HAVE COURT IN THE MORNING.

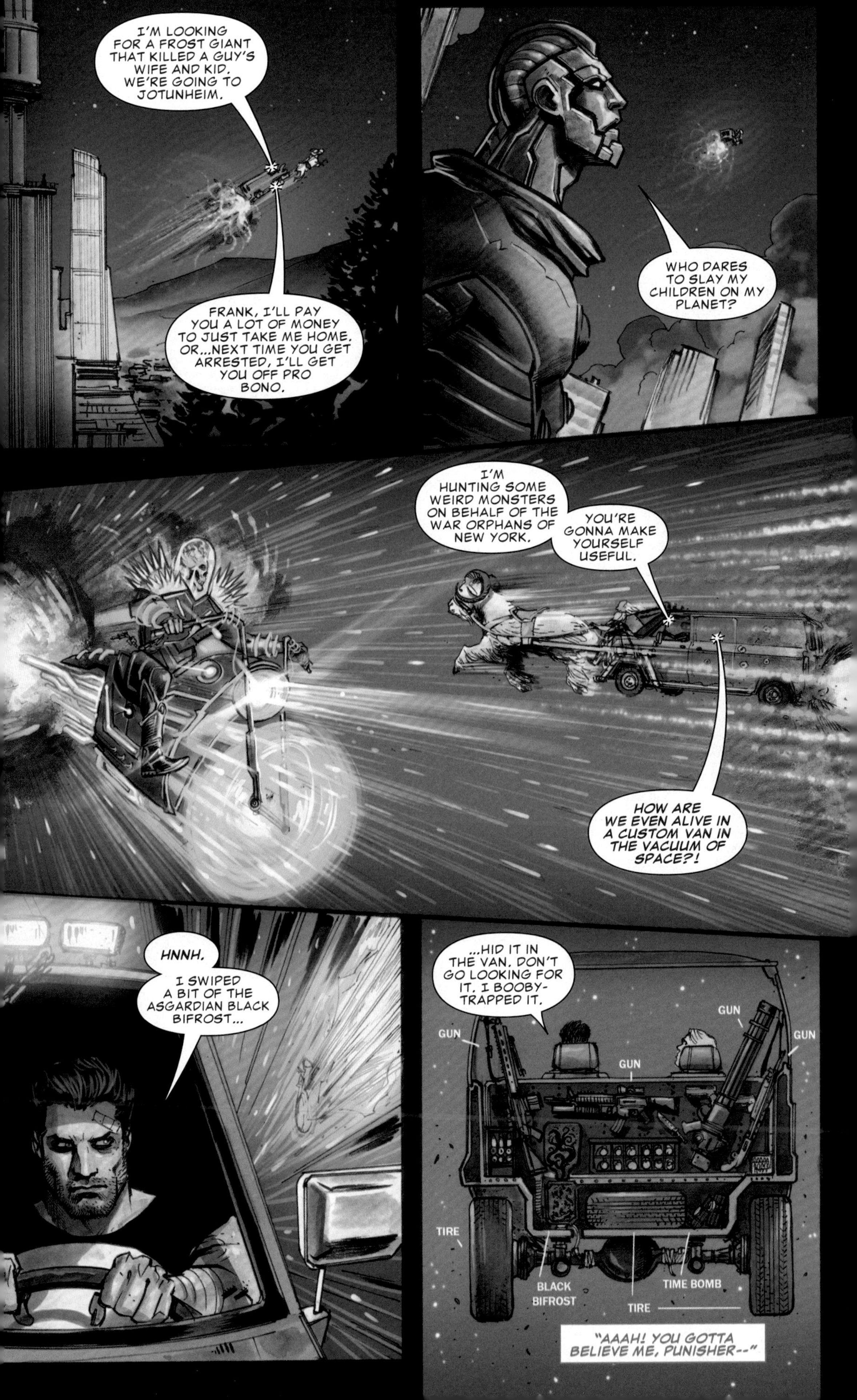
I'M LOOKING FOR A FROST GIANT THAT KILLED A GUY'S WIFE AND KID. WE'RE GOING TO JOTUNHEIM.
FRANK, I'LL PAY YOU A LOT OF MONEY TO JUST TAKE ME HOME. OR...NEXT TIME YOU GET ARRESTED, I'LL GET YOU OFF PRO BONO.
WHO DARES TO SLAY MY CHILDREN ON MY PLANET?
I'M HUNTING SOME WEIRD MONSTERS ON BEHALF OF THE WAR ORPHANS OF NEW YORK.
YOU'RE GONNA MAKE YOURSELF USEFUL.
HOW ARE WE EVEN ALIVE IN A CUSTOM VAN IN THE VACUUM OF SPACE?!
HNNH.
I SWIPED A BIT OF THE ASGARDIAN BLACK BIFROST...
...HID IT IN THE VAN. DON'T GO LOOKING FOR IT. I BOOBY-TRAPPED IT.
GUN
GUN
GUN
GUN
TIRE
BLACK BIFROST
TIRE
TIME BOMB
"AAAH! YOU GOTTA BELIEVE ME, PUNISHER--"

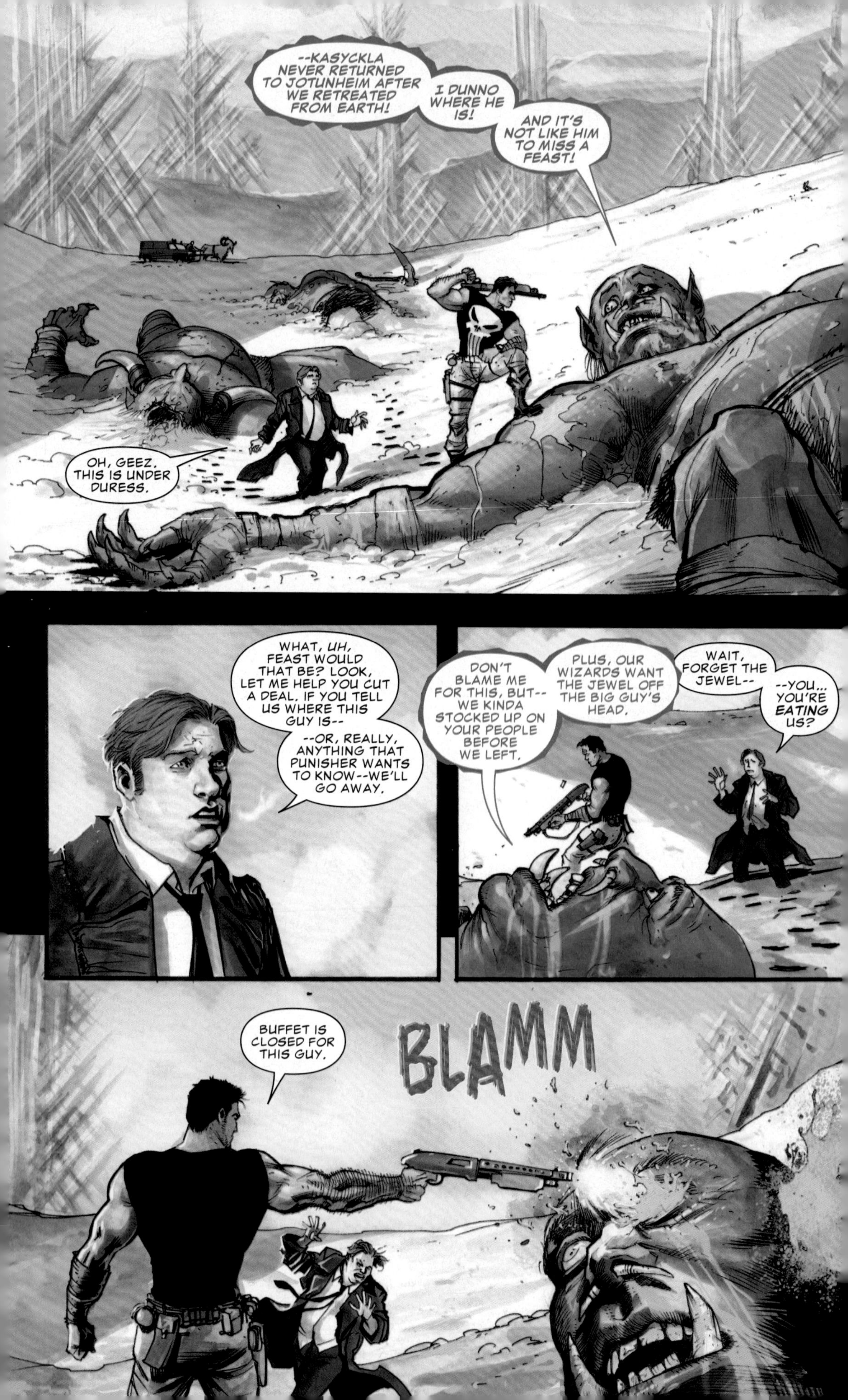
--KASYCKLA NEVER RETURNED TO JOTUNHEIM AFTER WE RETREATED FROM EARTH!
I DUNNO WHERE HE IS!
AND IT'S NOT LIKE HIM TO MISS A FEAST!
OH, GEEZ. THIS IS UNDER DURESS.
WHAT, UH, FEAST WOULD THAT BE? LOOK, LET ME HELP YOU CUT A DEAL. IF YOU TELL US WHERE THIS GUY IS--
--OR, REALLY, ANYTHING THAT PUNISHER WANTS TO KNOW--WE'LL GO AWAY.
DON'T BLAME ME FOR THIS, BUT--WE KINDA STOCKED UP ON YOUR PEOPLE BEFORE WE LEFT.
PLUS, OUR WIZARDS WANT THE JEWEL OFF THE BIG GUY'S HEAD.
WAIT, FORGET THE JEWEL--
--YOU... YOU'RE EATING US?
BUFFET IS CLOSED FOR THIS GUY.
BLAMM

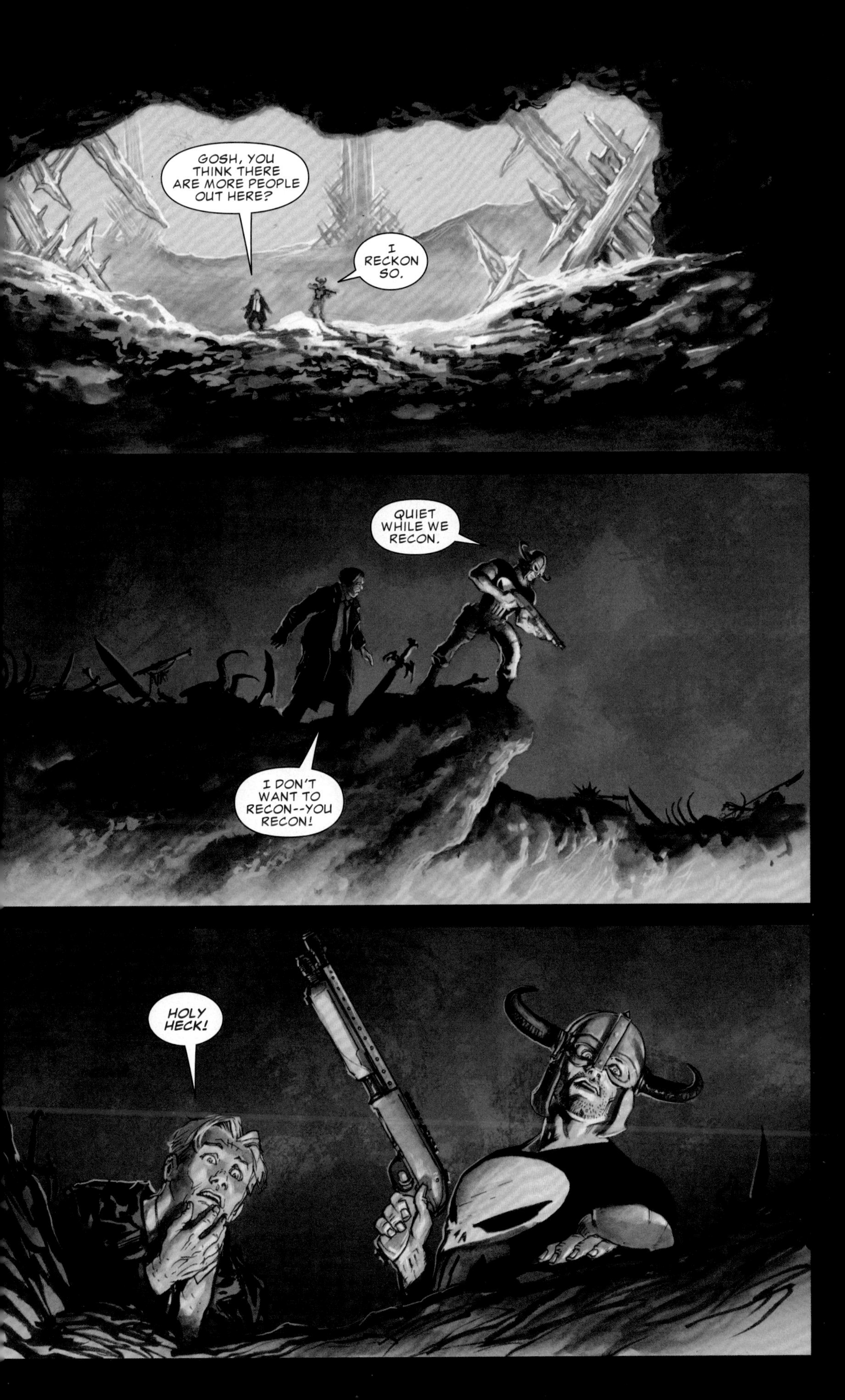
GOSH, YOU THINK THERE ARE MORE PEOPLE OUT HERE?
I RECKON SO.
QUIET WHILE WE RECON.
I DON'T WANT TO RECON--YOU RECON!
HOLY HECK!

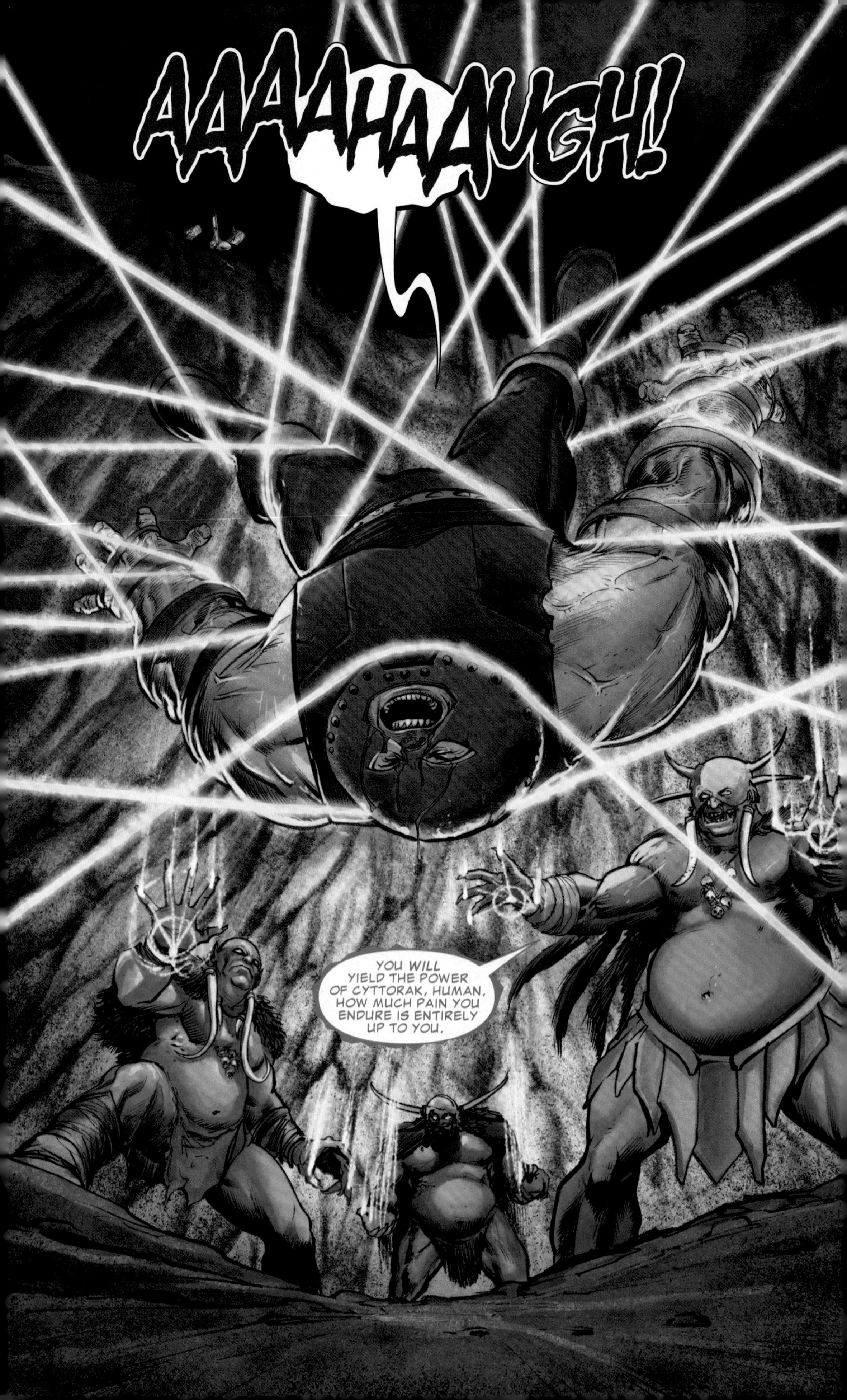
AAAAHAAAUGH!
YOU WILL YIELD THE POWER OF CYTTORAK, HUMAN. HOW MUCH PAIN YOU ENDURE IS ENTIRELY UP TO YOU.

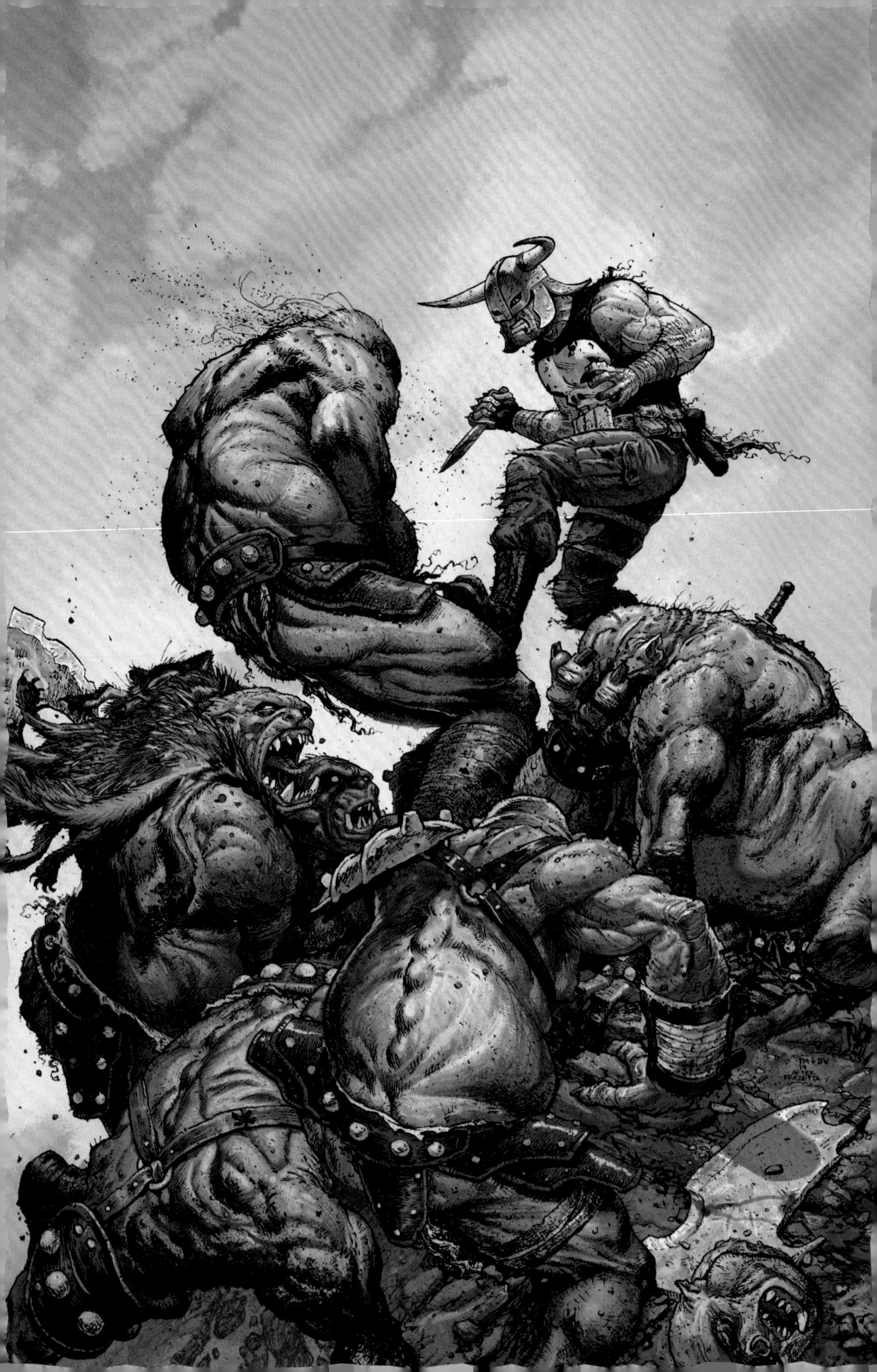
TM+DW
AFTER
FRAZETTA

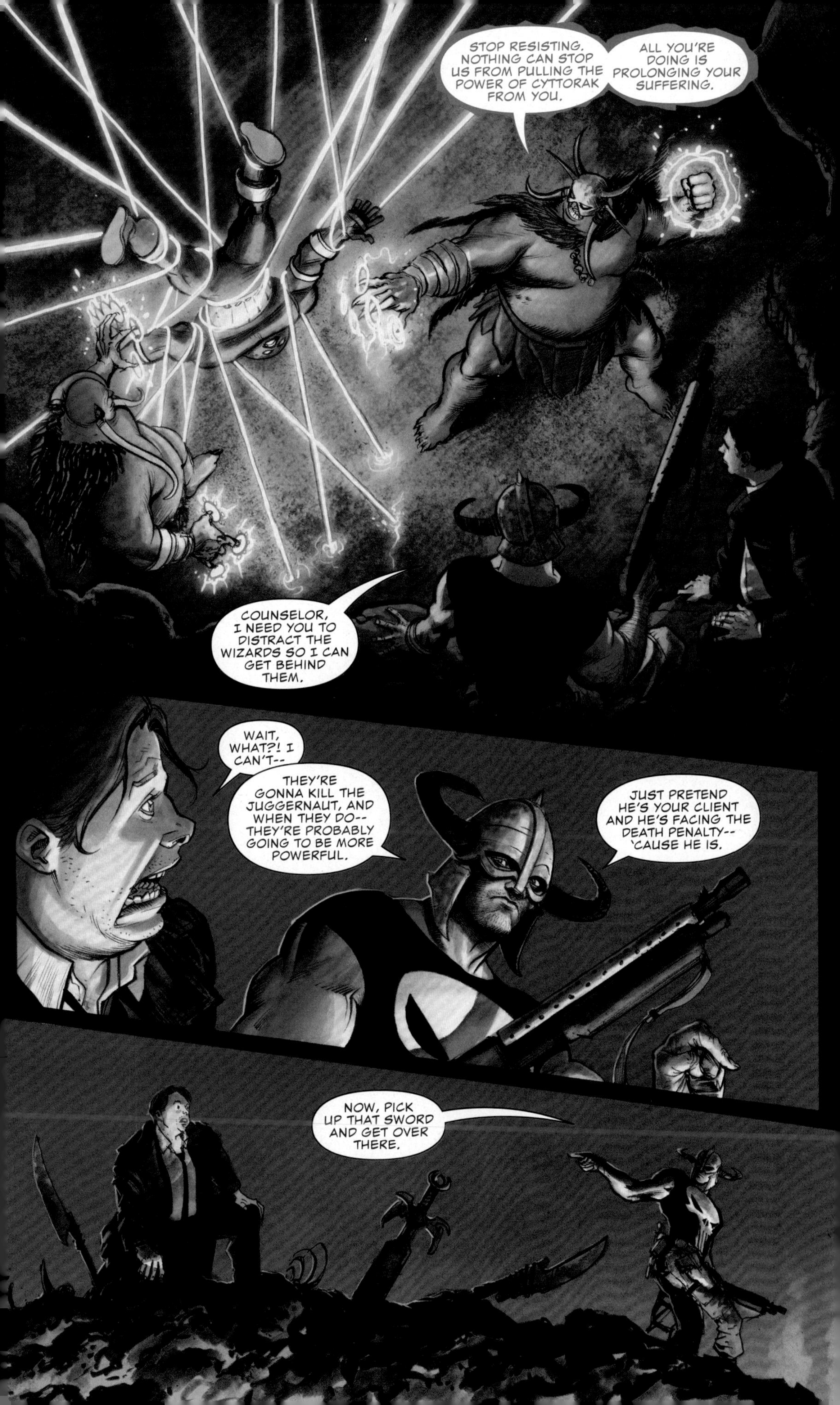
STOP RESISTING. NOTHING CAN STOP US FROM PULLING THE POWER OF CYTTORAK FROM YOU.
ALL YOU'RE DOING IS PROLONGING YOUR SUFFERING.
COUNSELOR, I NEED YOU TO DISTRACT THE WIZARDS SO I CAN GET BEHIND THEM.
WAIT, WHAT?! I CAN'T--
THEY'RE GONNA KILL THE JUGGERNAUT, AND WHEN THEY DO-- THEY'RE PROBABLY GOING TO BE MORE POWERFUL.
JUST PRETEND HE'S YOUR CLIENT AND HE'S FACING THE DEATH PENALTY-- 'CAUSE HE IS.
NOW, PICK UP THAT SWORD AND GET OVER THERE.

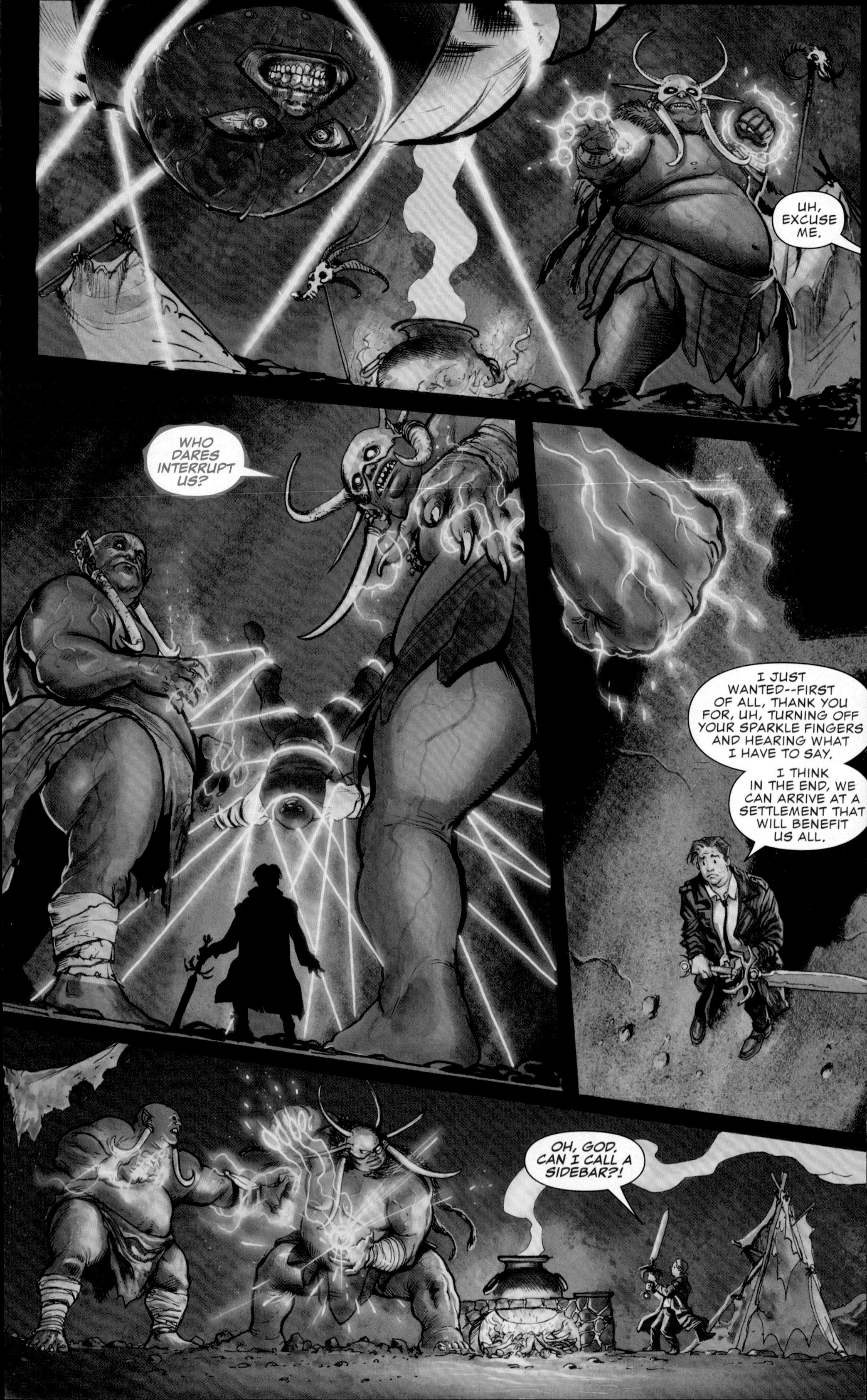
UH, EXCUSE ME.
WHO DARES INTERRUPT US?
I JUST WANTED--FIRST OF ALL, THANK YOU FOR, UH, TURNING OFF YOUR SPARKLE FINGERS AND HEARING WHAT I HAVE TO SAY.
I THINK IN THE END, WE CAN ARRIVE AT A SETTLEMENT THAT WILL BENEFIT US ALL.
OH, GOD. CAN I CALL A SIDEBAR?!

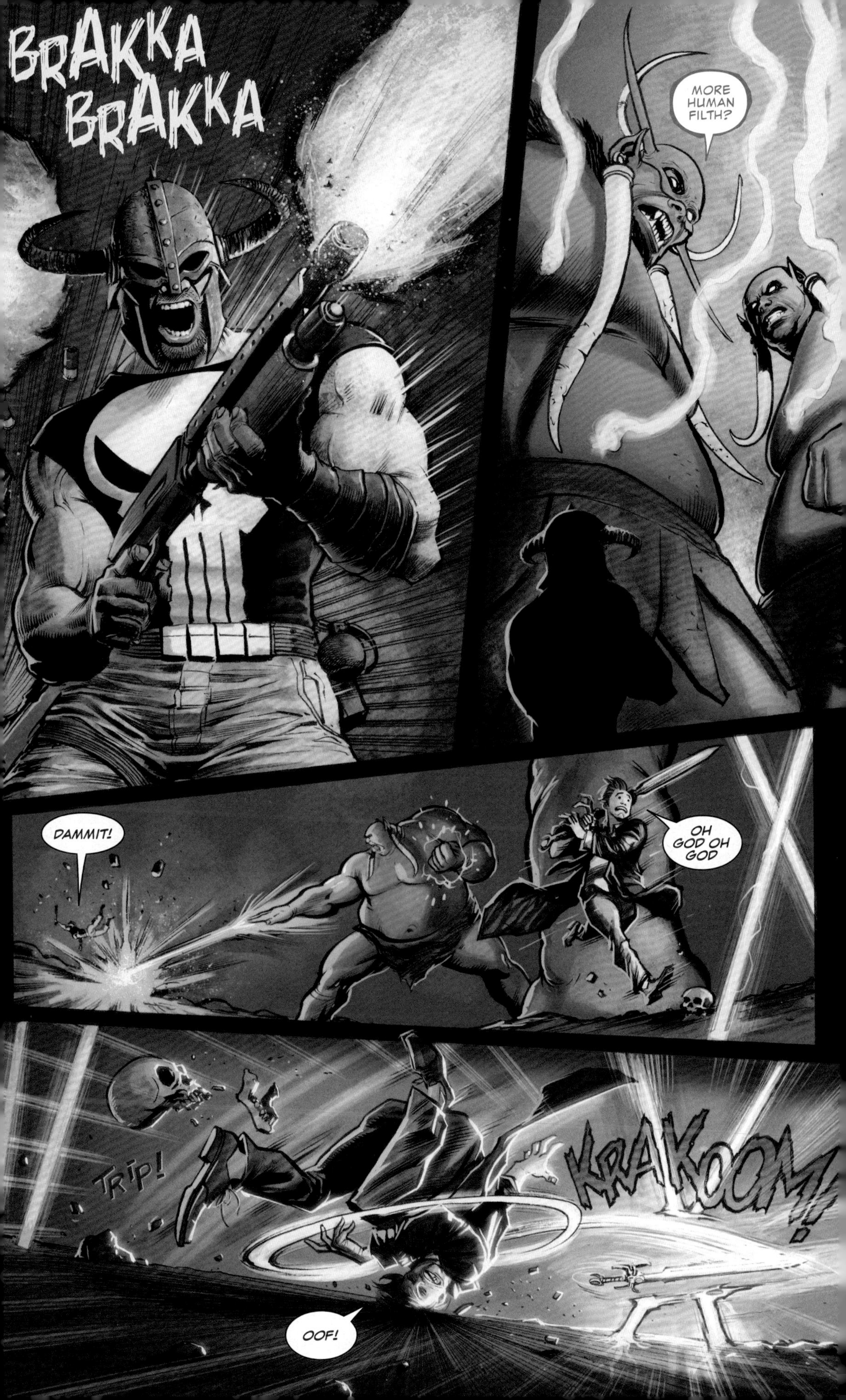
BRAKKA
BRAKKA
MORE HUMAN FILTH?
DAMMIT!
OH GOD OH GOD
TRIP!
KRAKOOM!
OOF!

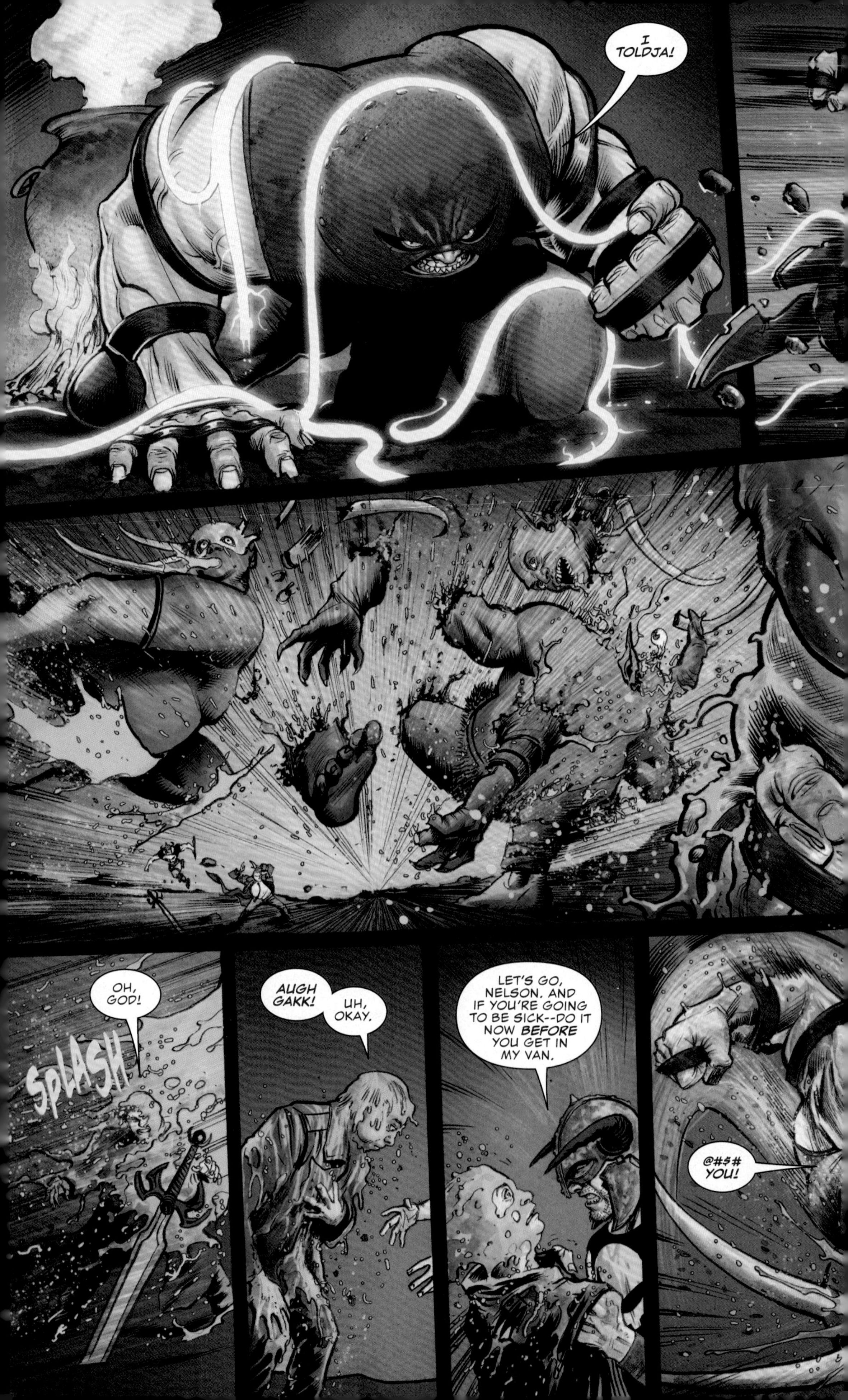
I TOLDJA!
OH, GOD!
SPLASH
AUGH GAKK!
UH, OKAY.
LET'S GO, NELSON. AND IF YOU'RE GOING TO BE SICK--DO IT NOW *BEFORE* YOU GET IN MY VAN.
@#$# YOU!

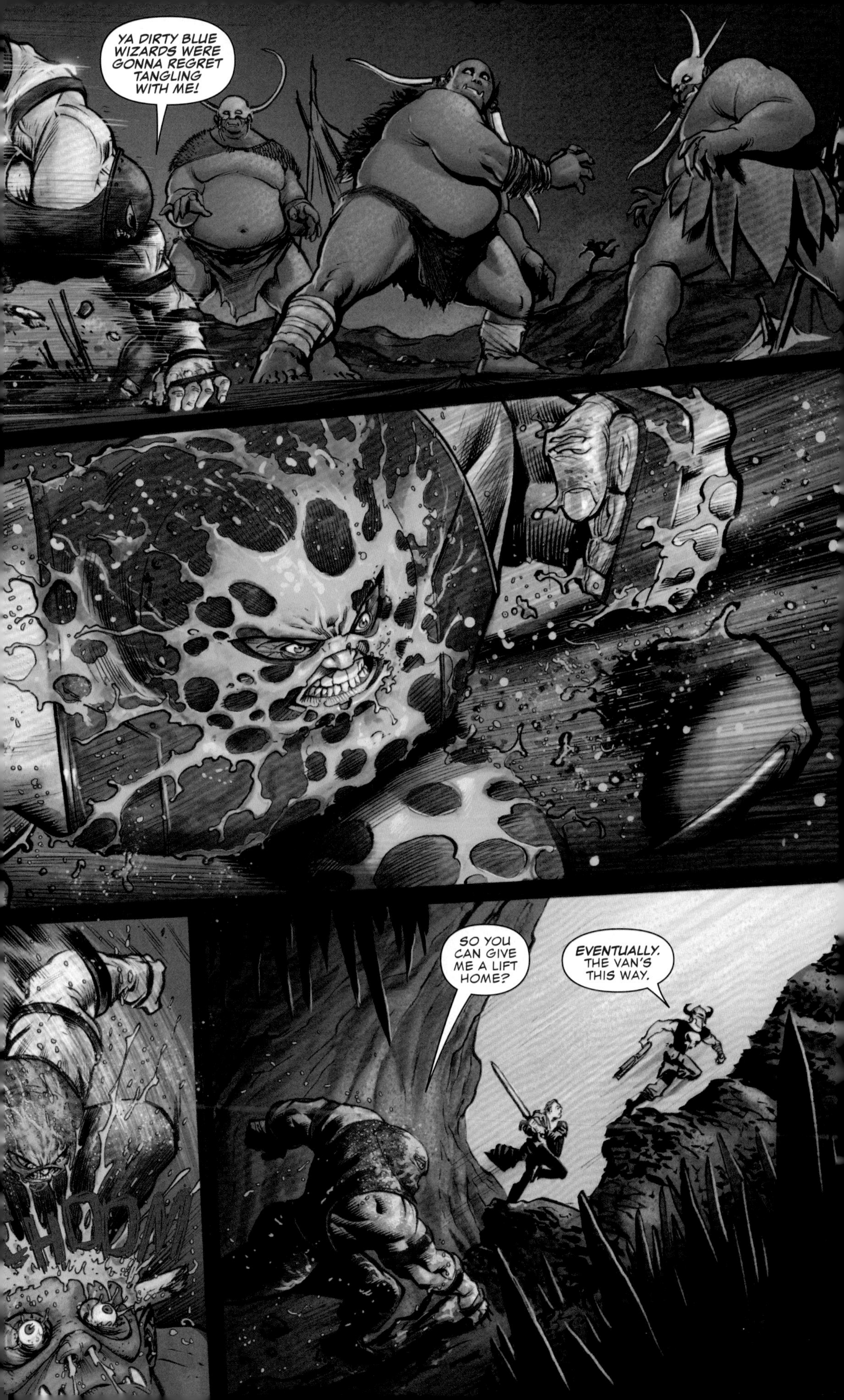
YA DIRTY BLUE WIZARDS WERE GONNA REGRET TANGLING WITH ME!
SO YOU CAN GIVE ME A LIFT HOME?
EVENTUALLY. THE VAN'S THIS WAY.

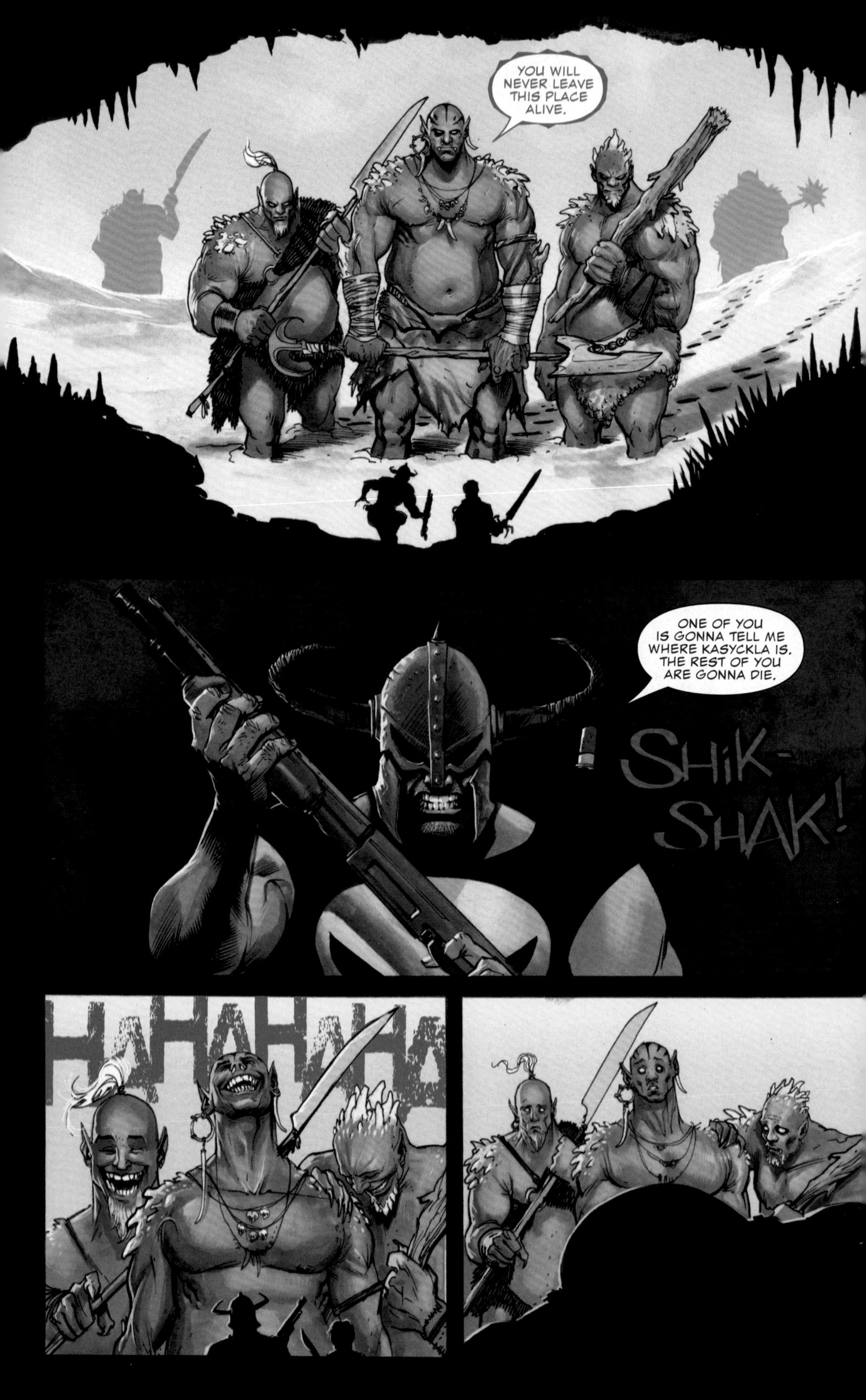
YOU WILL NEVER LEAVE THIS PLACE ALIVE.
ONE OF YOU IS GONNA TELL ME WHERE KASYCKLA IS. THE REST OF YOU ARE GONNA DIE.
SHIK-SHAK!
HAHAHAHA

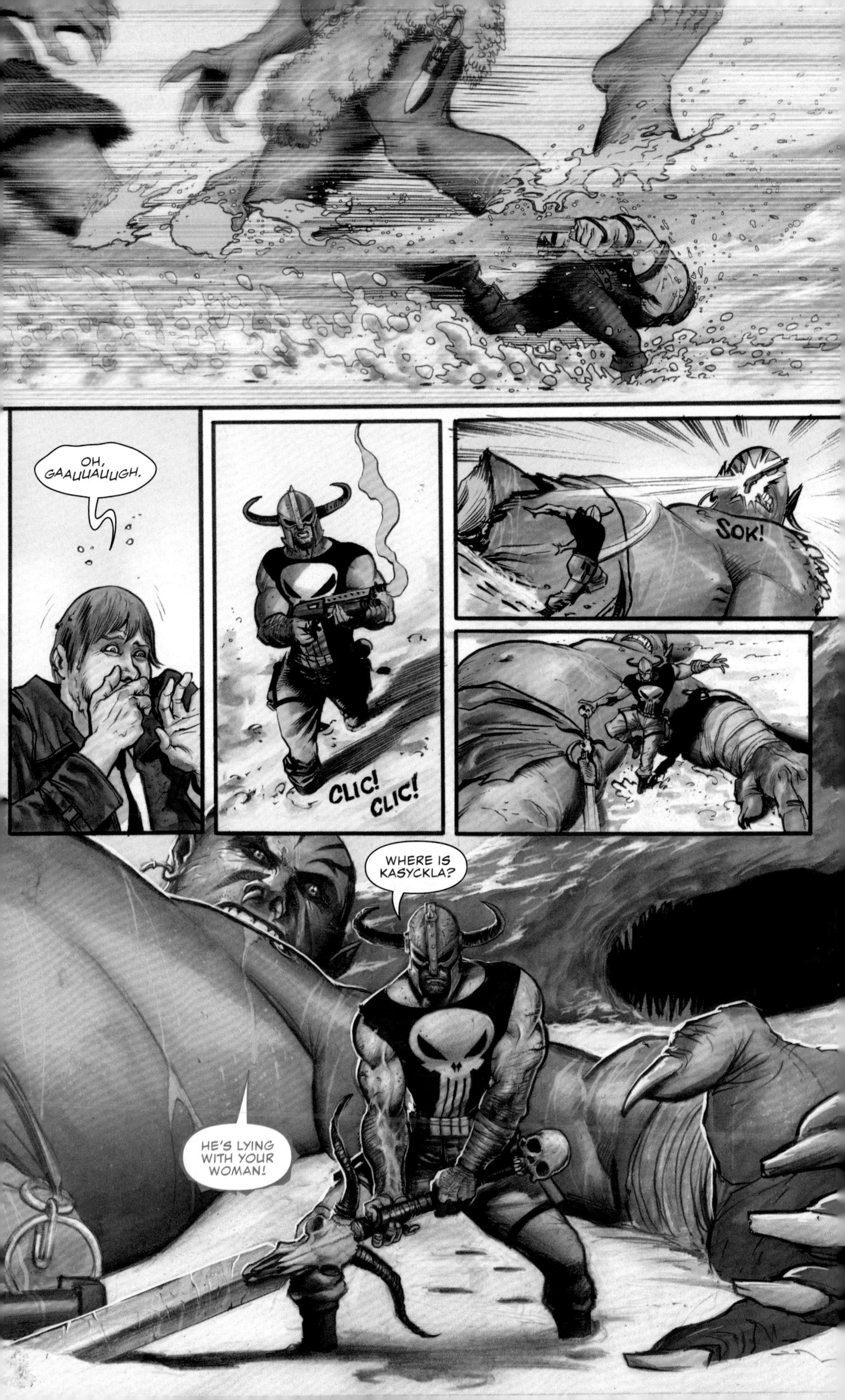
OH, GAAUUAUUGH.
CLIC! CLIC!
SOK!
WHERE IS KASYCKLA?
HE'S LYING WITH YOUR WOMAN!

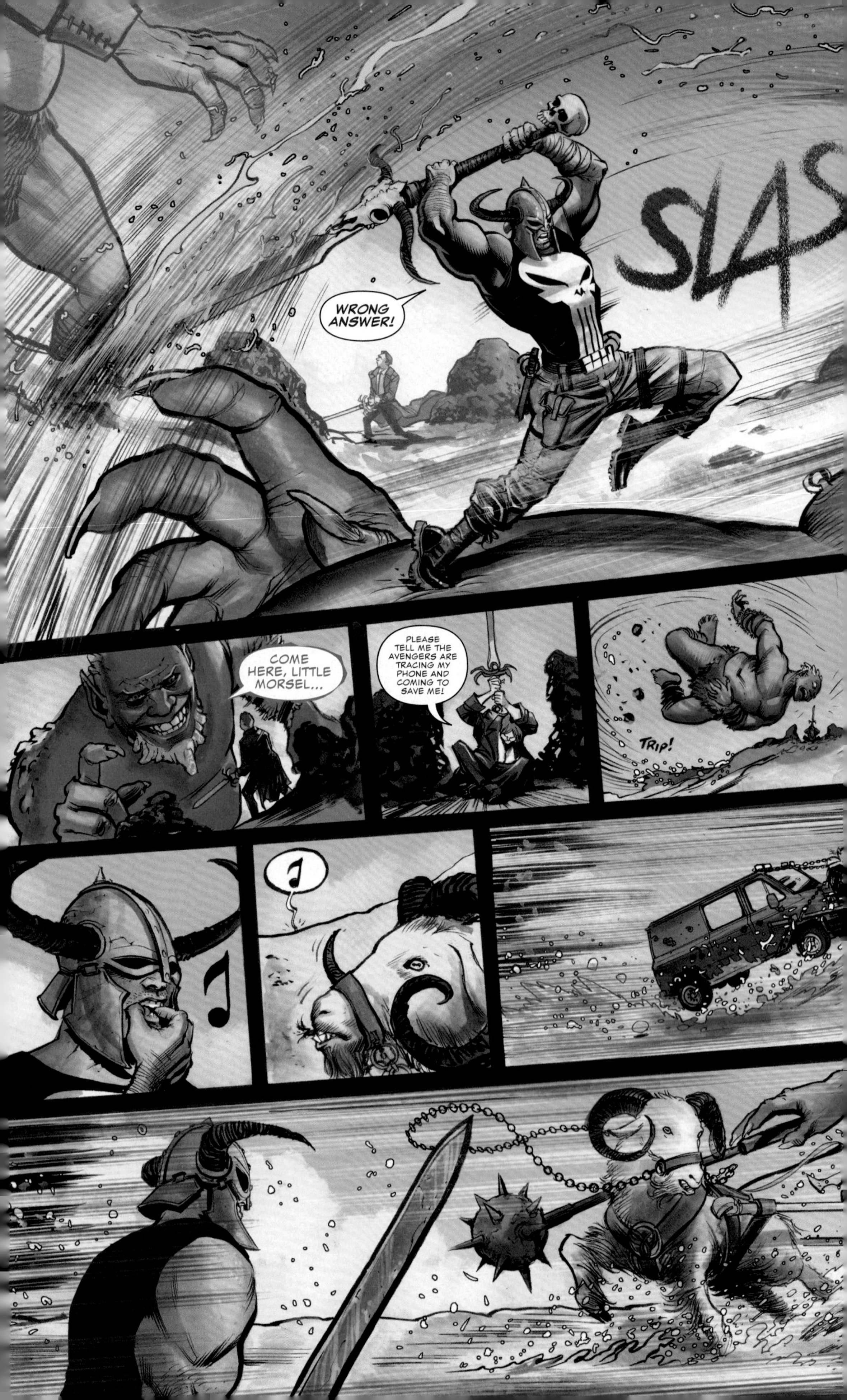
SLAS
WRONG ANSWER!
COME HERE, LITTLE MORSEL...
PLEASE TELL ME THE AVENGERS ARE TRACING MY PHONE AND COMING TO SAVE ME!
TRIP!

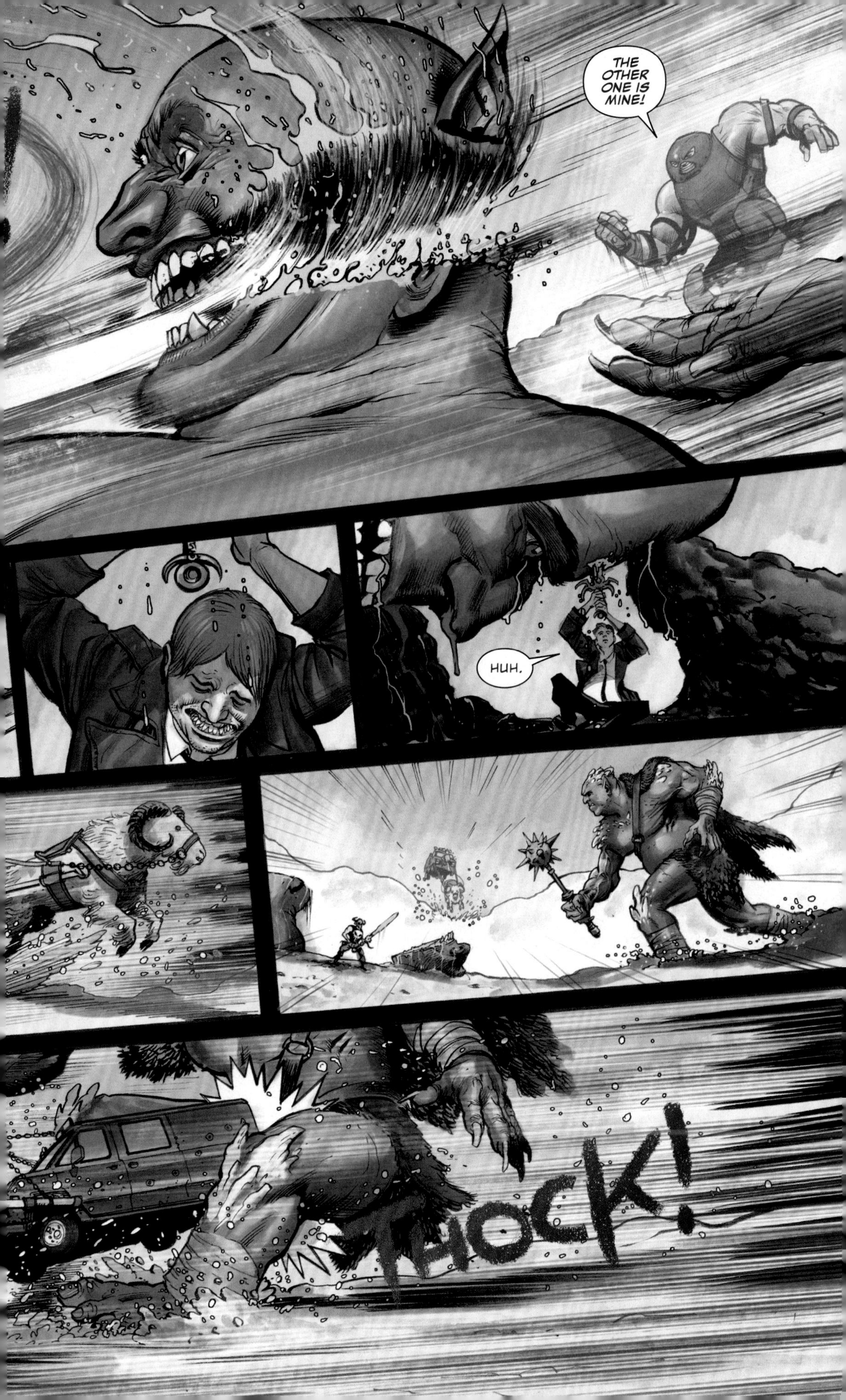
THE OTHER ONE IS MINE!
HUH.
THOCK!

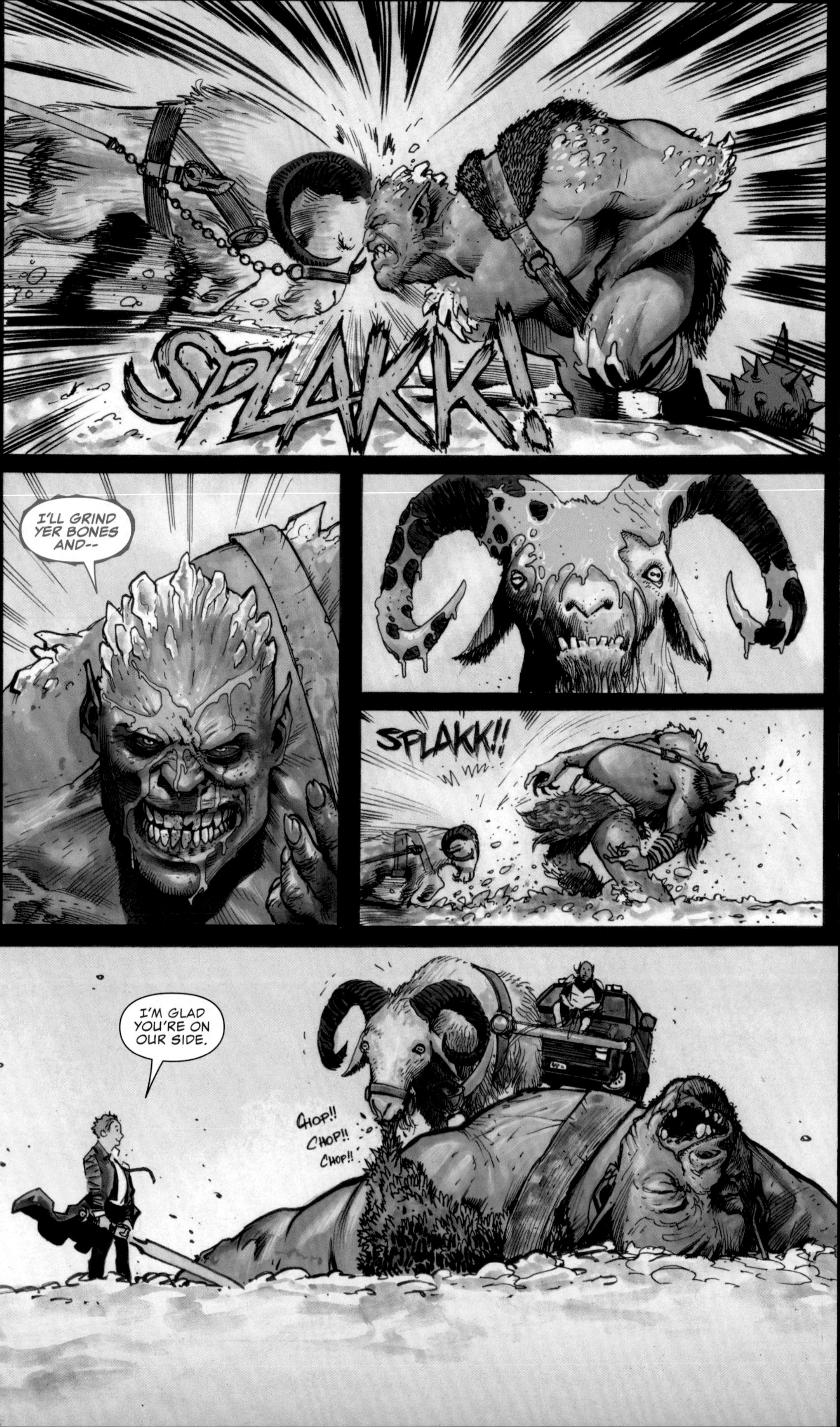
SPLAKK!!
I'LL GRIND YER BONES AND--
SPLAKK!!
I'M GLAD YOU'RE ON OUR SIDE.
CHOP!!
CHOP!!
CHOP!!

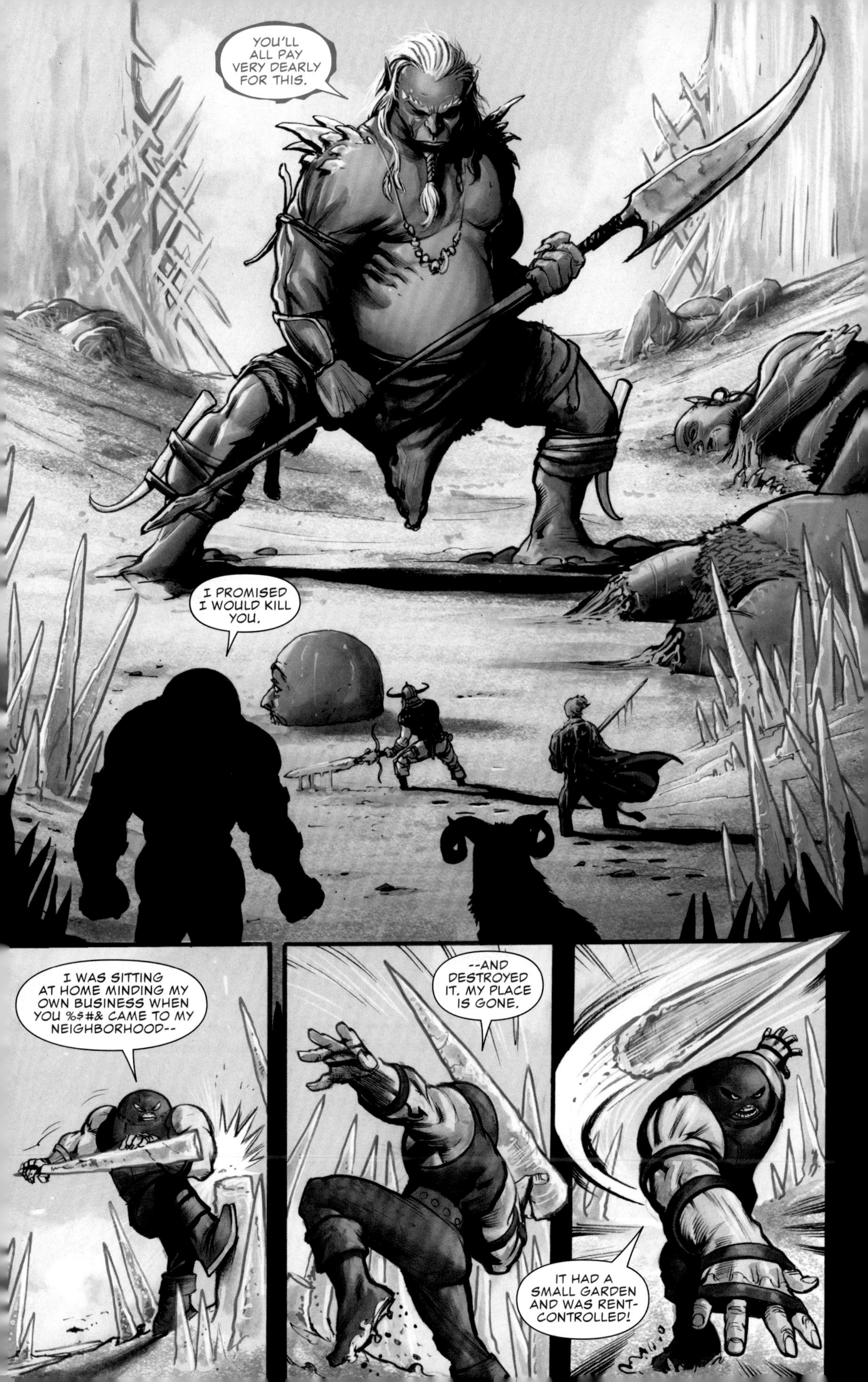
YOU'LL ALL PAY VERY DEARLY FOR THIS.
I PROMISED I WOULD KILL YOU.
I WAS SITTING AT HOME MINDING MY OWN BUSINESS WHEN YOU %$#& CAME TO MY NEIGHBORHOOD--
--AND DESTROYED IT. MY PLACE IS GONE.
IT HAD A SMALL GARDEN AND WAS RENT-CONTROLLED!

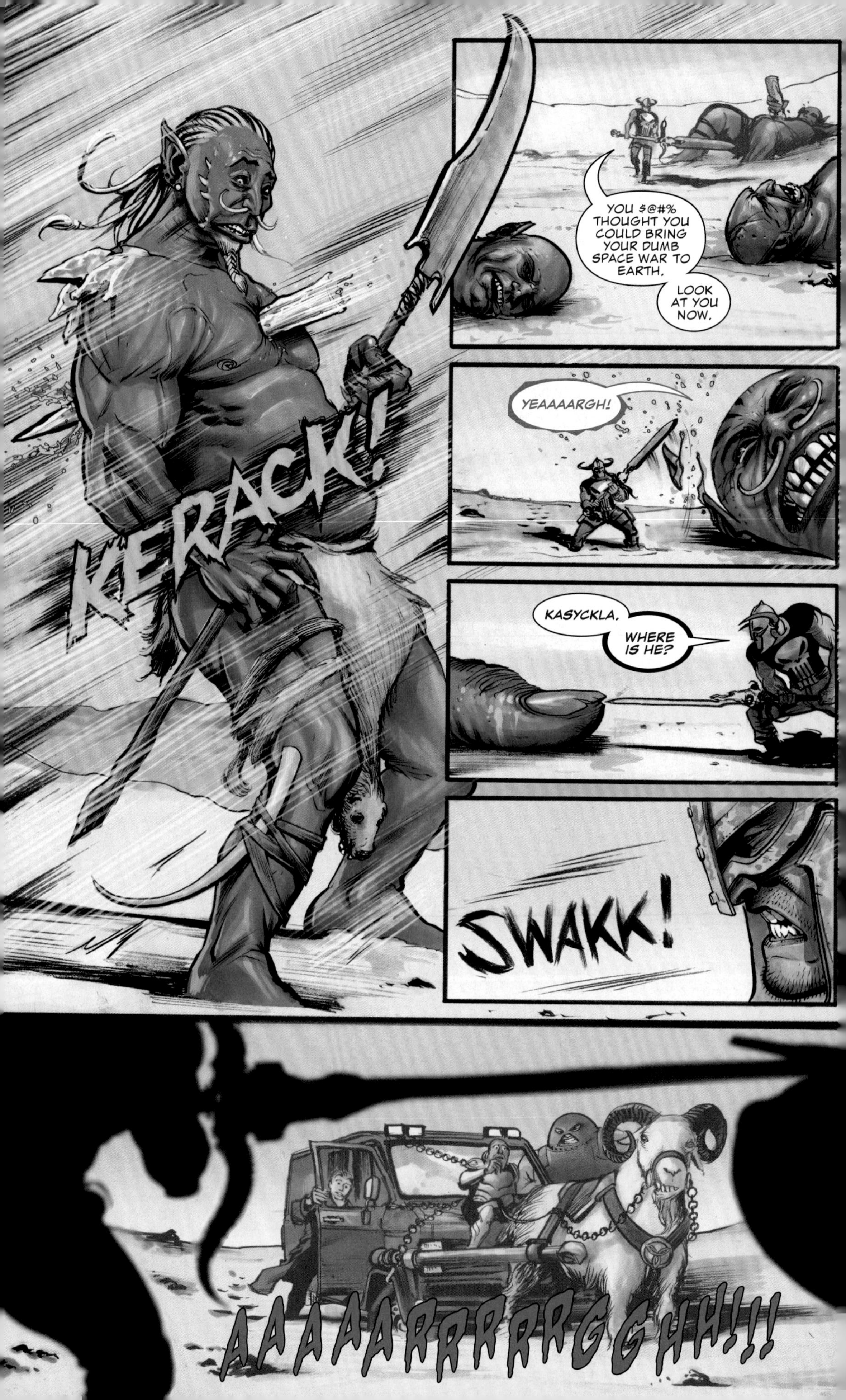
KERACK!
YOU $@#% THOUGHT YOU COULD BRING YOUR DUMB SPACE WAR TO EARTH.
LOOK AT YOU NOW.
YEAAAARGH!
KASYCKLA.
WHERE IS HE?
SWAKK!
AAAAARRRRRGGHH!!!

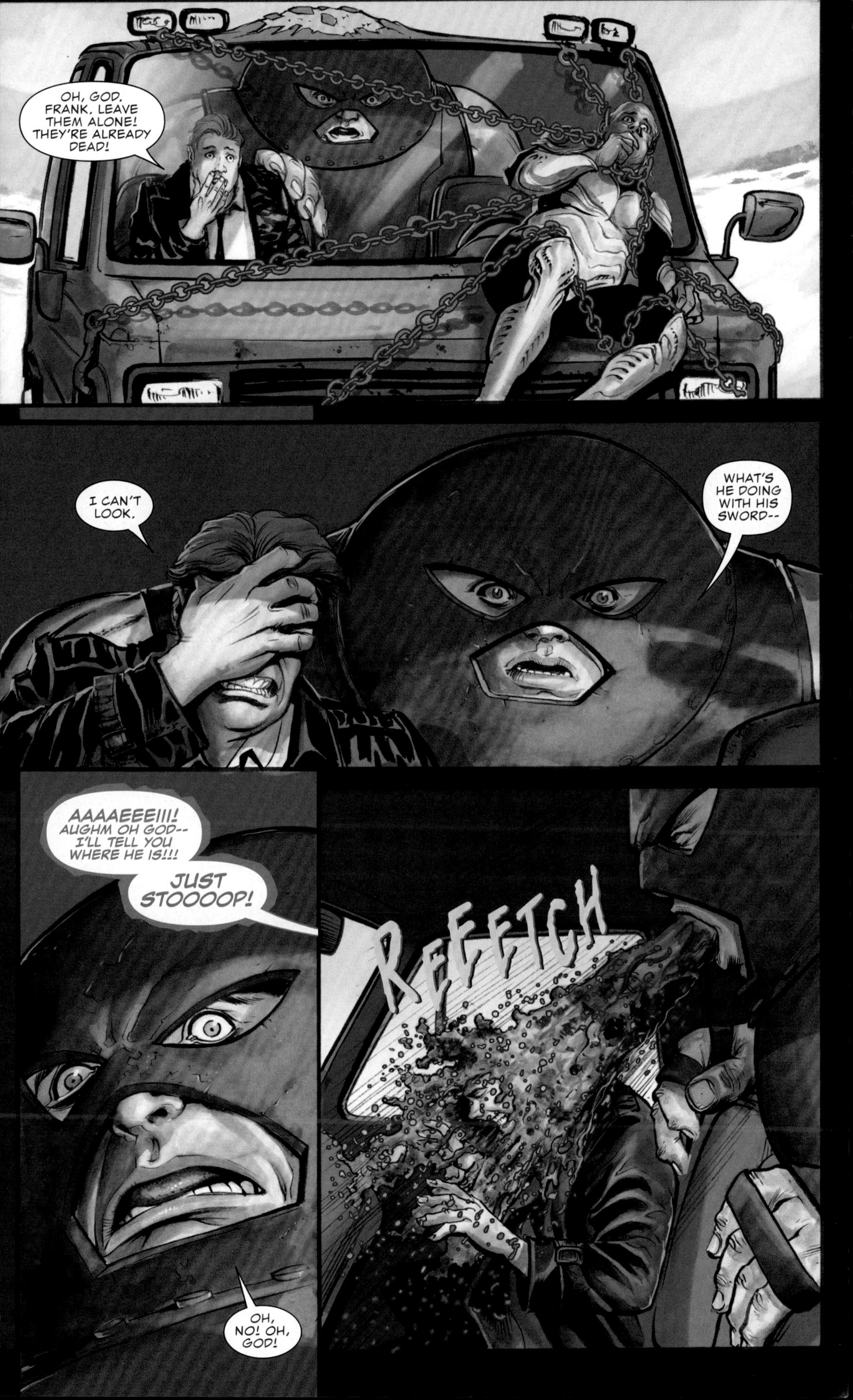

OH, GOD. FRANK. LEAVE THEM ALONE! THEY'RE ALREADY DEAD!
I CAN'T LOOK.
WHAT'S HE DOING WITH HIS SWORD--
AAAAEEE!!!! AUGHM OH GOD-- I'LL TELL YOU WHERE HE IS!!!
JUST STOOOOP!
REEETCH
OH, NO! OH, GOD!

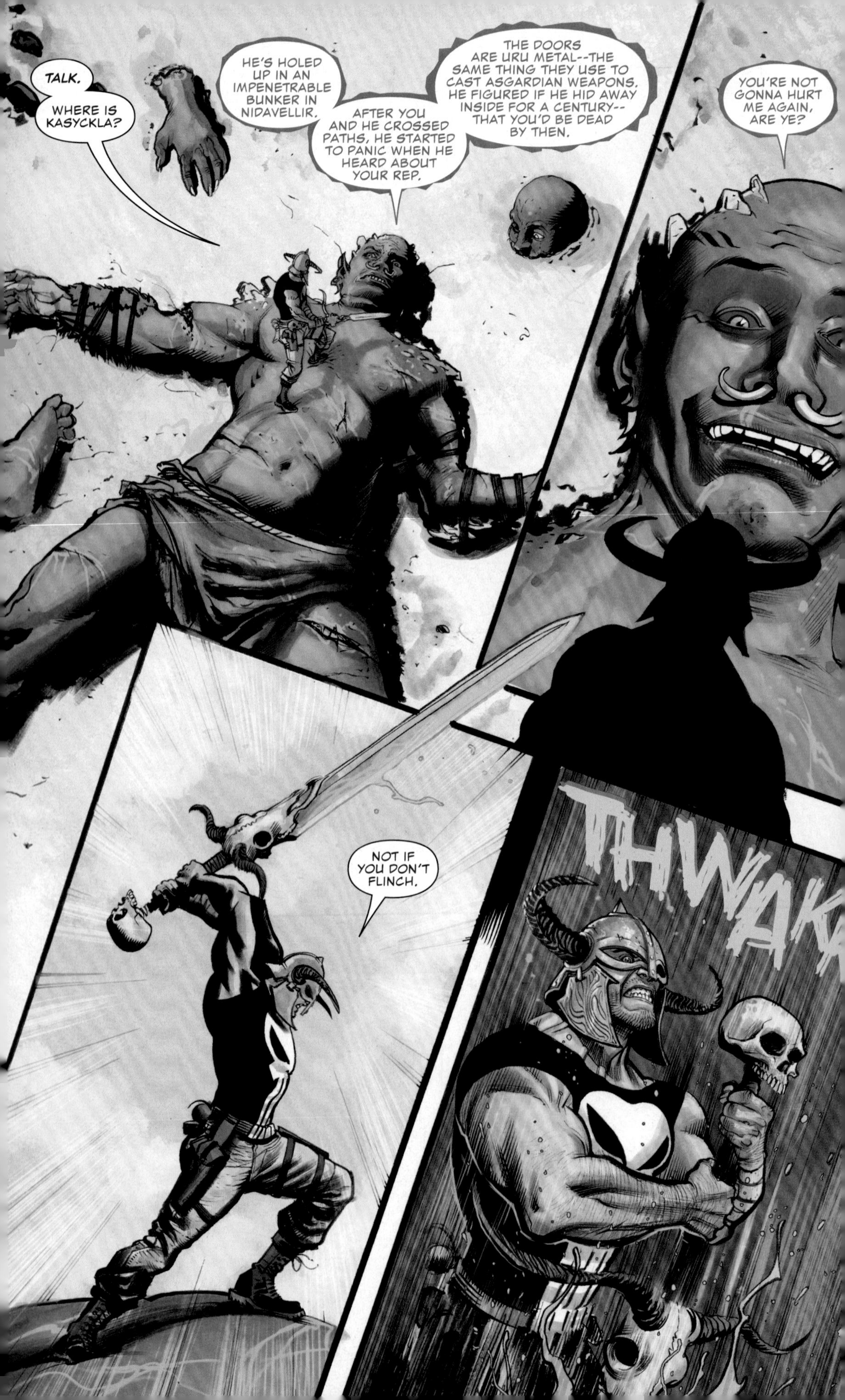
TALK.
WHERE IS KASYCKLA?
HE'S HOLED UP IN AN IMPENETRABLE BUNKER IN NIDAVELLIR.
AFTER YOU AND HE CROSSED PATHS, HE STARTED TO PANIC WHEN HE HEARD ABOUT YOUR REP.
THE DOORS ARE URU METAL--THE SAME THING THEY USE TO CAST ASGARDIAN WEAPONS. HE FIGURED IF HE HID AWAY INSIDE FOR A CENTURY--THAT YOU'D BE DEAD BY THEN.
YOU'RE NOT GONNA HURT ME AGAIN, ARE YE?
NOT IF YOU DON'T FLINCH.
THWAK

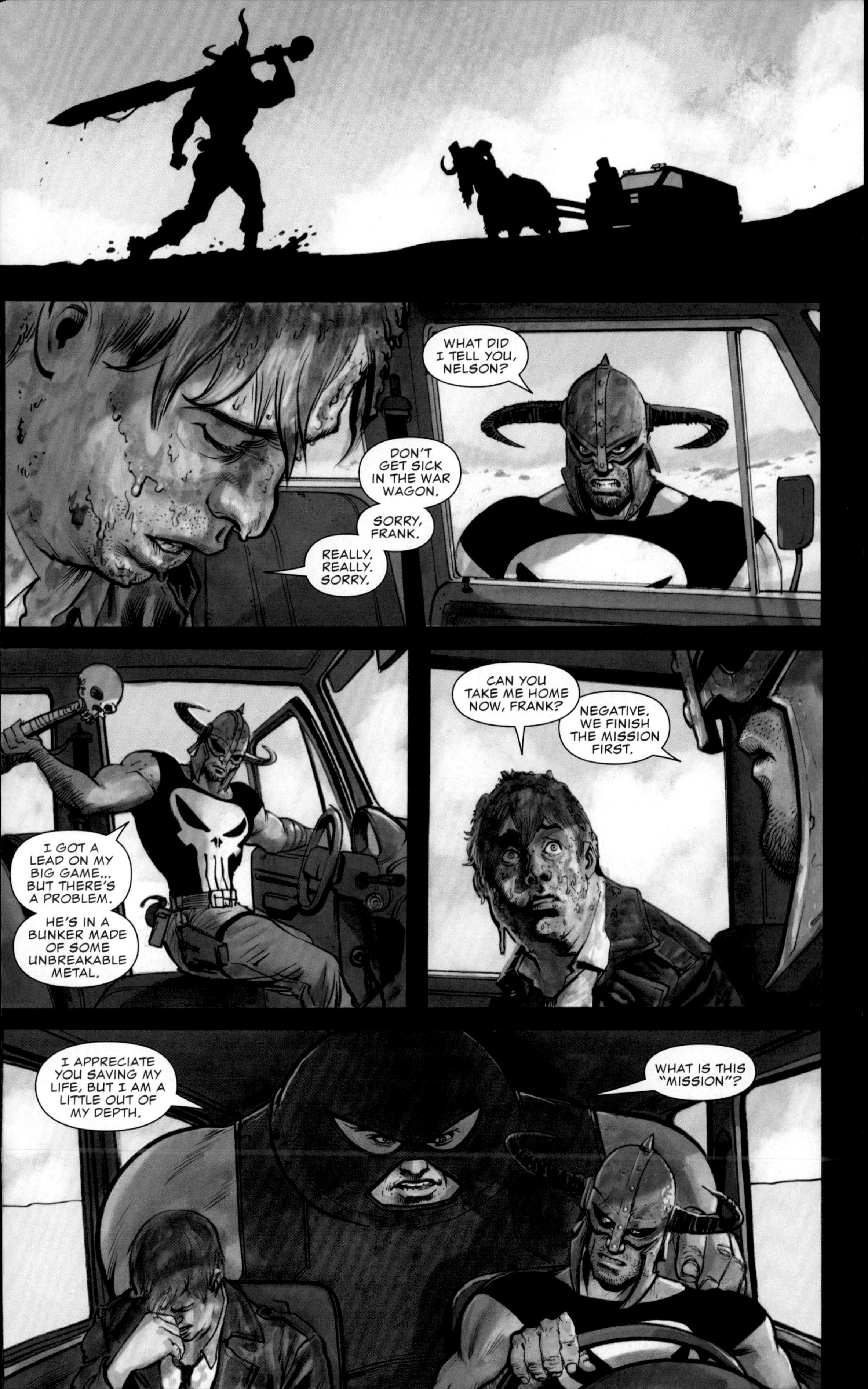
WHAT DID I TELL YOU, NELSON?
DON'T GET SICK IN THE WAR WAGON.
SORRY, FRANK.
REALLY. REALLY. SORRY.
I GOT A LEAD ON MY BIG GAME... BUT THERE'S A PROBLEM.
HE'S IN A BUNKER MADE OF SOME UNBREAKABLE METAL.
CAN YOU TAKE ME HOME NOW, FRANK?
NEGATIVE. WE FINISH THE MISSION FIRST.
I APPRECIATE YOU SAVING MY LIFE, BUT I AM A LITTLE OUT OF MY DEPTH.
WHAT IS THIS "MISSION"?

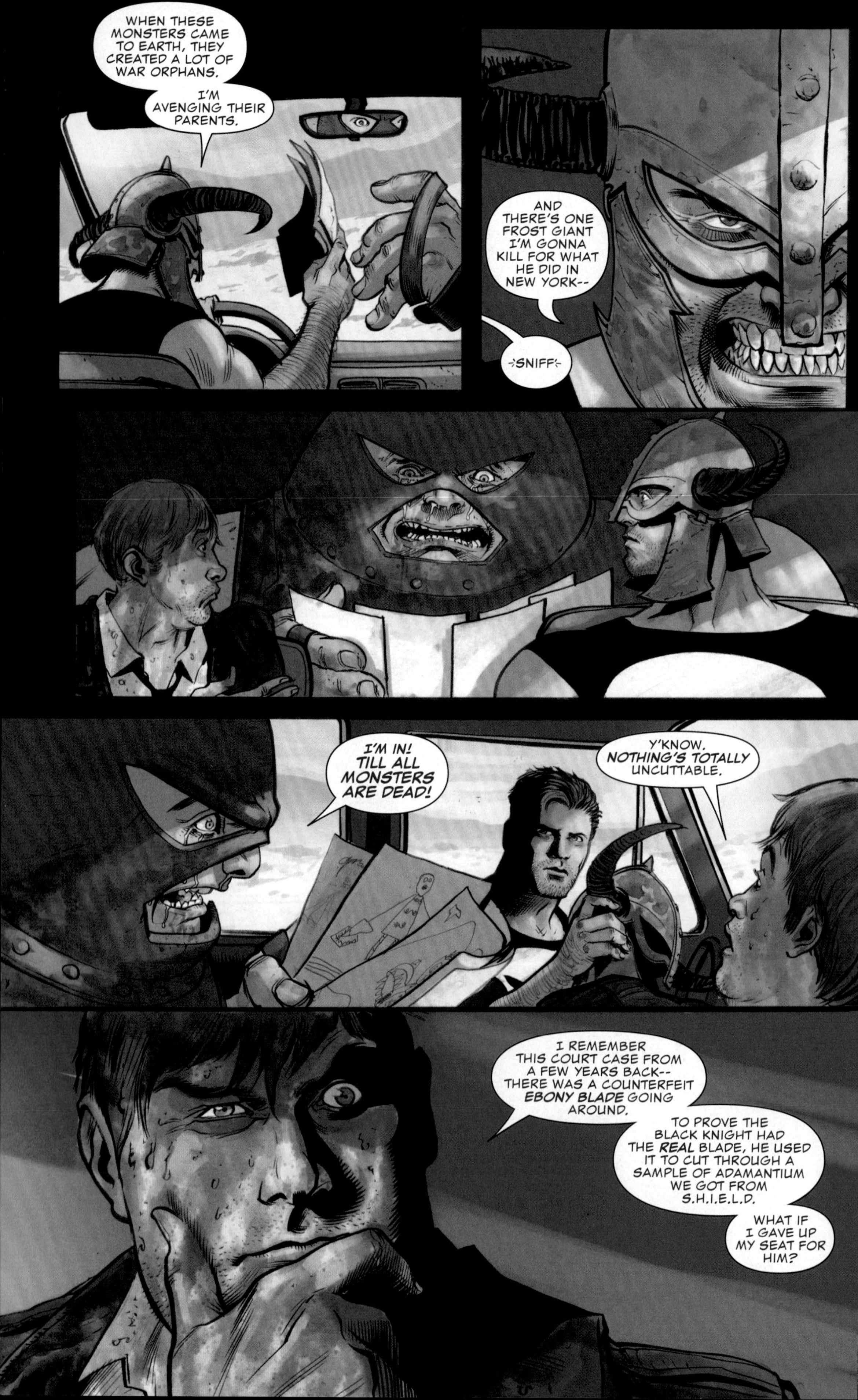
WHEN THESE MONSTERS CAME TO EARTH, THEY CREATED A LOT OF WAR ORPHANS.
I'M AVENGING THEIR PARENTS.
AND THERE'S ONE FROST GIANT I'M GONNA KILL FOR WHAT HE DID IN NEW YORK--
SNIFF
I'M IN! TILL ALL MONSTERS ARE DEAD!
Y'KNOW. NOTHING'S TOTALLY UNCUTTABLE.
I REMEMBER THIS COURT CASE FROM A FEW YEARS BACK-- THERE WAS A COUNTERFEIT EBONY BLADE GOING AROUND.
TO PROVE THE BLACK KNIGHT HAD THE REAL BLADE, HE USED IT TO CUT THROUGH A SAMPLE OF ADAMANTIUM WE GOT FROM S.H.I.E.L.D.
WHAT IF I GAVE UP MY SEAT FOR HIM?

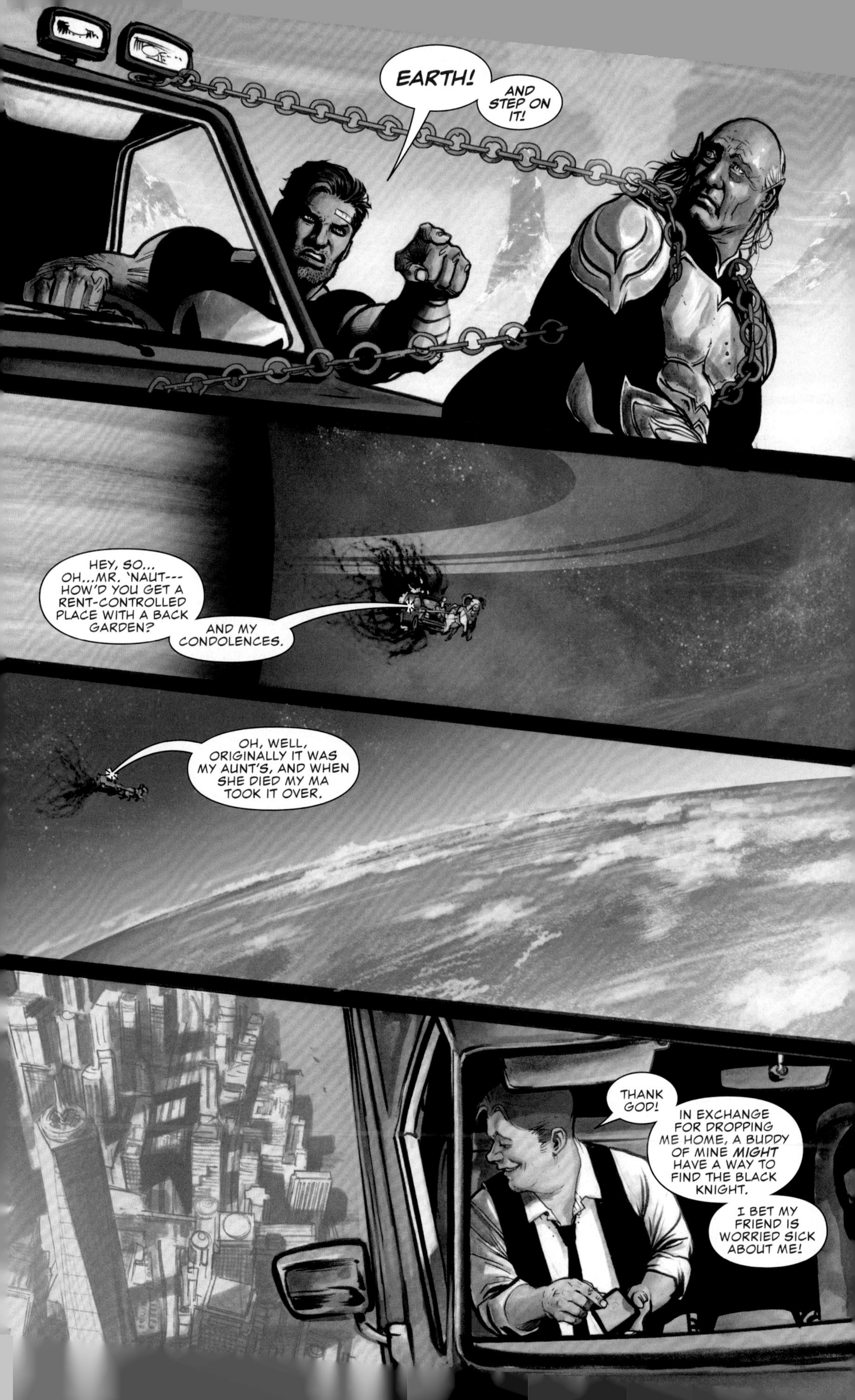
EARTH!
AND STEP ON IT!
HEY, SO... OH...MR. 'NAUT--- HOW'D YOU GET A RENT-CONTROLLED PLACE WITH A BACK GARDEN?
AND MY CONDOLENCES.
OH, WELL, ORIGINALLY IT WAS MY AUNT'S, AND WHEN SHE DIED MY MA TOOK IT OVER.
THANK GOD!
IN EXCHANGE FOR DROPPING ME HOME, A BUDDY OF MINE *MIGHT* HAVE A WAY TO FIND THE BLACK KNIGHT.
I BET MY FRIEND IS WORRIED SICK ABOUT ME!

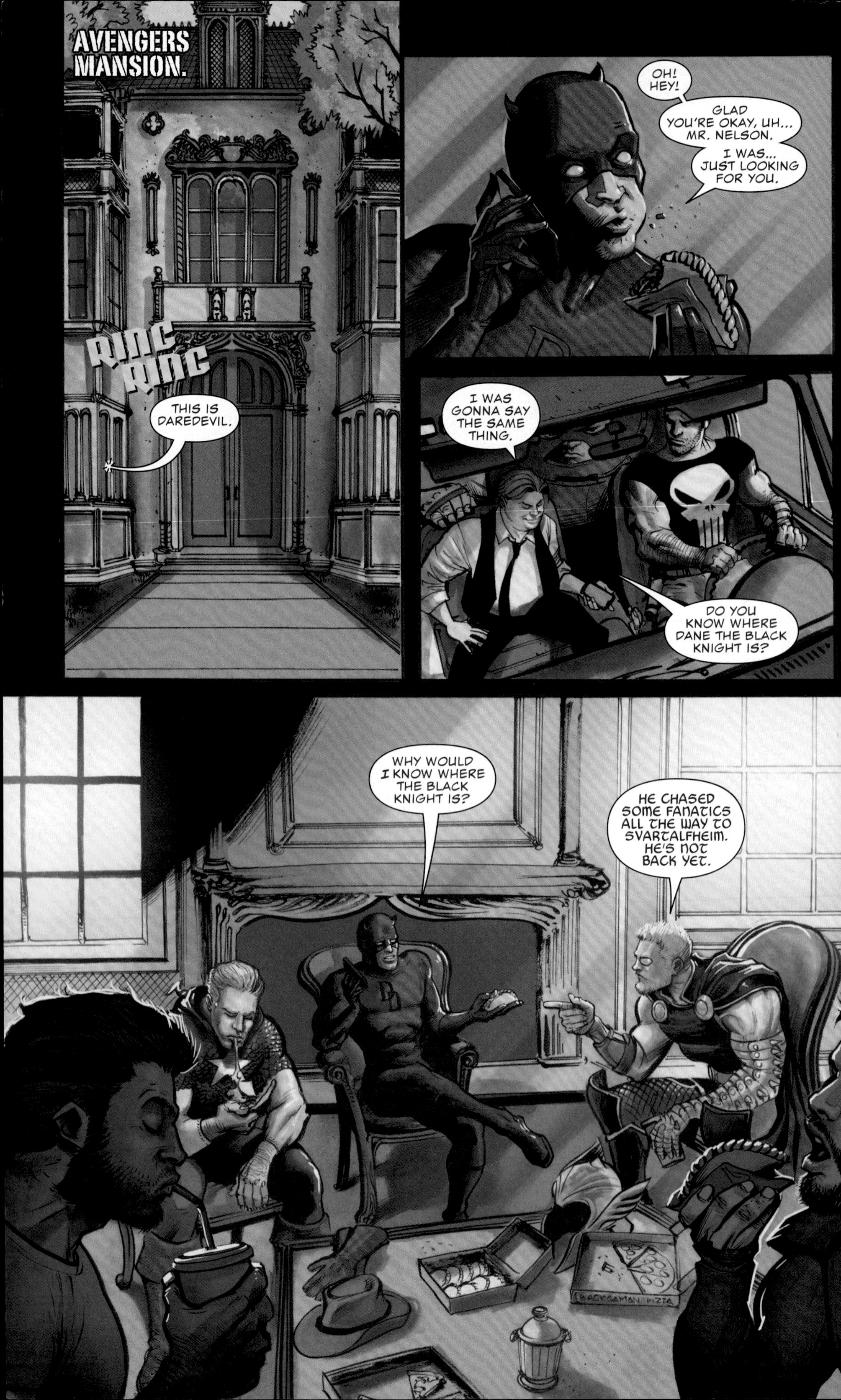
AVENGERS MANSION.
RING RING
THIS IS DAREDEVIL.
OH! HEY!
GLAD YOU'RE OKAY, UH... MR. NELSON.
I WAS... JUST LOOKING FOR YOU.
I WAS GONNA SAY THE SAME THING.
DO YOU KNOW WHERE DANE THE BLACK KNIGHT IS?
WHY WOULD I KNOW WHERE THE BLACK KNIGHT IS?
HE CHASED SOME FANATICS ALL THE WAY TO SVARTALFHEIM. HE'S NOT BACK YET.
BACKGAMON PIZZA

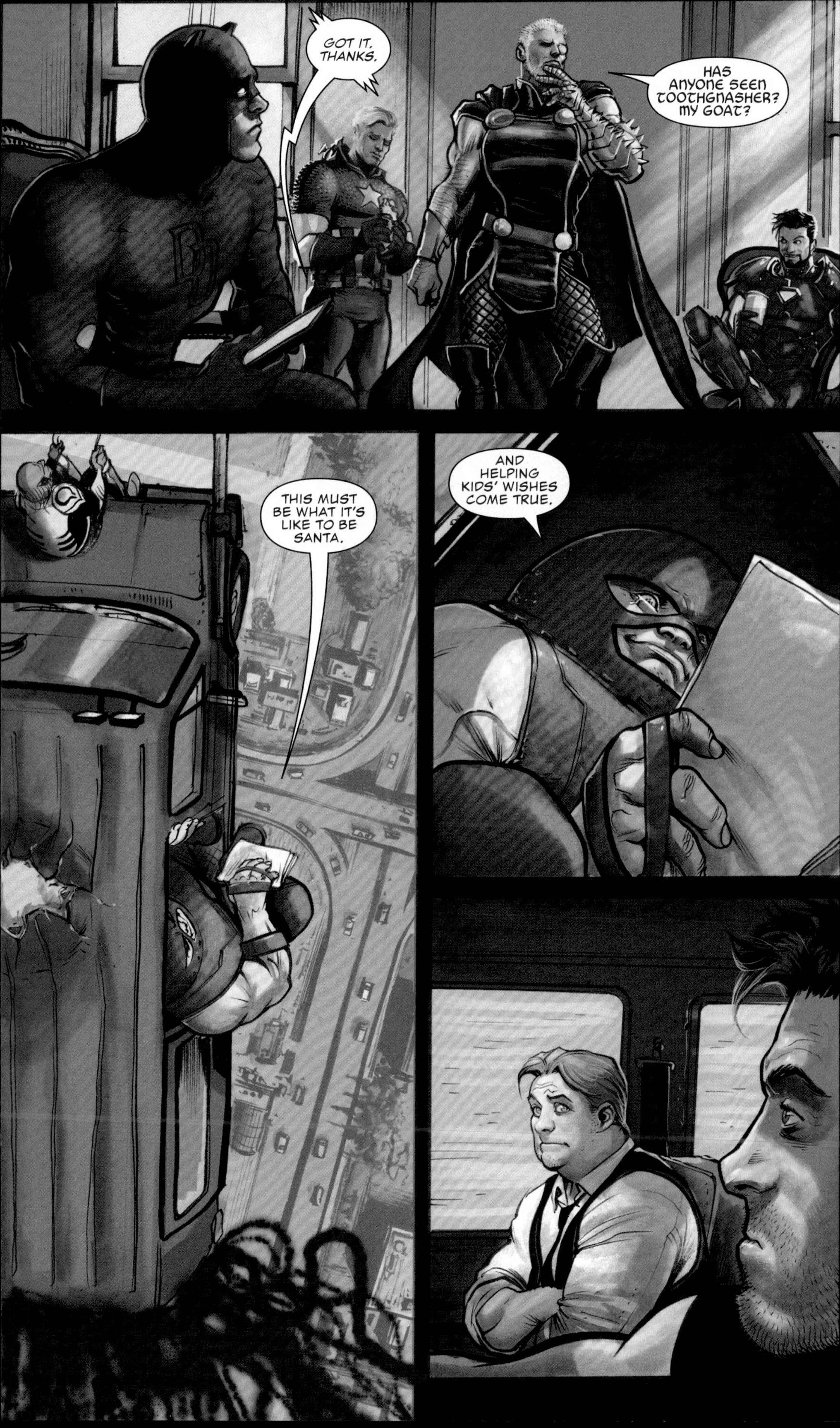
GOT IT. THANKS.
HAS ANYONE SEEN TOOTHGNASHER? MY GOAT?
THIS MUST BE WHAT IT'S LIKE TO BE SANTA.
AND HELPING KIDS' WISHES COME TRUE.

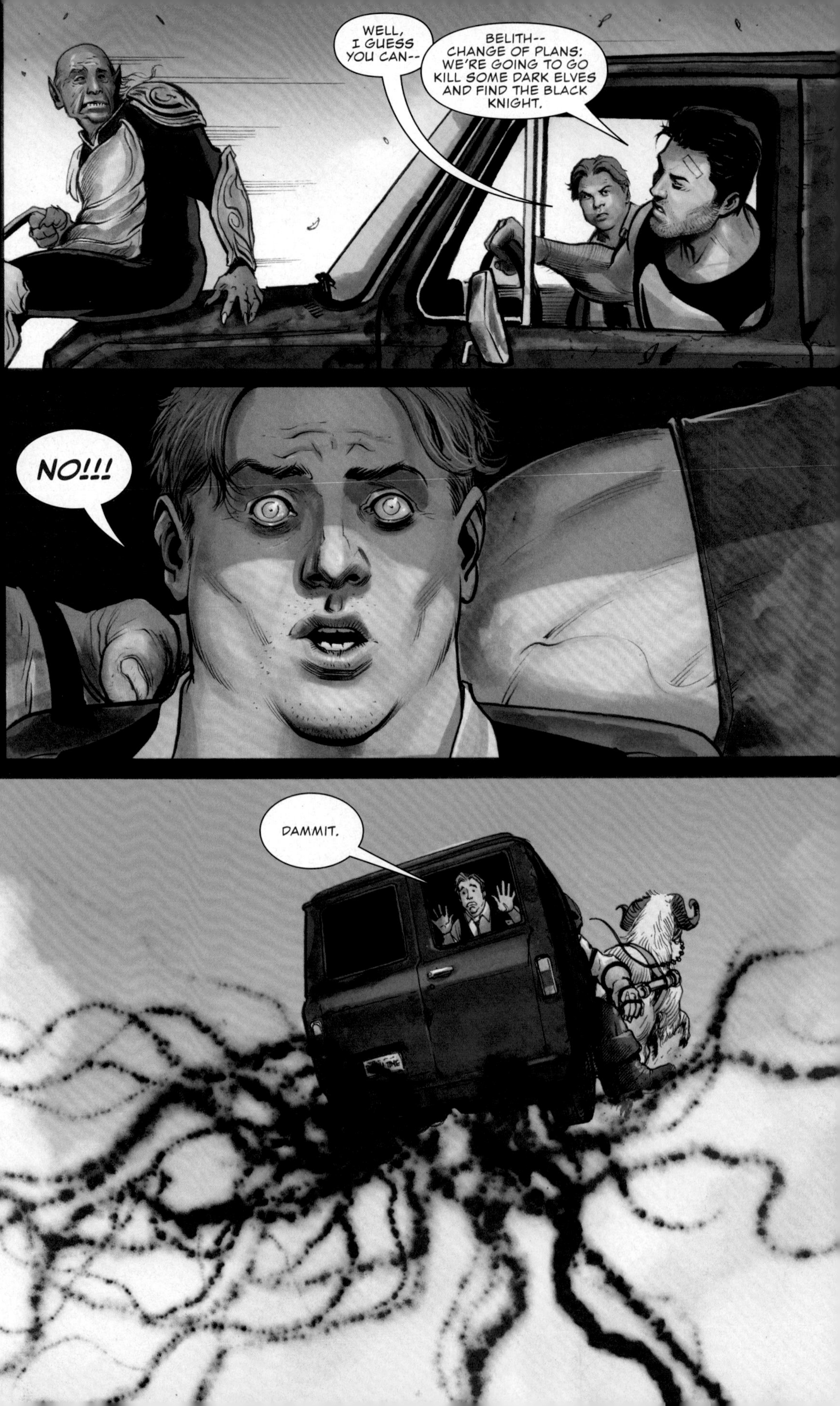
WELL, I GUESS YOU CAN--
BELITH-- CHANGE OF PLANS: WE'RE GOING TO GO KILL SOME DARK ELVES AND FIND THE BLACK KNIGHT.
NO!!!
DAMMIT.

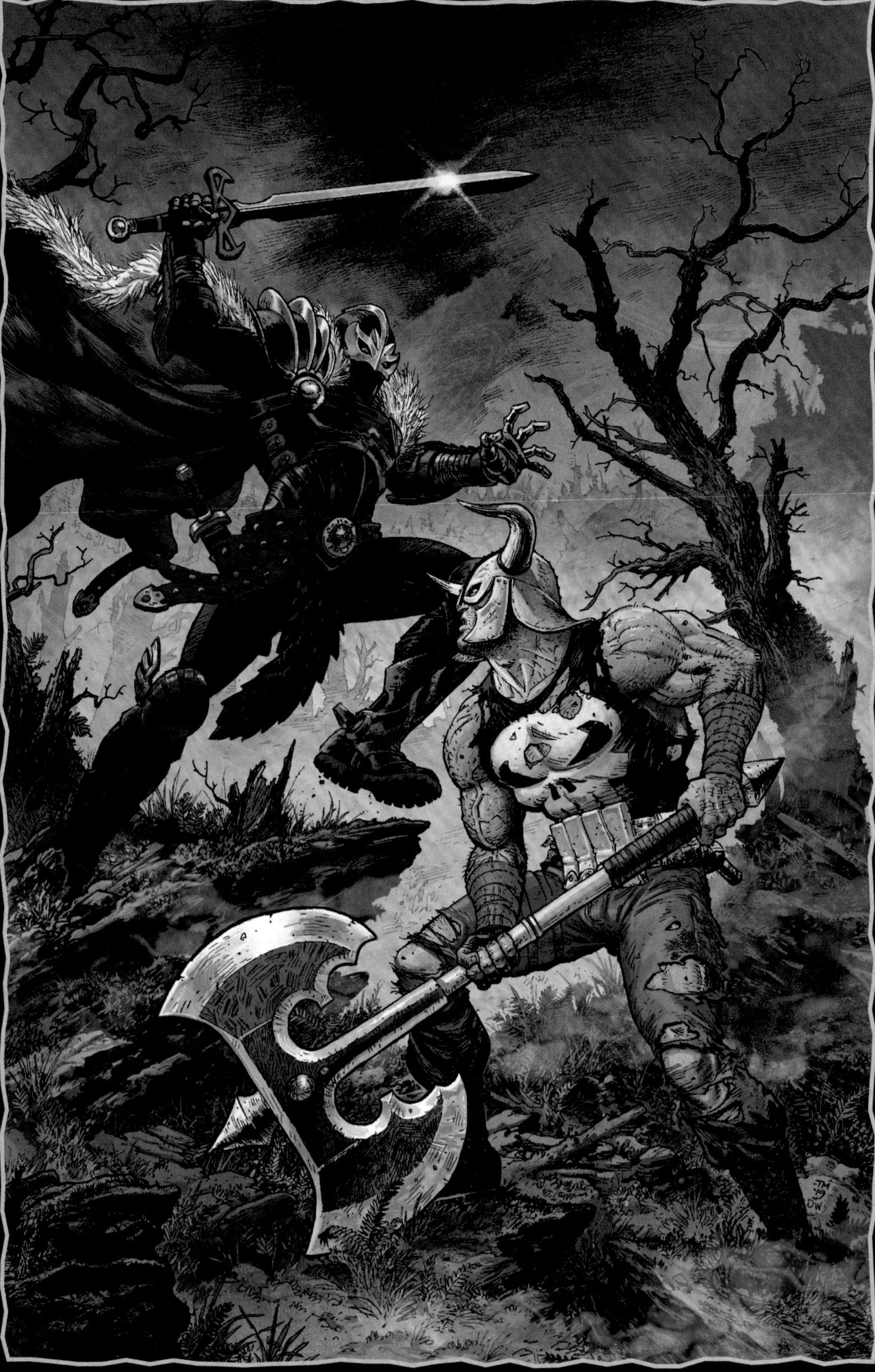

FOUR

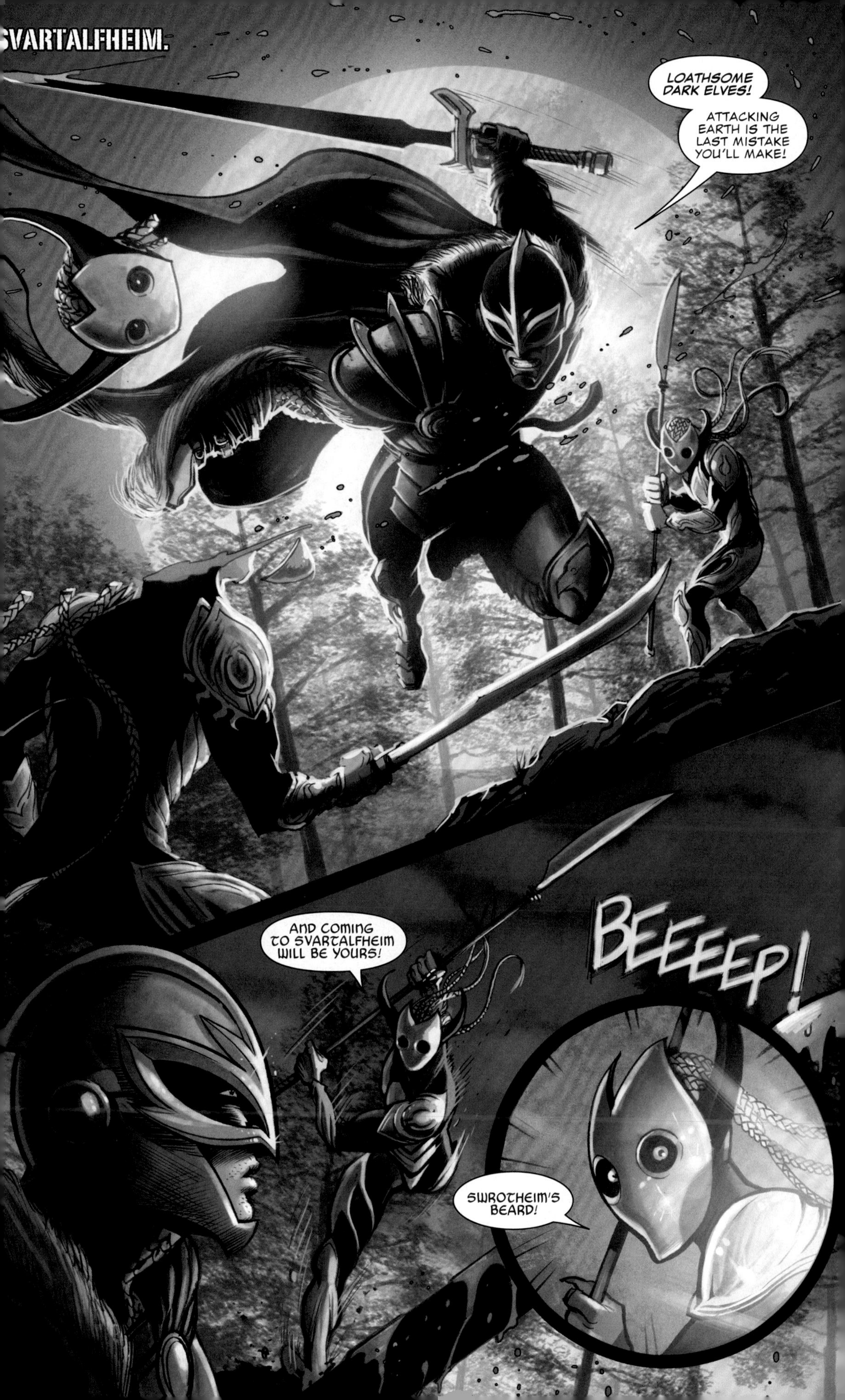
SVARTALFHEIM.
LOATHSOME DARK ELVES!
ATTACKING EARTH IS THE LAST MISTAKE YOU'LL MAKE!
AND COMING TO SVARTALFHEIM WILL BE YOURS!
BEEEEP!
SWROTHEIM'S BEARD!

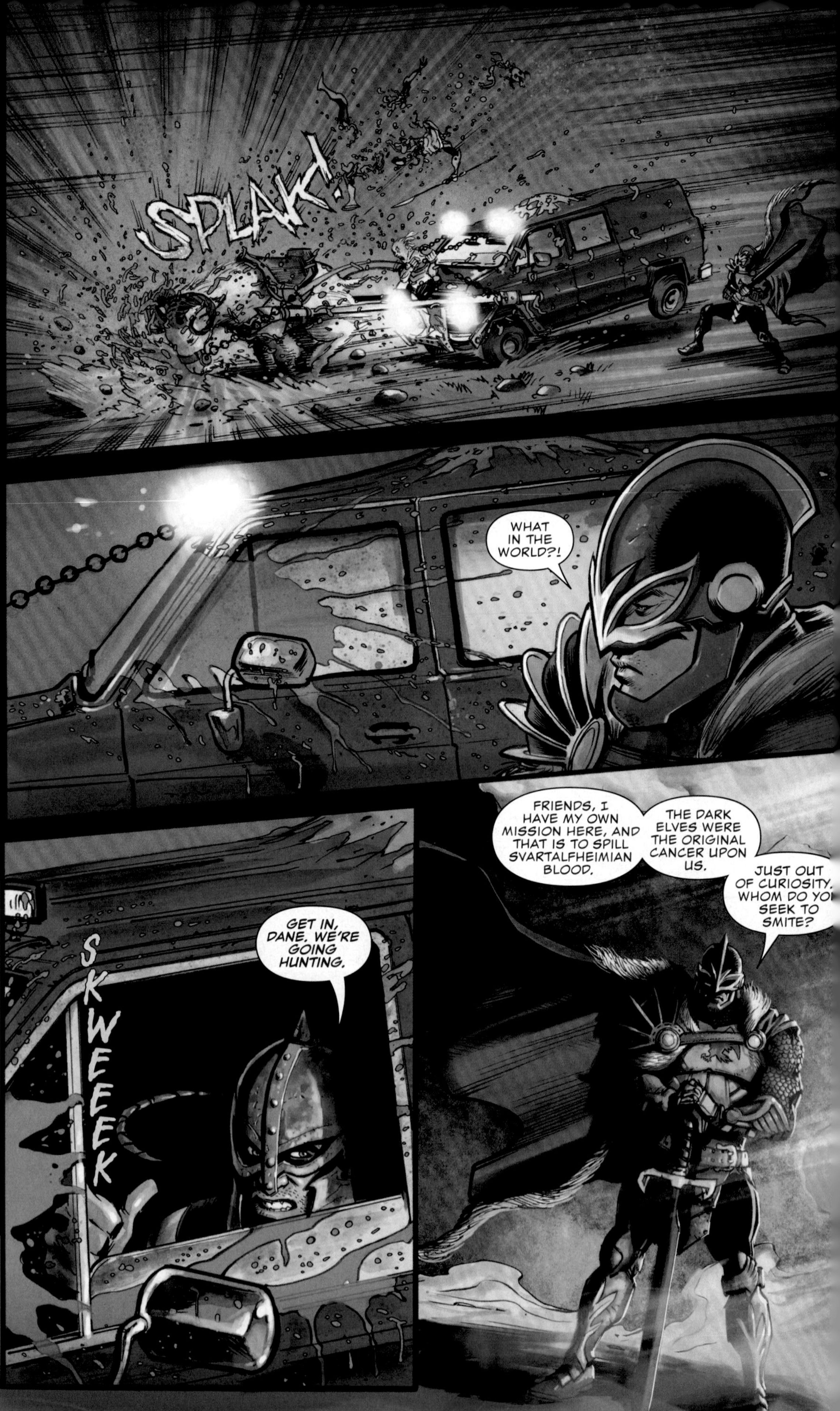
SPLAK!
WHAT IN THE WORLD?!
GET IN, DANE. WE'RE GOING HUNTING.
SKWEEEK
FRIENDS, I HAVE MY OWN MISSION HERE, AND THAT IS TO SPILL SVARTALFHEIMIAN BLOOD.
THE DARK ELVES WERE THE ORIGINAL CANCER UPON US.
JUST OUT OF CURIOSITY, WHOM DO YO SEEK TO SMITE?

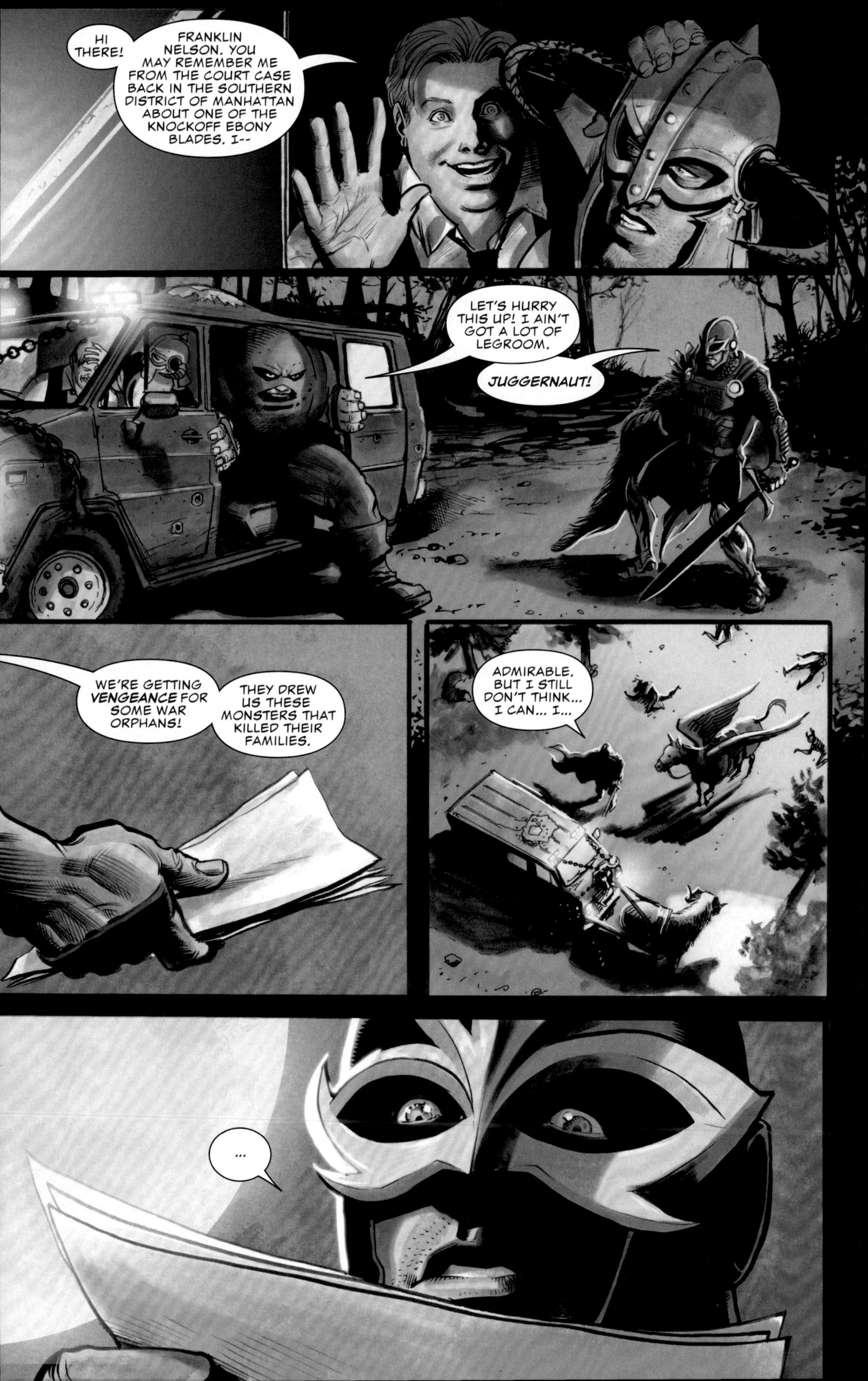

HI THERE!
FRANKLIN NELSON. YOU MAY REMEMBER ME FROM THE COURT CASE BACK IN THE SOUTHERN DISTRICT OF MANHATTAN ABOUT ONE OF THE KNOCKOFF EBONY BLADES. I--
LET'S HURRY THIS UP! I AIN'T GOT A LOT OF LEGROOM.
JUGGERNAUT!
WE'RE GETTING VENGEANCE FOR SOME WAR ORPHANS!
THEY DREW US THESE MONSTERS THAT KILLED THEIR FAMILIES.
ADMIRABLE, BUT I STILL DON'T THINK... I CAN... I...
...

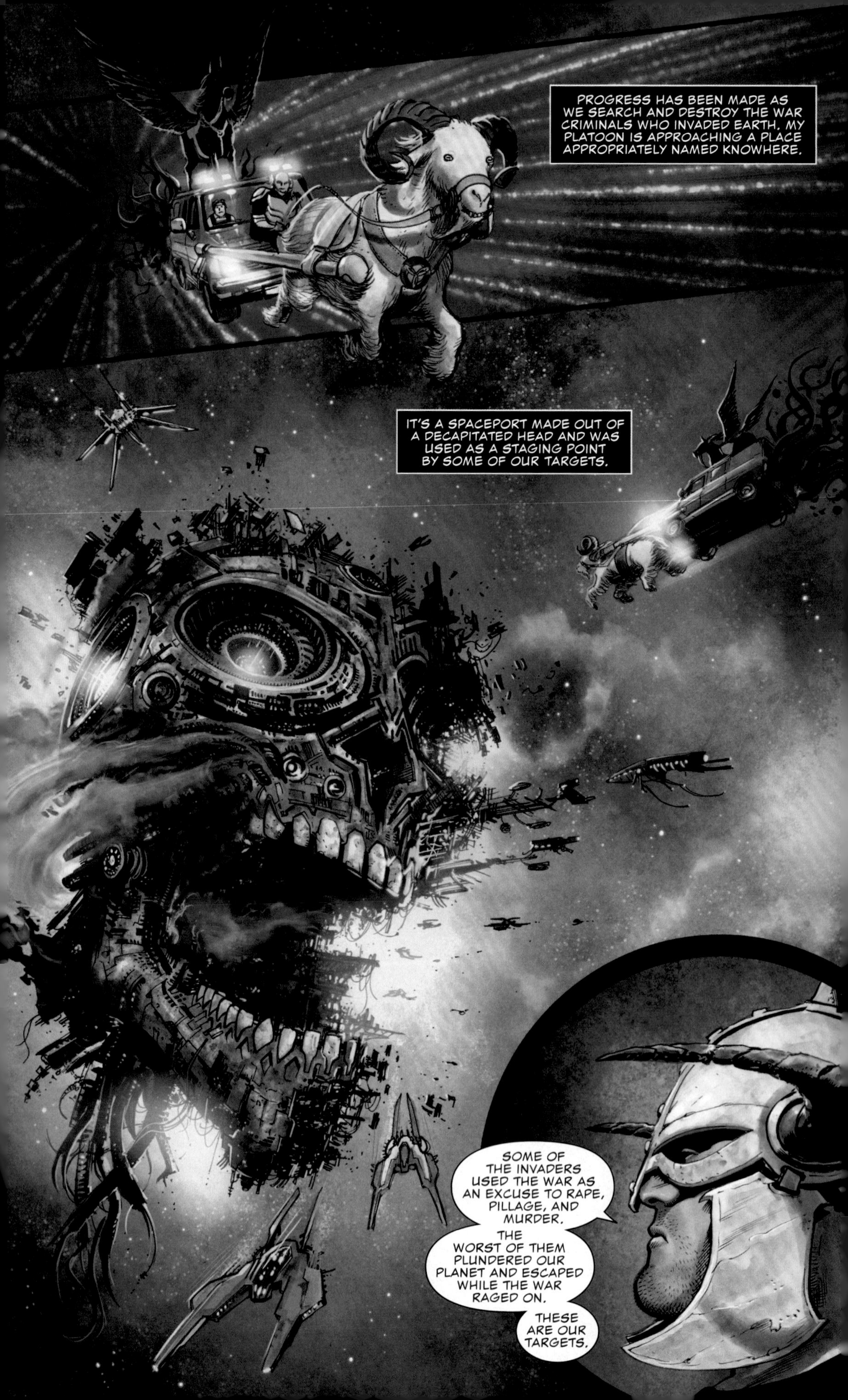

PROGRESS HAS BEEN MADE AS WE SEARCH AND DESTROY THE WAR CRIMINALS WHO INVADED EARTH. MY PLATOON IS APPROACHING A PLACE APPROPRIATELY NAMED KNOWHERE.
IT'S A SPACEPORT MADE OUT OF A DECAPITATED HEAD AND WAS USED AS A STAGING POINT BY SOME OF OUR TARGETS.
SOME OF THE INVADERS USED THE WAR AS AN EXCUSE TO RAPE, PILLAGE, AND MURDER.
THE WORST OF THEM PLUNDERED OUR PLANET AND ESCAPED WHILE THE WAR RAGED ON.
THESE ARE OUR TARGETS.

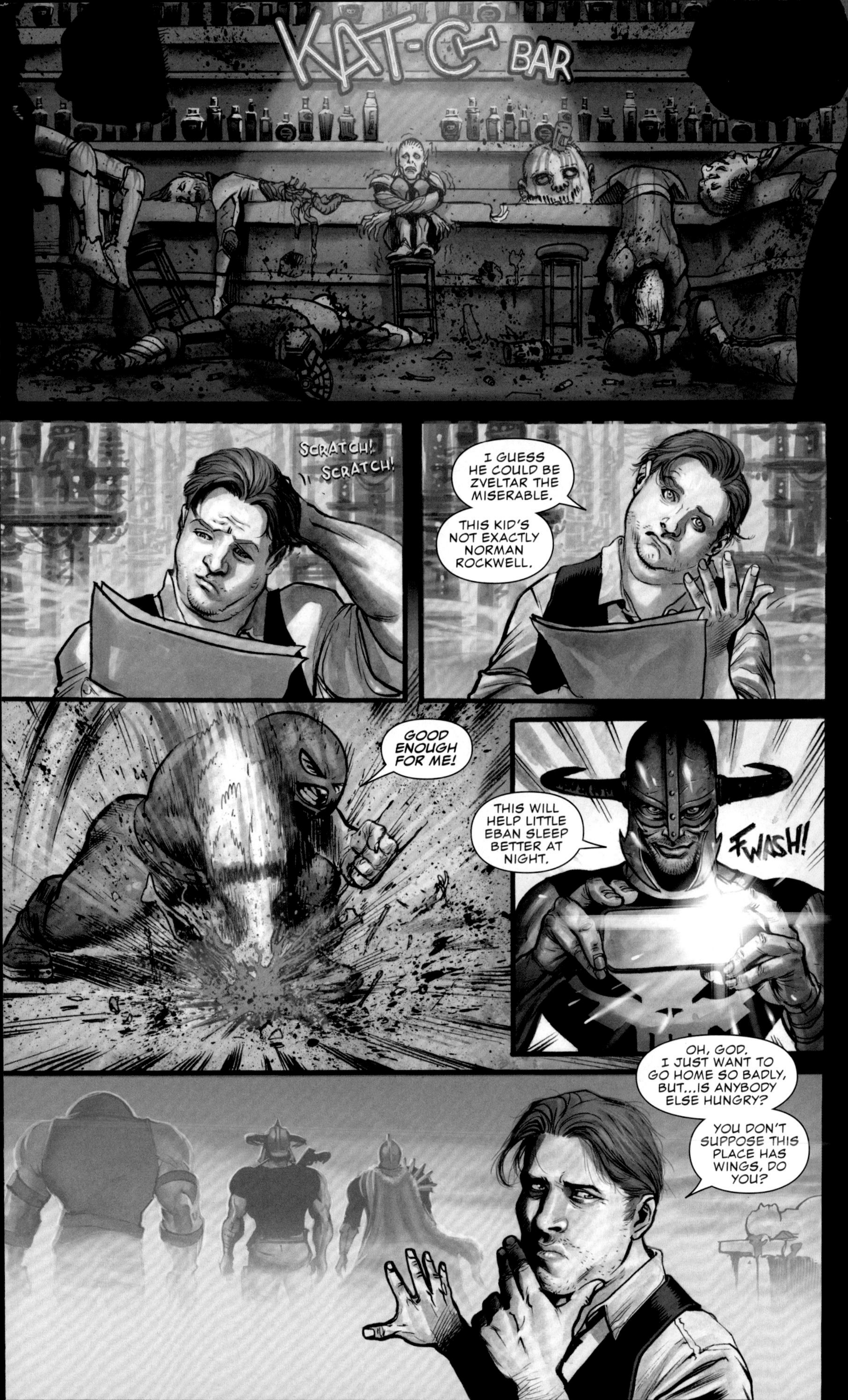
KAT-C BAR
SCRATCH!
SCRATCH!
I GUESS HE COULD BE ZVELTAR THE MISERABLE.
THIS KID'S NOT EXACTLY NORMAN ROCKWELL.
GOOD ENOUGH FOR ME!
THIS WILL HELP LITTLE EBAN SLEEP BETTER AT NIGHT.
FWASH!
OH, GOD. I JUST WANT TO GO HOME SO BADLY, BUT...IS ANYBODY ELSE HUNGRY?
YOU DON'T SUPPOSE THIS PLACE HAS WINGS, DO YOU?

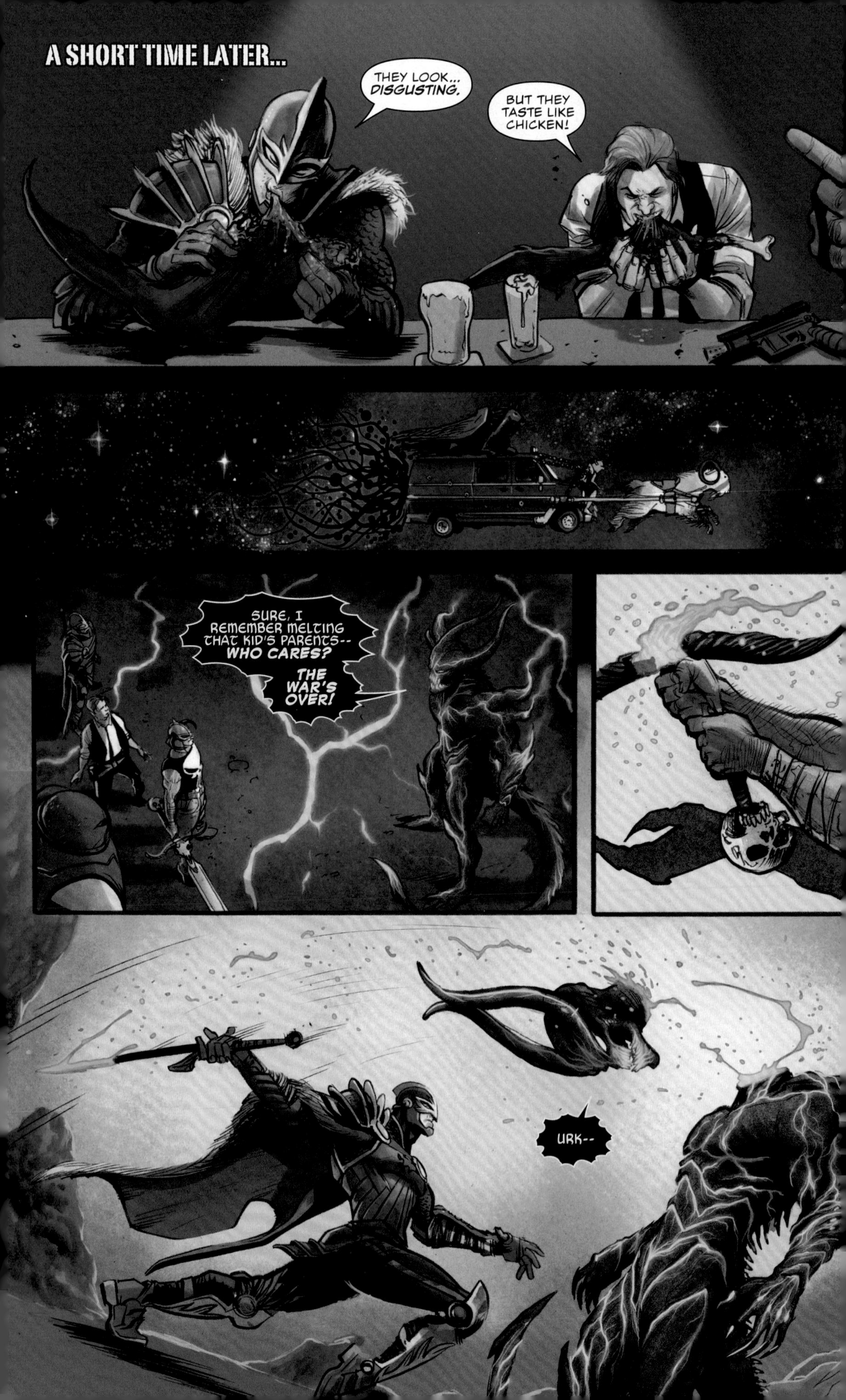
A SHORT TIME LATER...
THEY LOOK... DISGUSTING.
BUT THEY TASTE LIKE CHICKEN!
SURE, I REMEMBER MELTING THAT KID'S PARENTS-- WHO CARES?
THE WAR'S OVER!
URK--

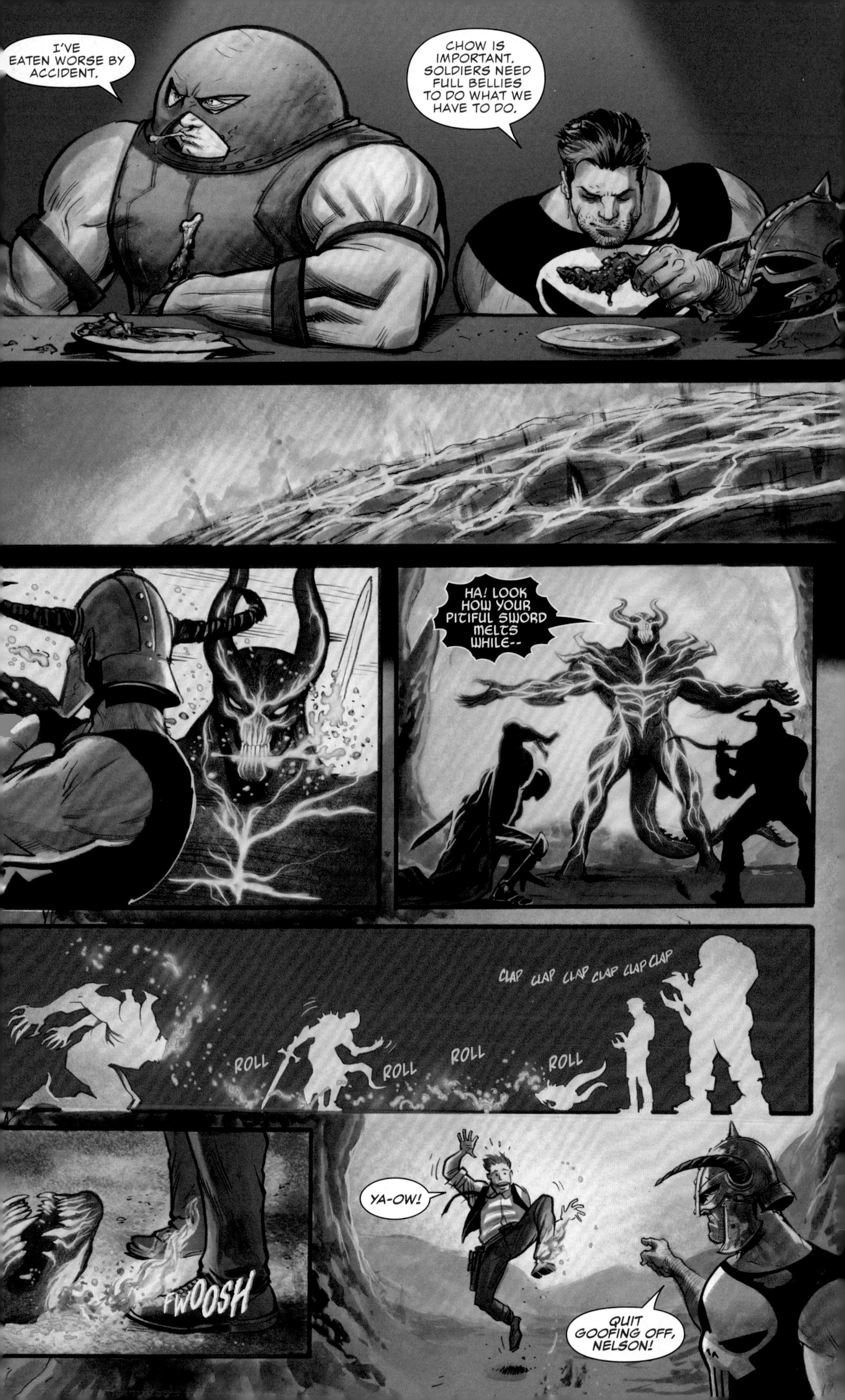
I'VE EATEN WORSE BY ACCIDENT.
CHOW IS IMPORTANT. SOLDIERS NEED FULL BELLIES TO DO WHAT WE HAVE TO DO.
HA! LOOK HOW YOUR PITIFUL SWORD MELTS WHILE--
CLAP CLAP CLAP CLAP CLAP CLAP
ROLL
ROLL
ROLL
ROLL
FWOOSH
YA-OW!
QUIT GOOFING OFF, NELSON!

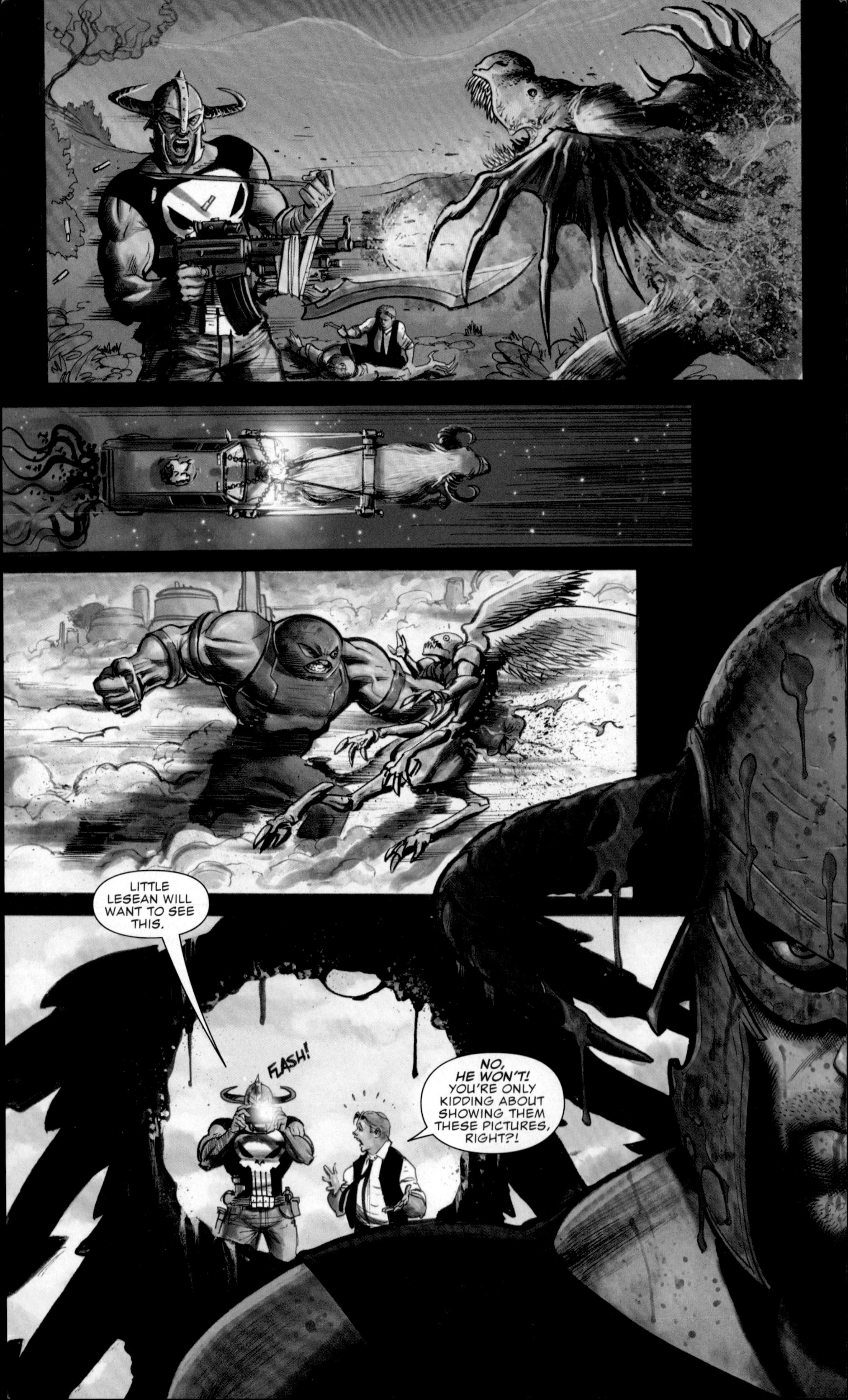
LITTLE LESEAN WILL WANT TO SEE THIS.
FLASH!
NO, HE WON'T! YOU'RE ONLY KIDDING ABOUT SHOWING THEM THESE PICTURES, RIGHT?!

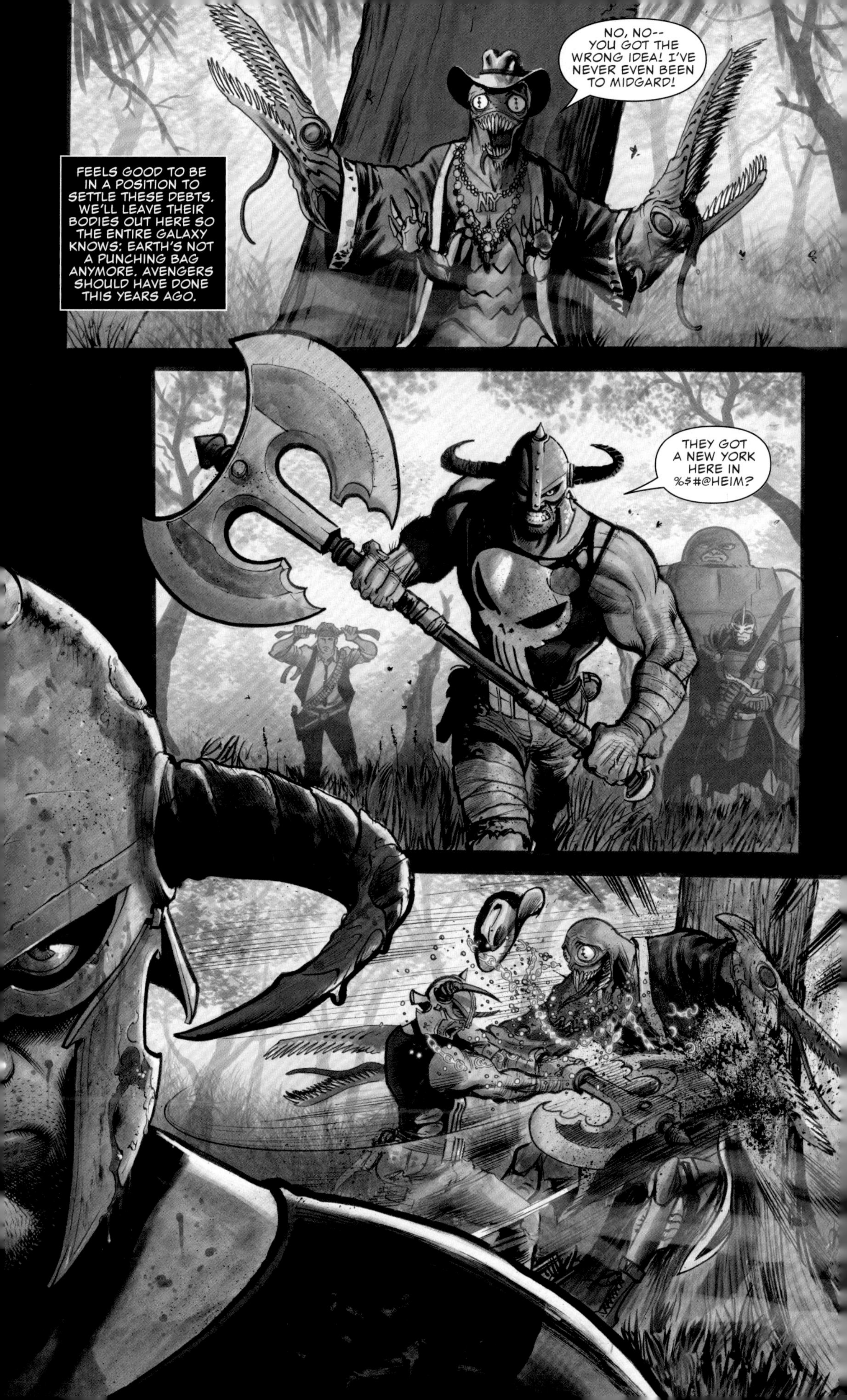
NO, NO-- YOU GOT THE WRONG IDEA! I'VE NEVER EVEN BEEN TO MIDGARD!
FEELS GOOD TO BE IN A POSITION TO SETTLE THESE DEBTS. WE'LL LEAVE THEIR BODIES OUT HERE SO THE ENTIRE GALAXY KNOWS: EARTH'S NOT A PUNCHING BAG ANYMORE. AVENGERS SHOULD HAVE DONE THIS YEARS AGO.
THEY GOT A NEW YORK HERE IN %$#@HEIM?

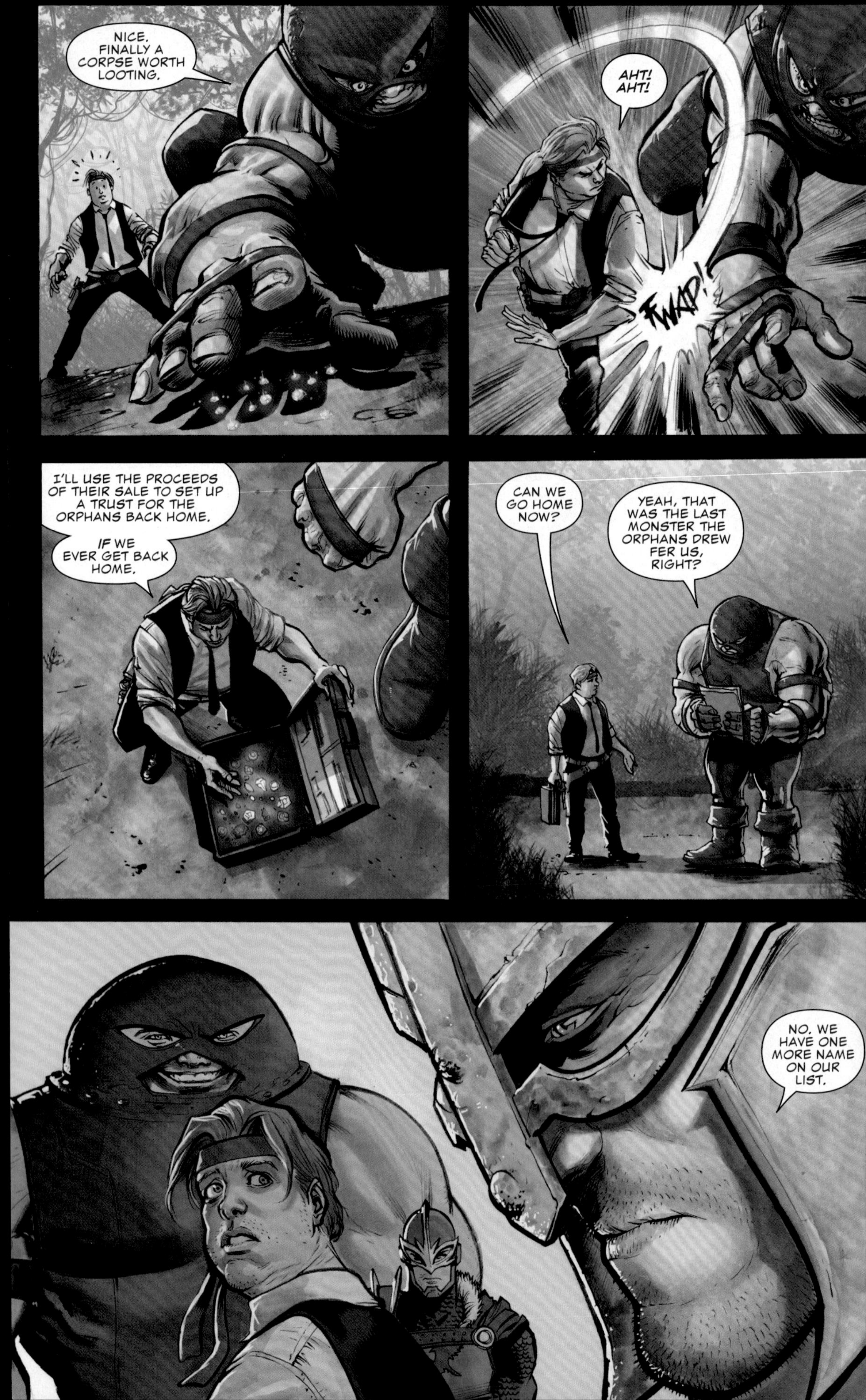
NICE. FINALLY A CORPSE WORTH LOOTING.
AHT! AHT!
FWAP!
I'LL USE THE PROCEEDS OF THEIR SALE TO SET UP A TRUST FOR THE ORPHANS BACK HOME.
IF WE EVER GET BACK HOME.
CAN WE GO HOME NOW?
YEAH, THAT WAS THE LAST MONSTER THE ORPHANS DREW FER US, RIGHT?
NO. WE HAVE ONE MORE NAME ON OUR LIST.

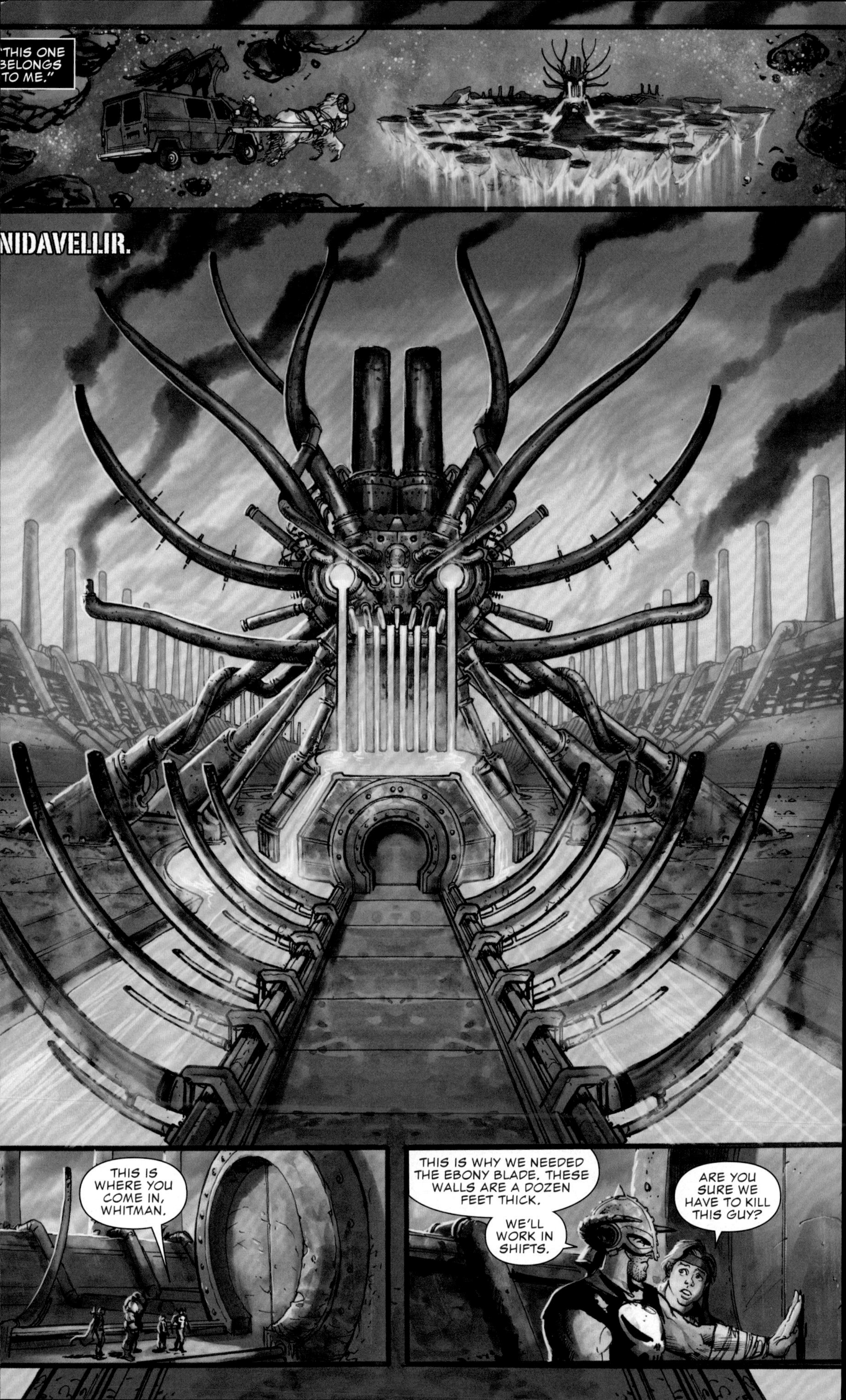
"THIS ONE BELONGS TO ME."
NIDAVELLIR.
THIS IS WHERE YOU COME IN, WHITMAN.
THIS IS WHY WE NEEDED THE EBONY BLADE. THESE WALLS ARE A DOZEN FEET THICK.
WE'LL WORK IN SHIFTS.
ARE YOU SURE WE HAVE TO KILL THIS GUY?

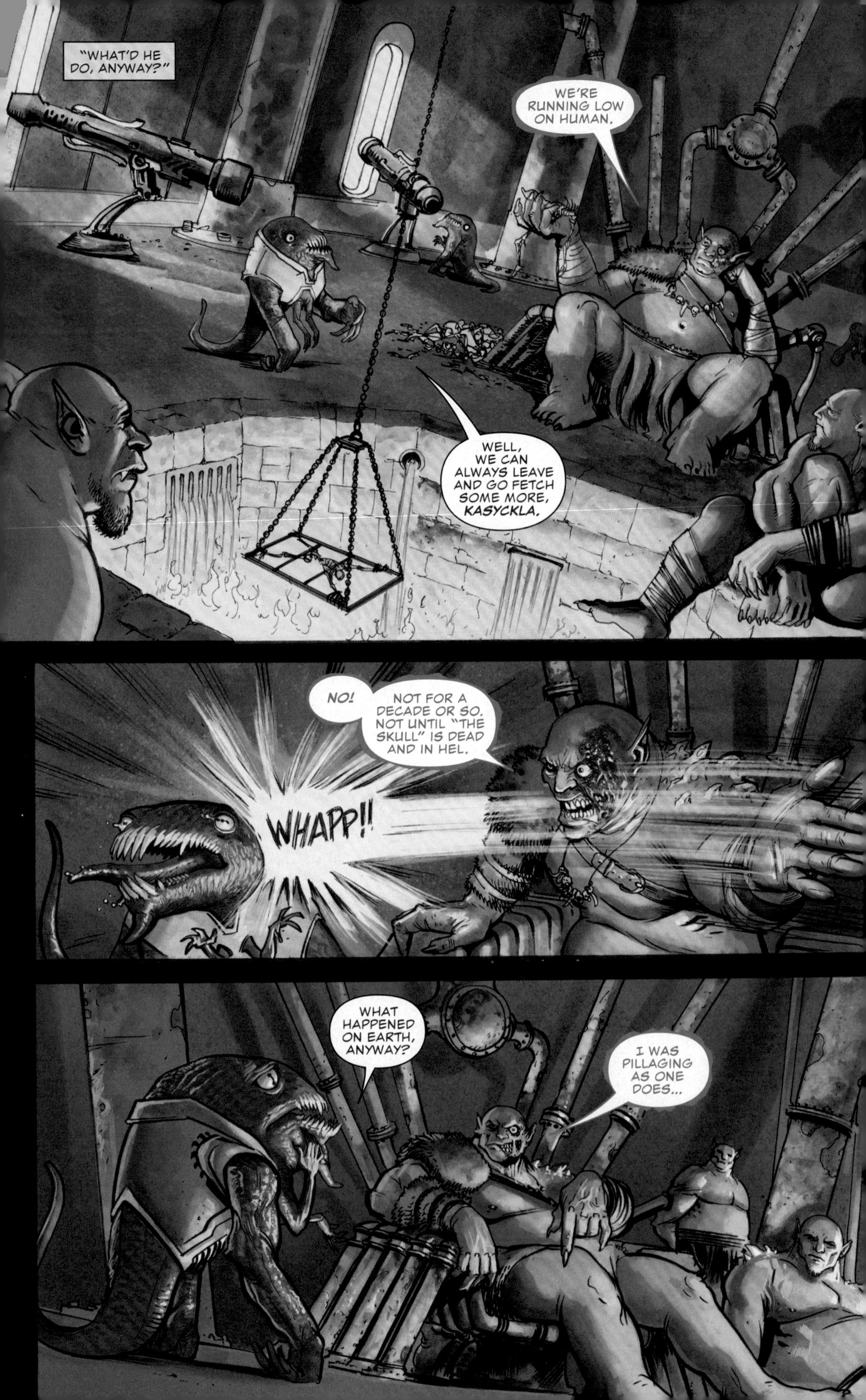
"WHAT'D HE DO, ANYWAY?"
WE'RE RUNNING LOW ON HUMAN.
WELL, WE CAN ALWAYS LEAVE AND GO FETCH SOME MORE, KASYCKLA.
NO!
NOT FOR A DECADE OR SO. NOT UNTIL "THE SKULL" IS DEAD AND IN HEL.
WHAPP!!
WHAT HAPPENED ON EARTH, ANYWAY?
I WAS PILLAGING AS ONE DOES...

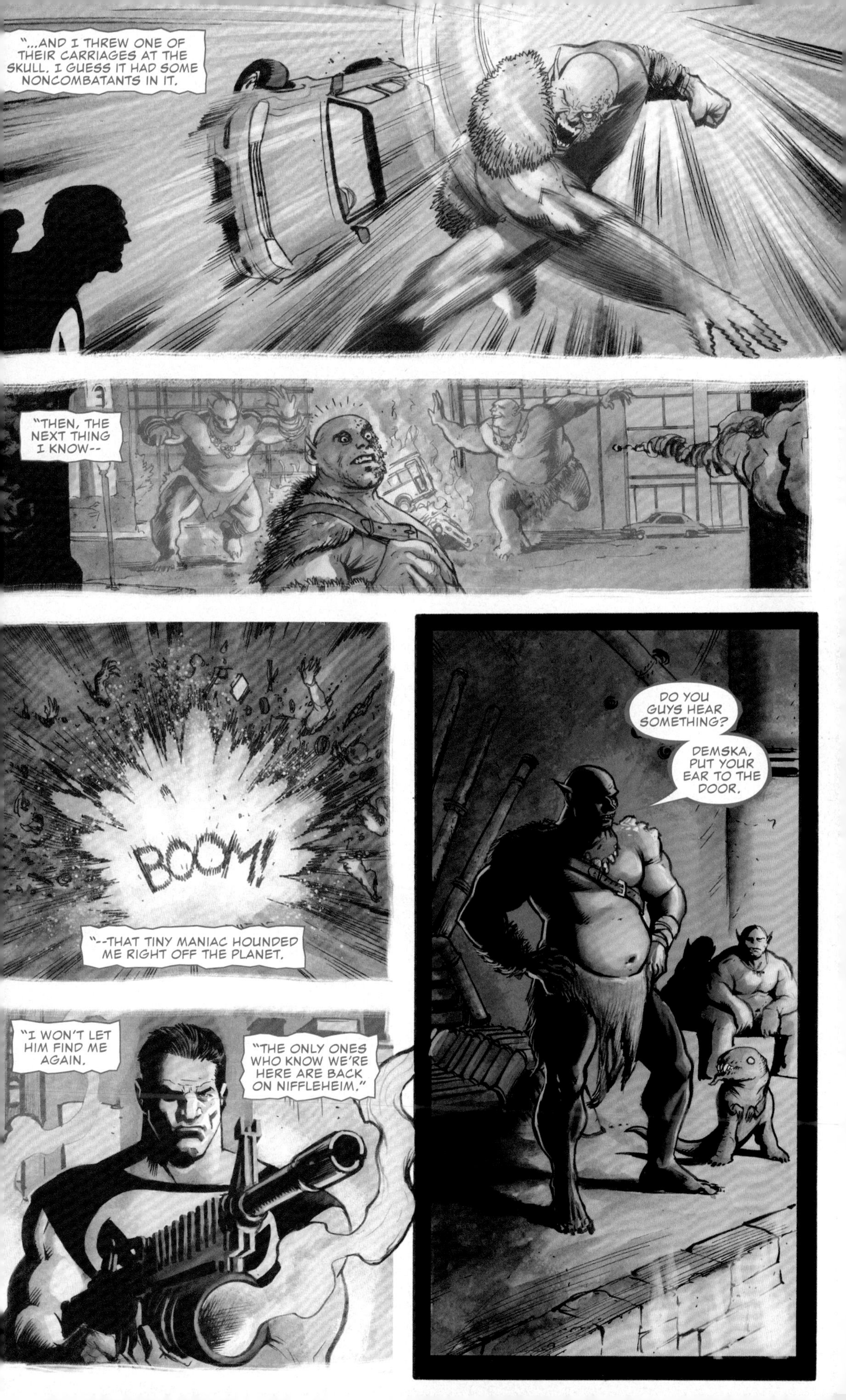
"...AND I THREW ONE OF THEIR CARRIAGES AT THE SKULL. I GUESS IT HAD SOME NONCOMBATANTS IN IT.
"THEN, THE NEXT THING I KNOW--
BOOM!
"--THAT TINY MANIAC HOUNDED ME RIGHT OFF THE PLANET.
"I WON'T LET HIM FIND ME AGAIN.
"THE ONLY ONES WHO KNOW WE'RE HERE ARE BACK ON NIFFLEHEIM."
DO YOU GUYS HEAR SOMETHING?
DEMSKA, PUT YOUR EAR TO THE DOOR.

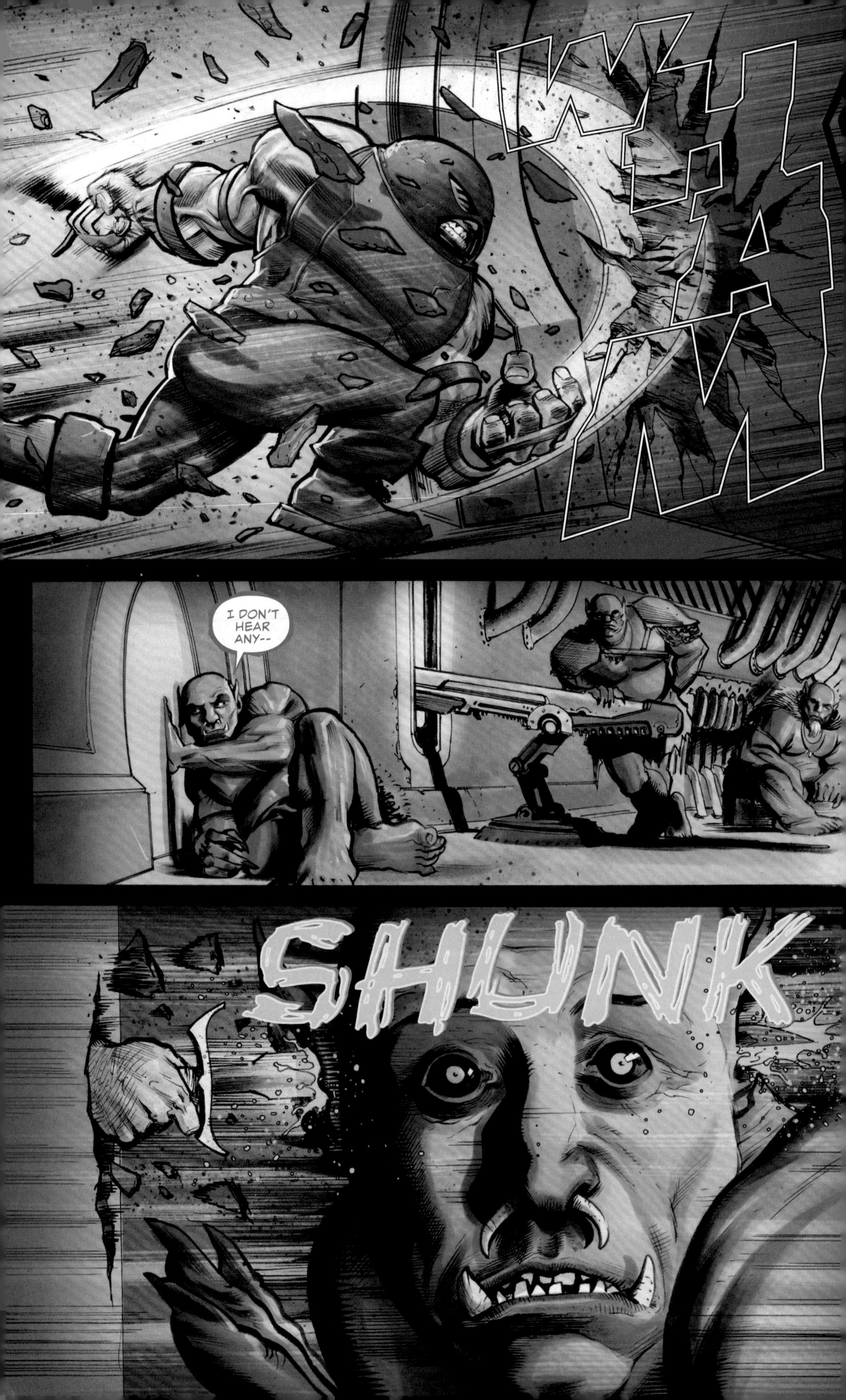
WHAM
I DON'T HEAR ANY--
SHUNK

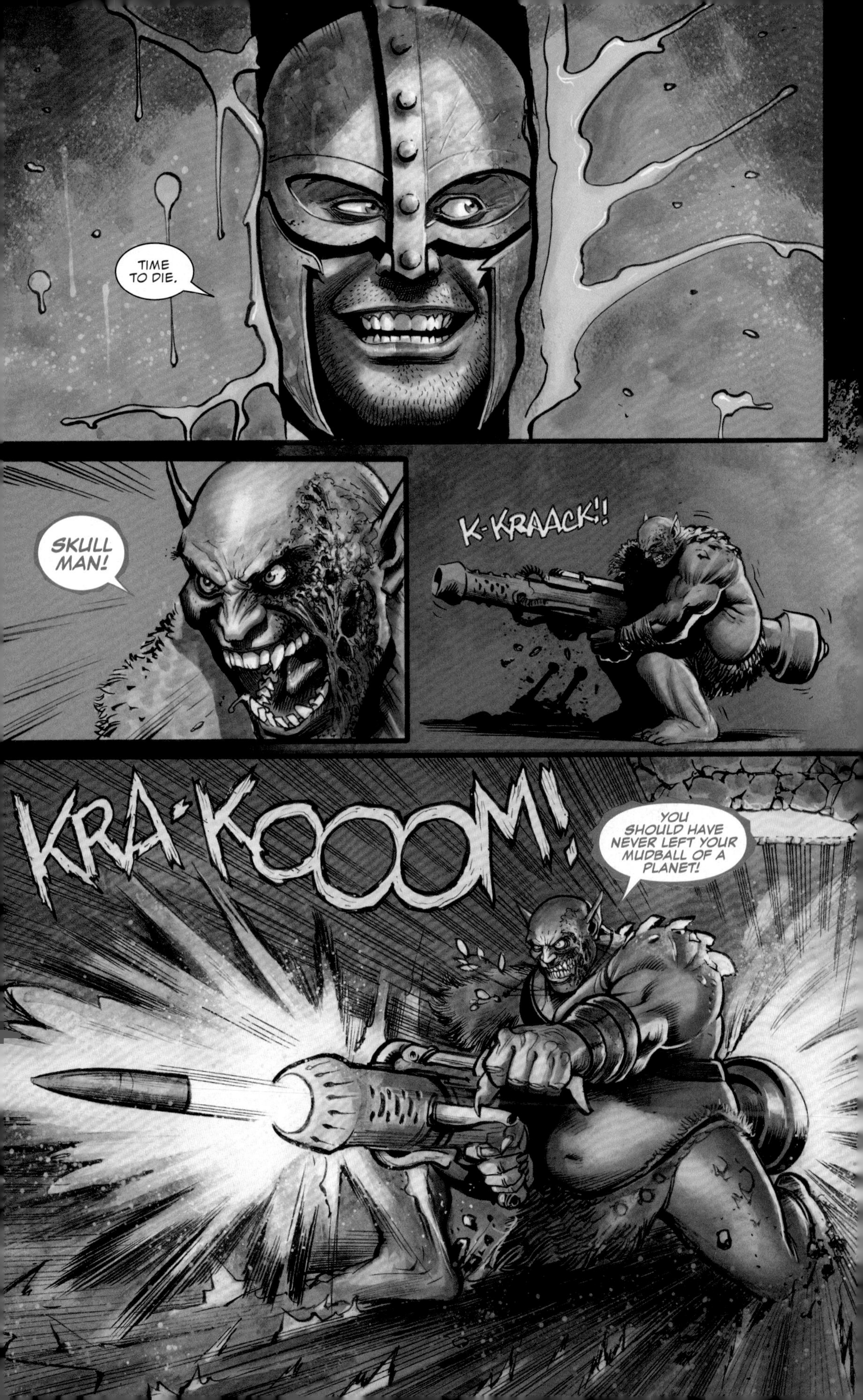
TIME TO DIE.
SKULL MAN!
K-KRAACK!!
KRA-KOOOM!
YOU SHOULD HAVE NEVER LEFT YOUR MUDBALL OF A PLANET!

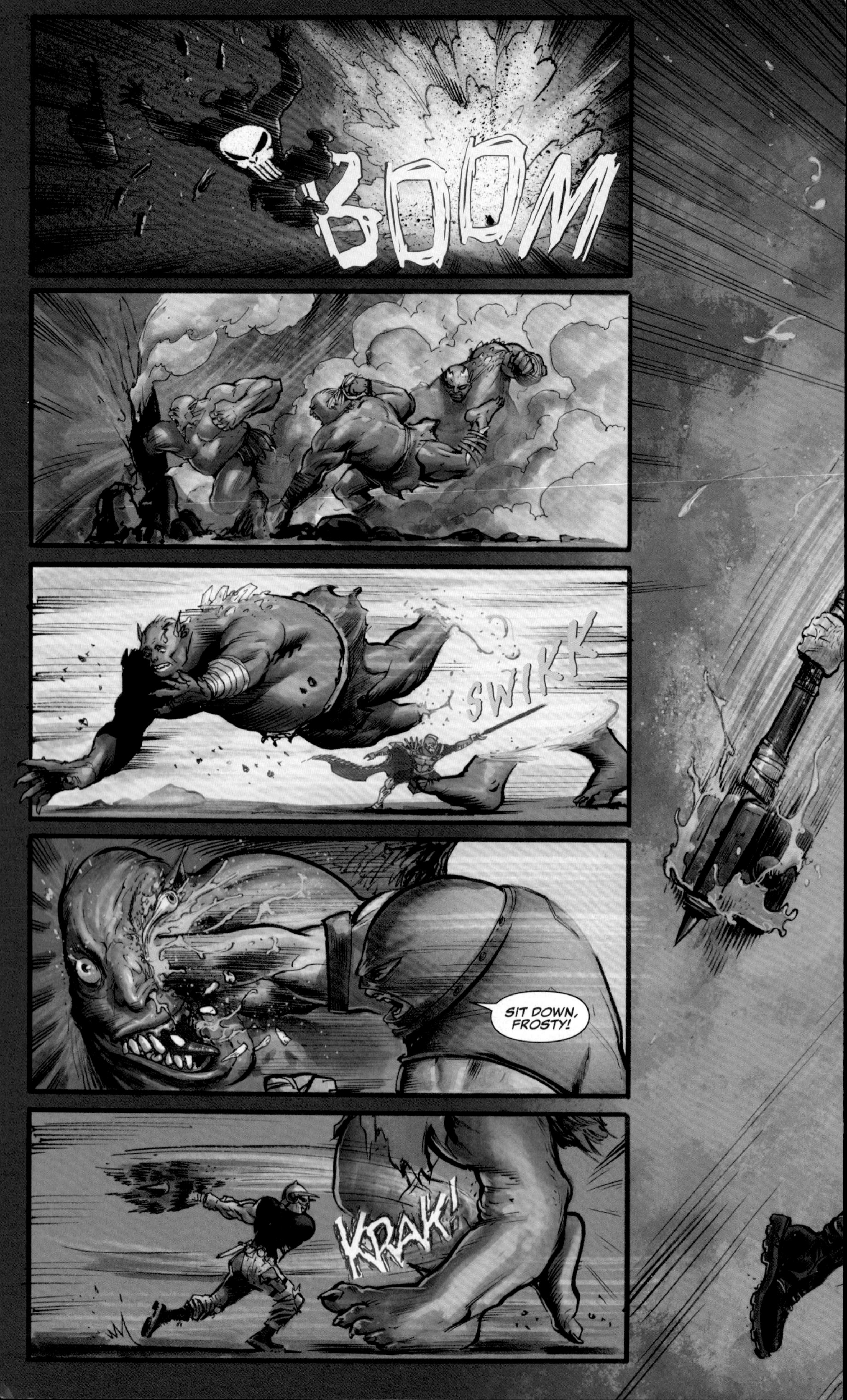
BOOM
SWIKK
SIT DOWN, FROSTY!
KRAK!

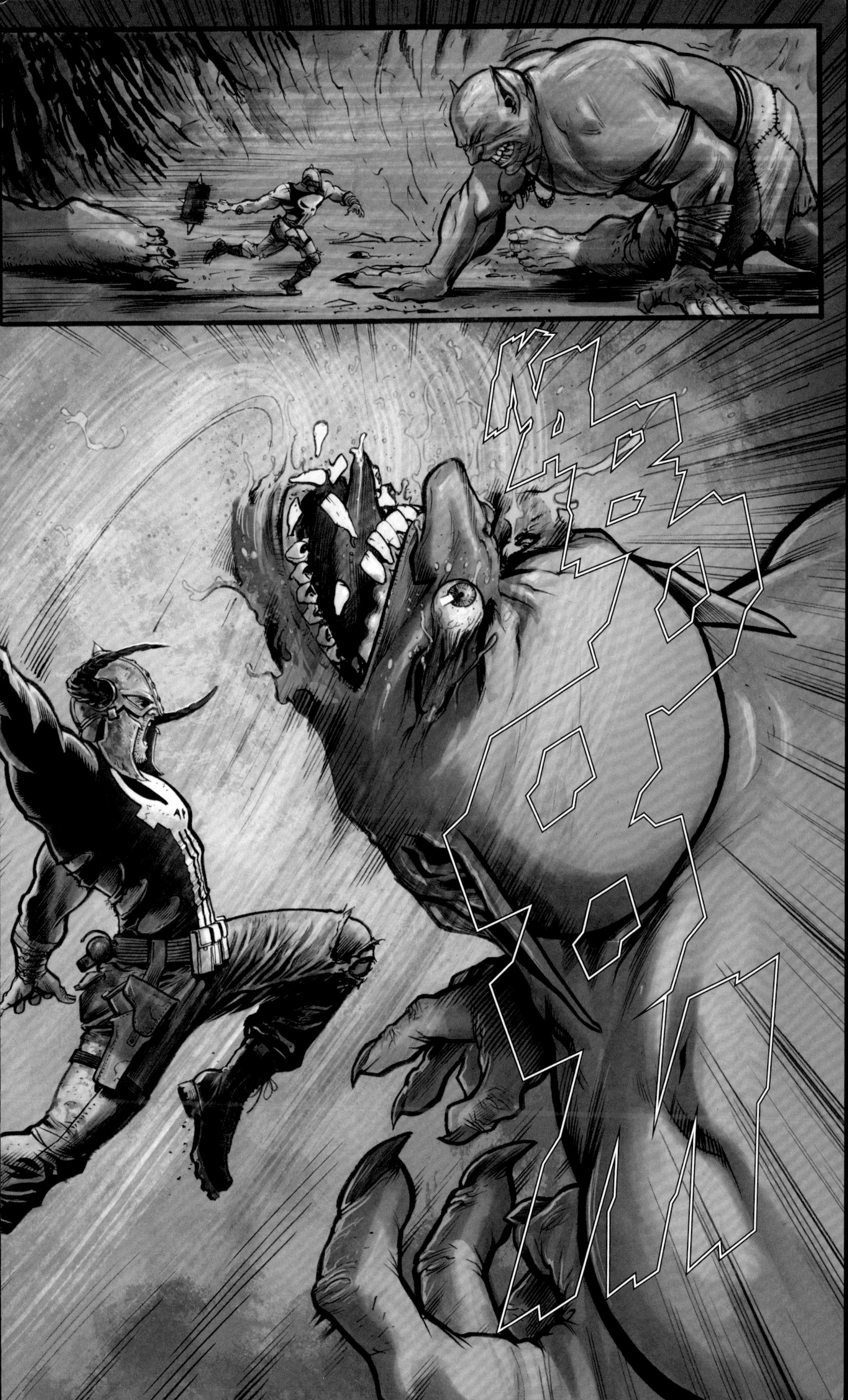
KABOOOM

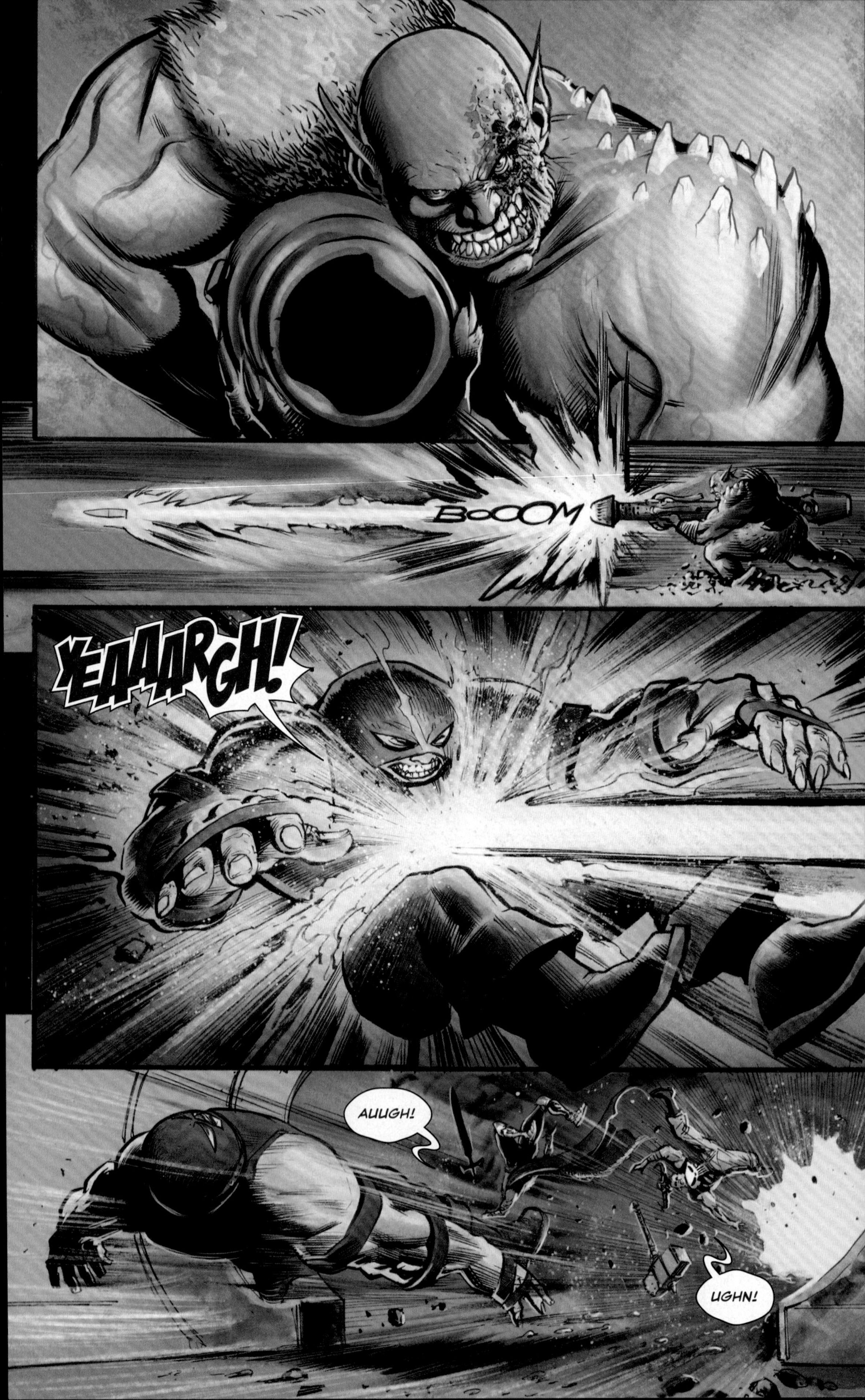
BOOOM
YEAAARGH!
AUUGH!
UGHN!

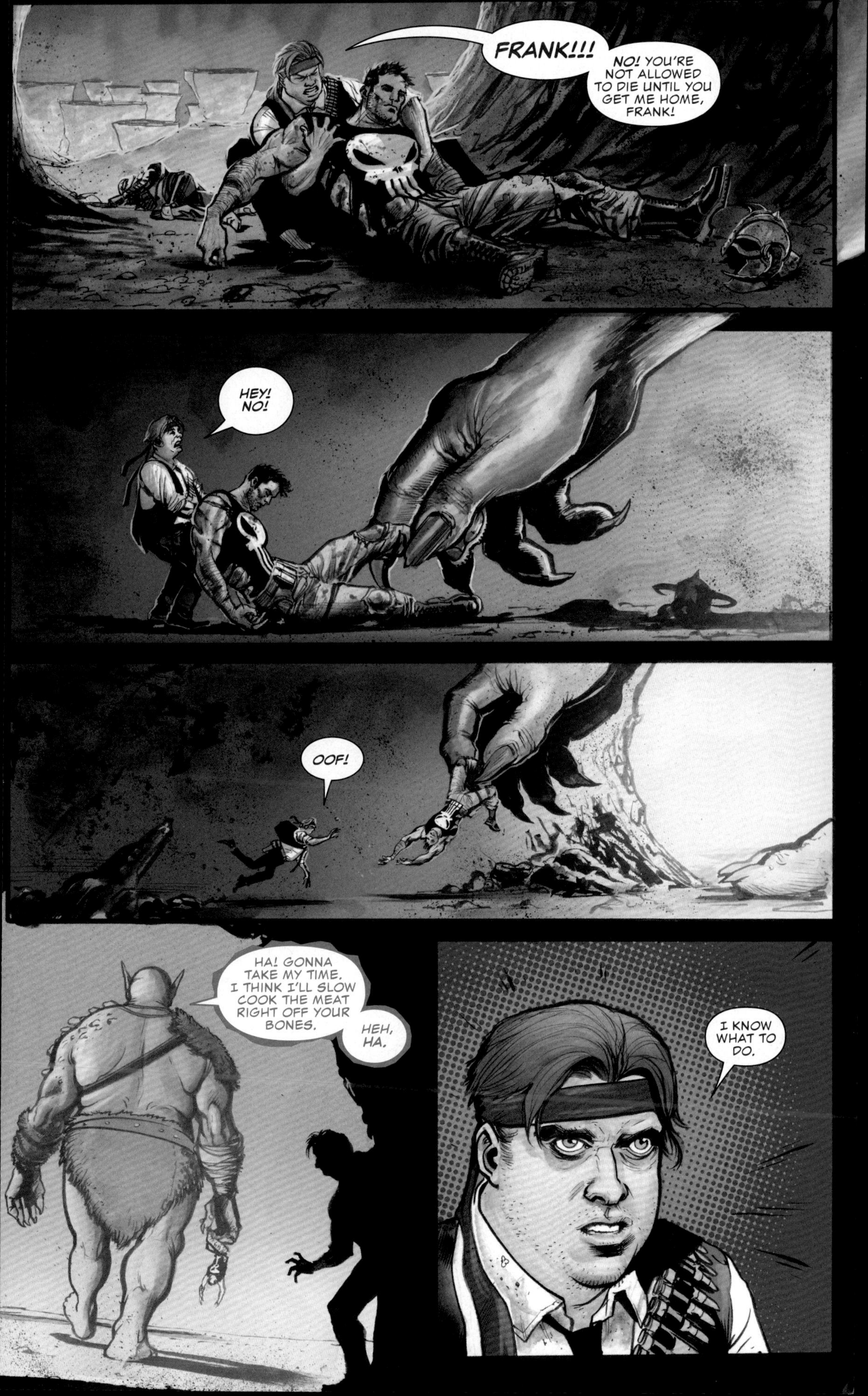
FRANK!!!
NO! YOU'RE NOT ALLOWED TO DIE UNTIL YOU GET ME HOME, FRANK!
HEY! NO!
OOF!
HA! GONNA TAKE MY TIME. I THINK I'LL SLOW COOK THE MEAT RIGHT OFF YOUR BONES.
HEH, HA.
I KNOW WHAT TO DO.

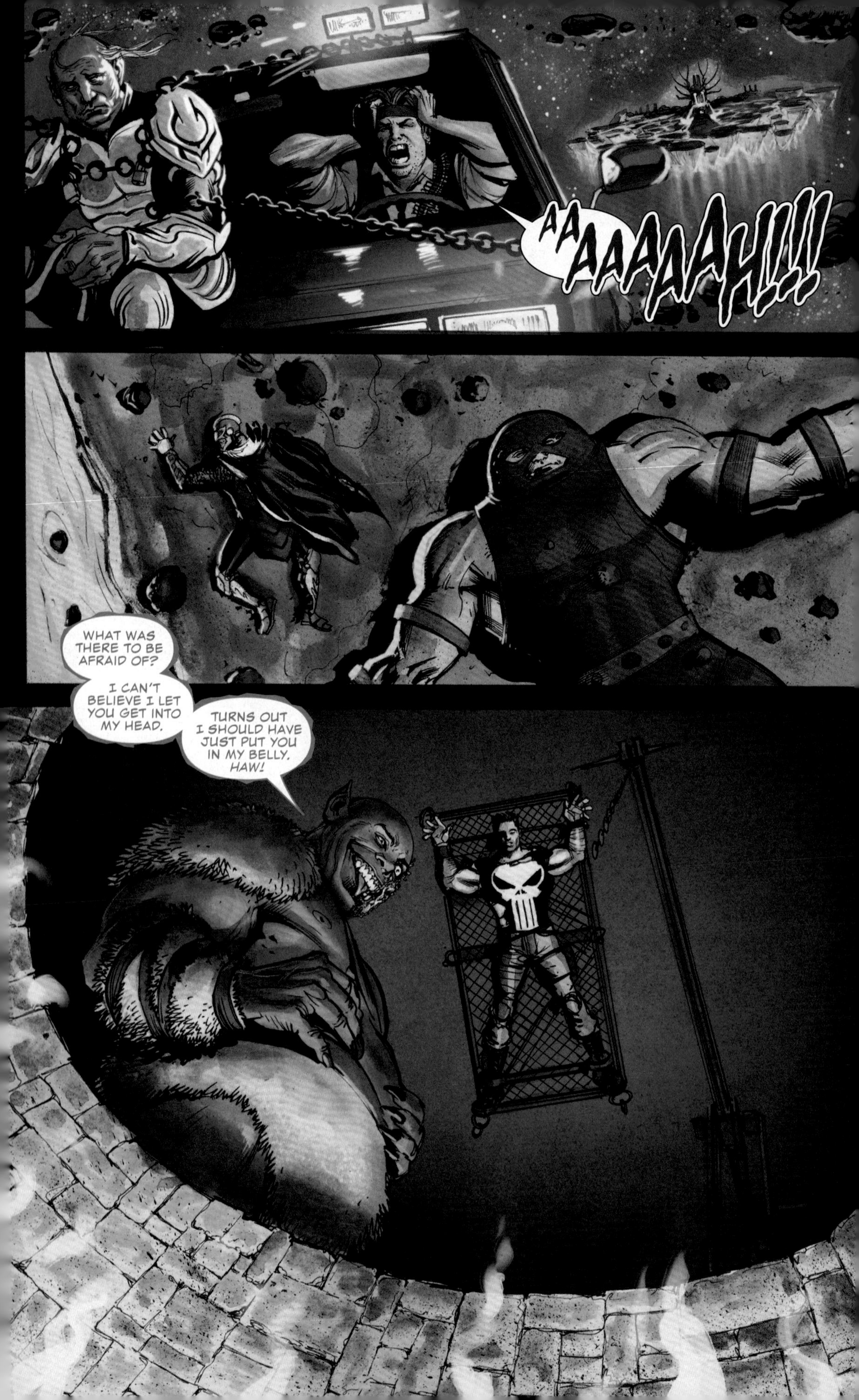
AAAAAAAH!!!
WHAT WAS THERE TO BE AFRAID OF?
I CAN'T BELIEVE I LET YOU GET INTO MY HEAD.
TURNS OUT I SHOULD HAVE JUST PUT YOU IN MY BELLY. HAW!

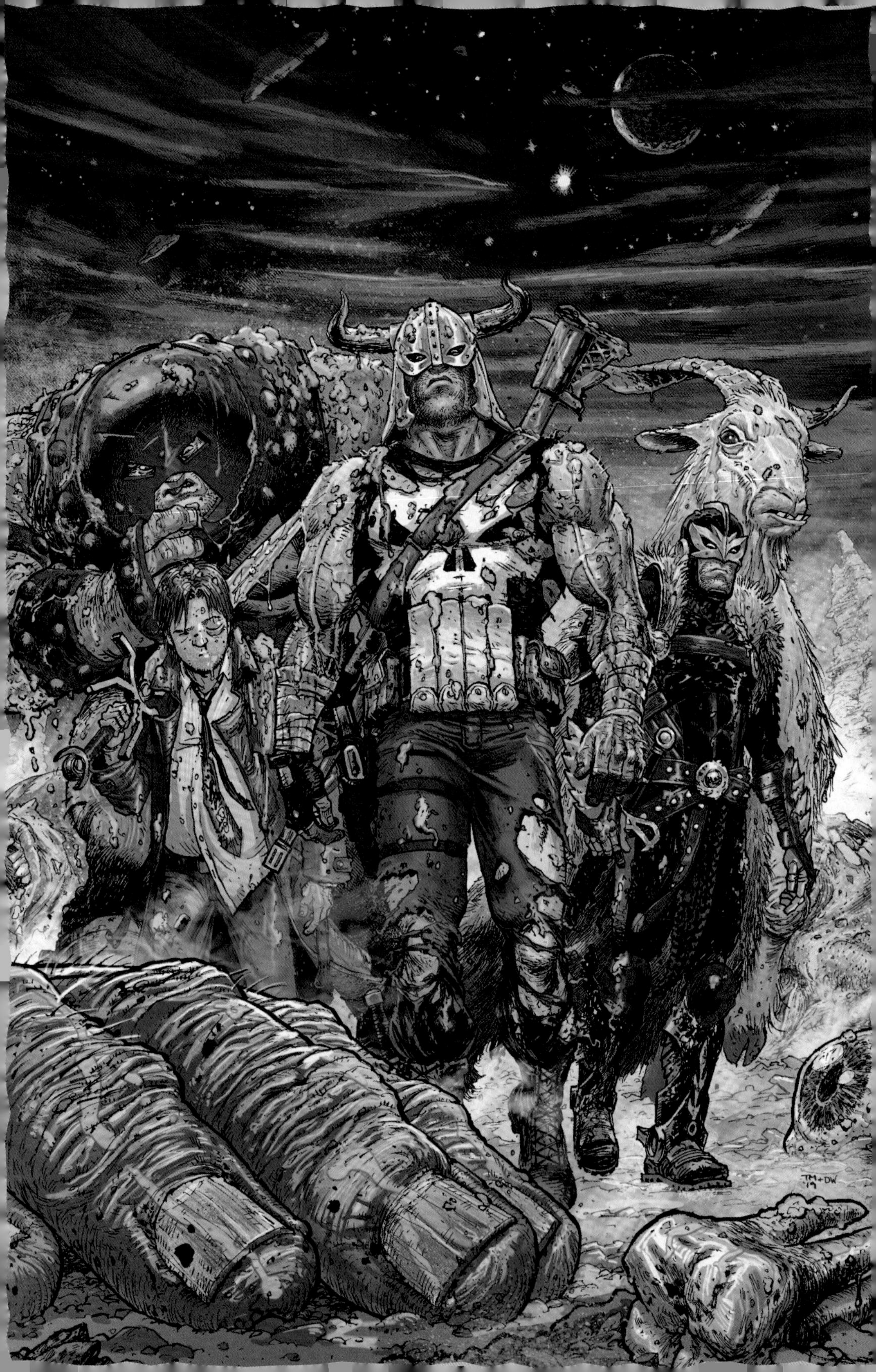

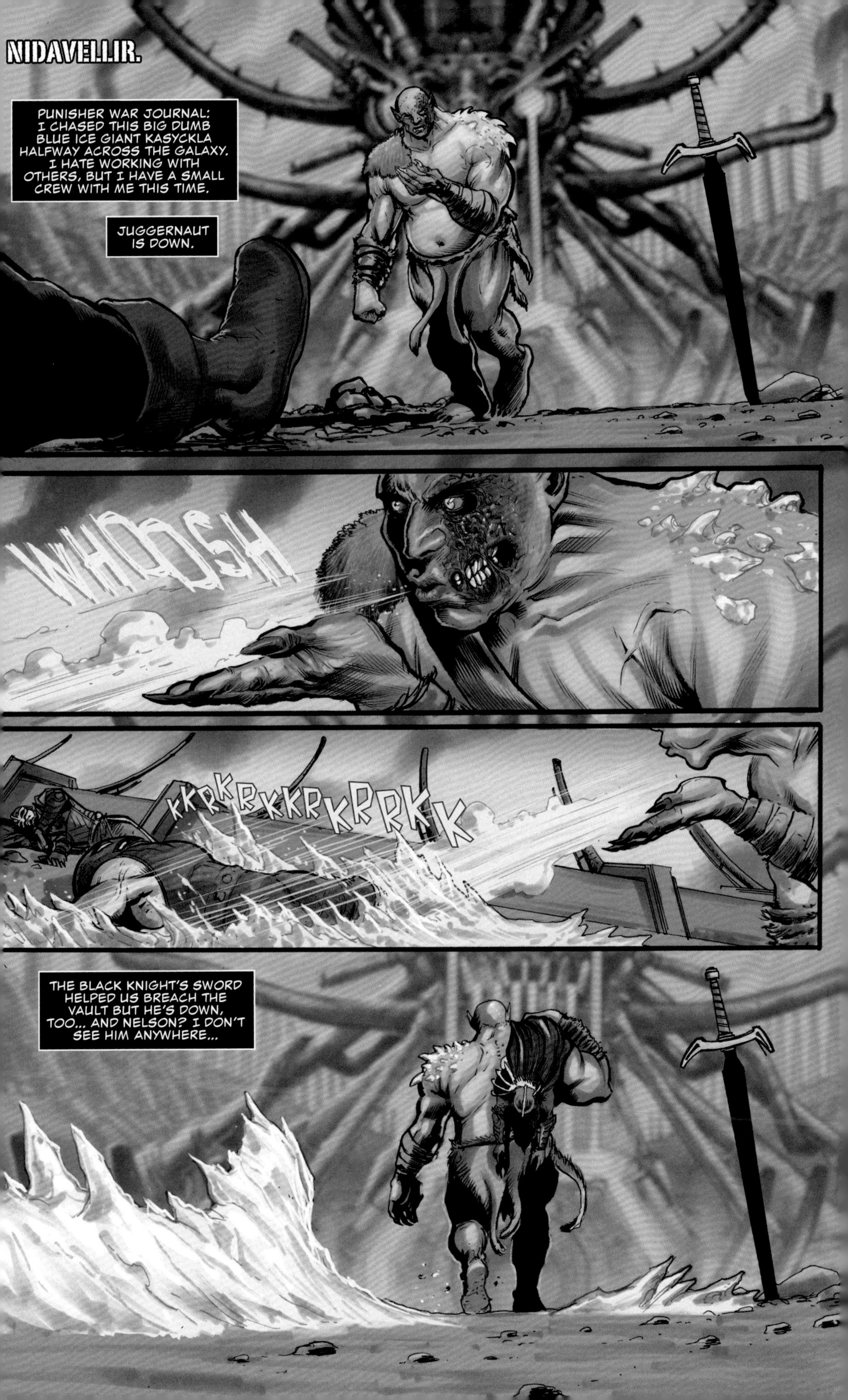
NIDAVELLIR.
PUNISHER WAR JOURNAL: I CHASED THIS BIG DUMB BLUE ICE GIANT KASYCKLA HALFWAY ACROSS THE GALAXY. I HATE WORKING WITH OTHERS, BUT I HAVE A SMALL CREW WITH ME THIS TIME.
JUGGERNAUT IS DOWN.
WHOOSH
KKRKRKKRKRRKK
THE BLACK KNIGHT'S SWORD HELPED US BREACH THE VAULT BUT HE'S DOWN, TOO... AND NELSON? I DON'T SEE HIM ANYWHERE...

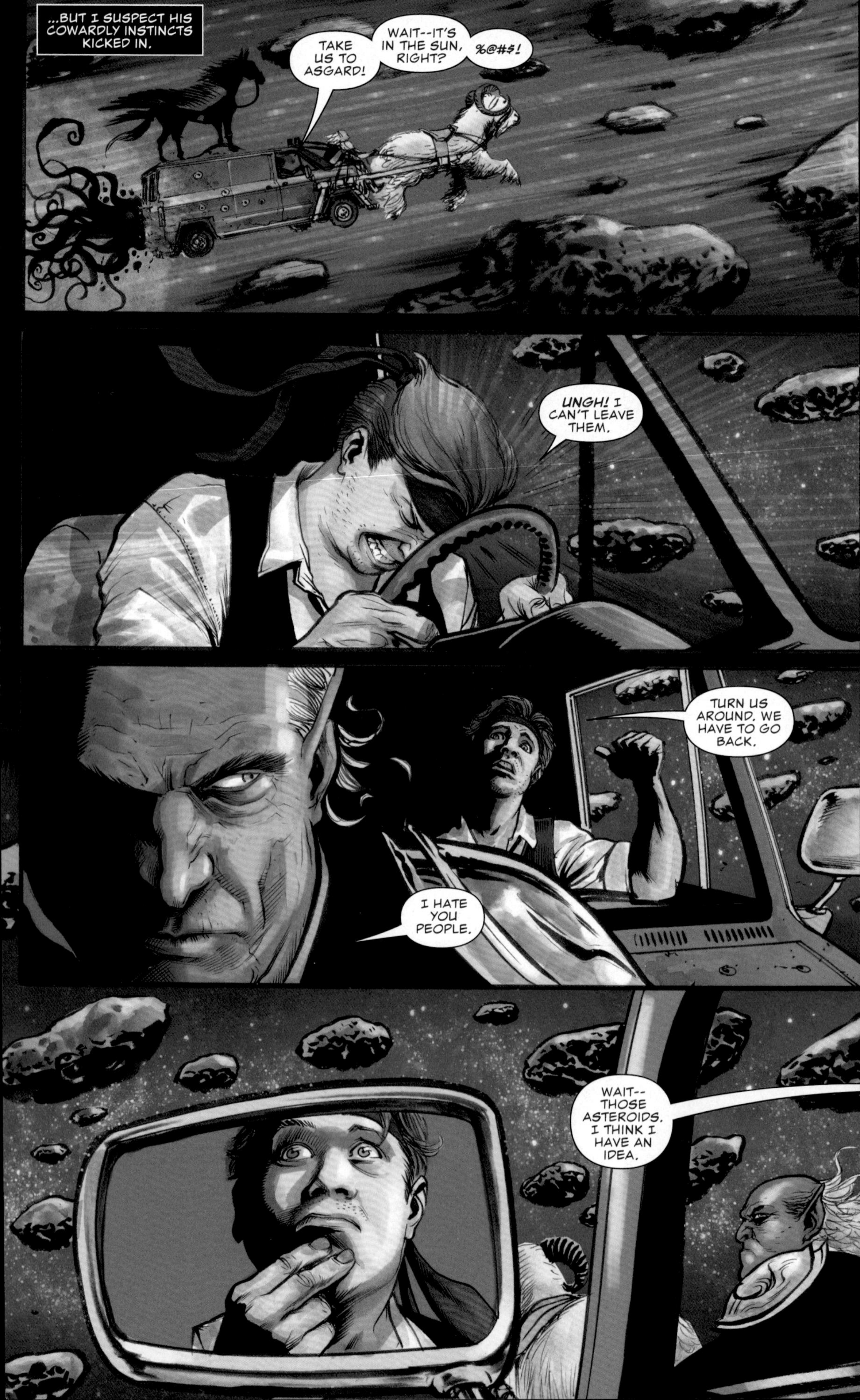
...BUT I SUSPECT HIS COWARDLY INSTINCTS KICKED IN.
TAKE US TO ASGARD!
WAIT--IT'S IN THE SUN, RIGHT?
%@#$!
UNGH! I CAN'T LEAVE THEM.
TURN US AROUND. WE HAVE TO GO BACK.
I HATE YOU PEOPLE.
WAIT-- THOSE ASTEROIDS. I THINK I HAVE AN IDEA.

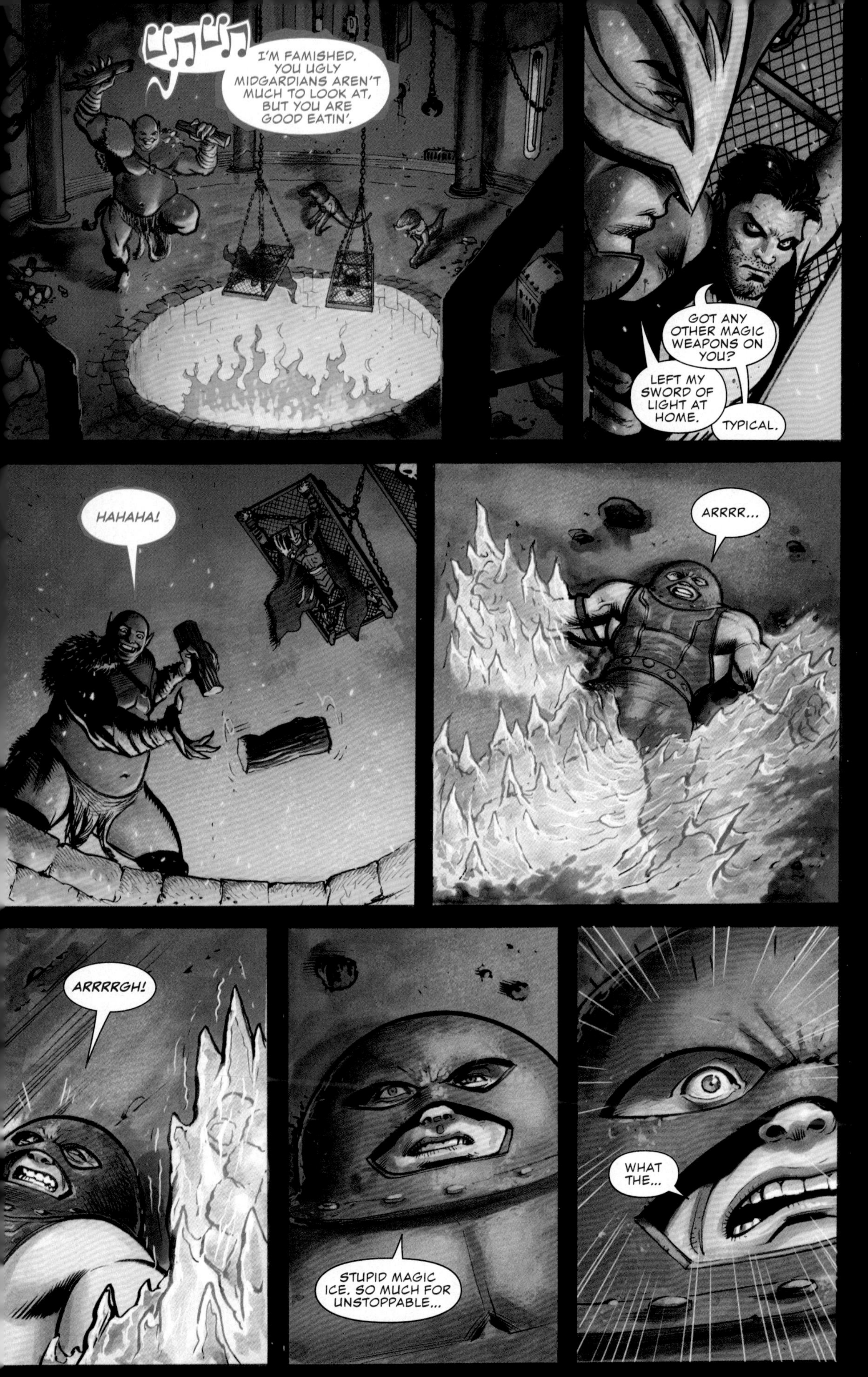
I'M FAMISHED. YOU UGLY MIDGARDIANS AREN'T MUCH TO LOOK AT, BUT YOU ARE GOOD EATIN'.
GOT ANY OTHER MAGIC WEAPONS ON YOU?
LEFT MY SWORD OF LIGHT AT HOME.
TYPICAL.
HAHAHA!
ARRRR...
ARRRRGH!
STUPID MAGIC ICE. SO MUCH FOR UNSTOPPABLE...
WHAT THE...

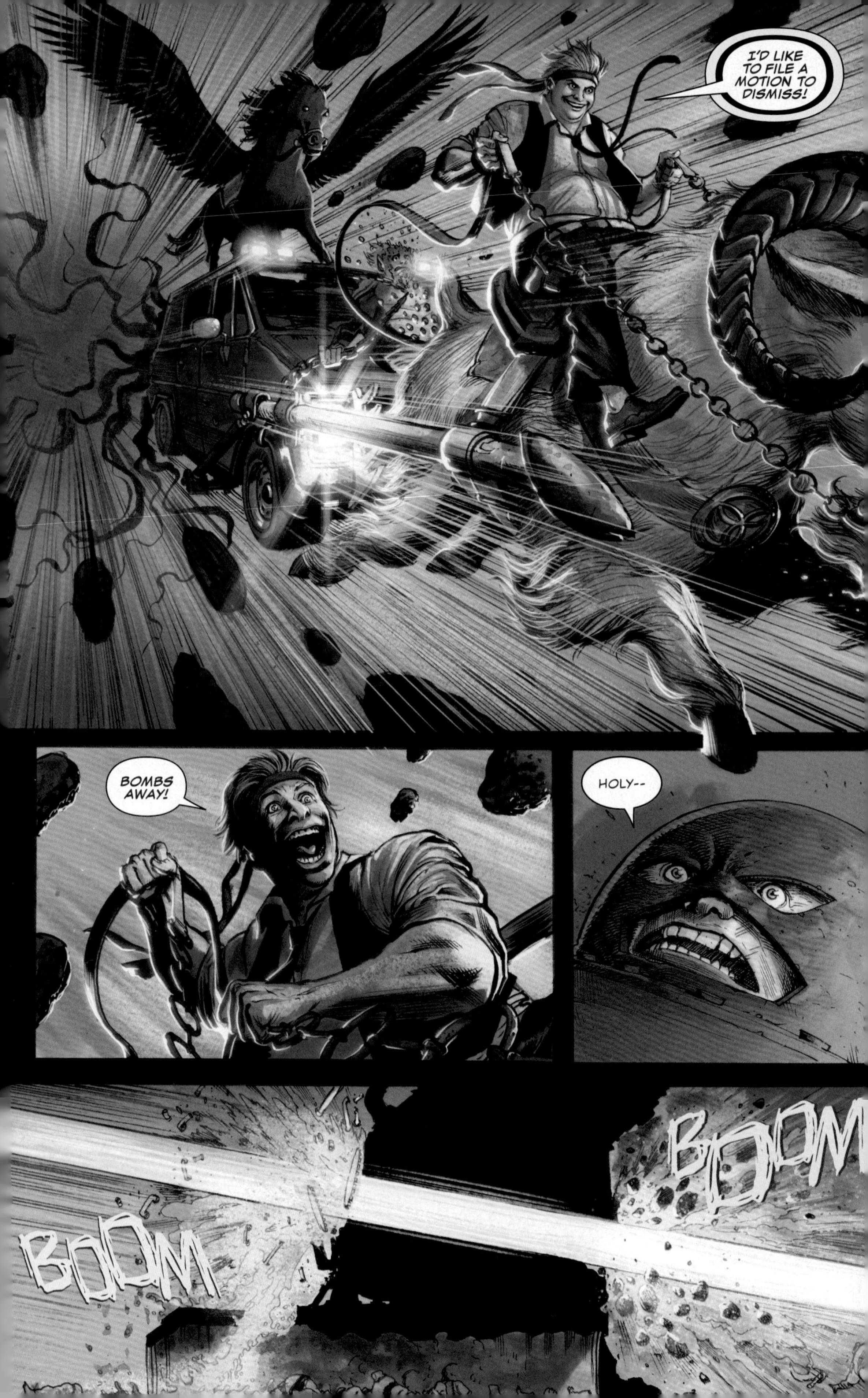
I'D LIKE TO FILE A MOTION TO DISMISS!
BOMBS AWAY!
HOLY--
BOOM
BOOM

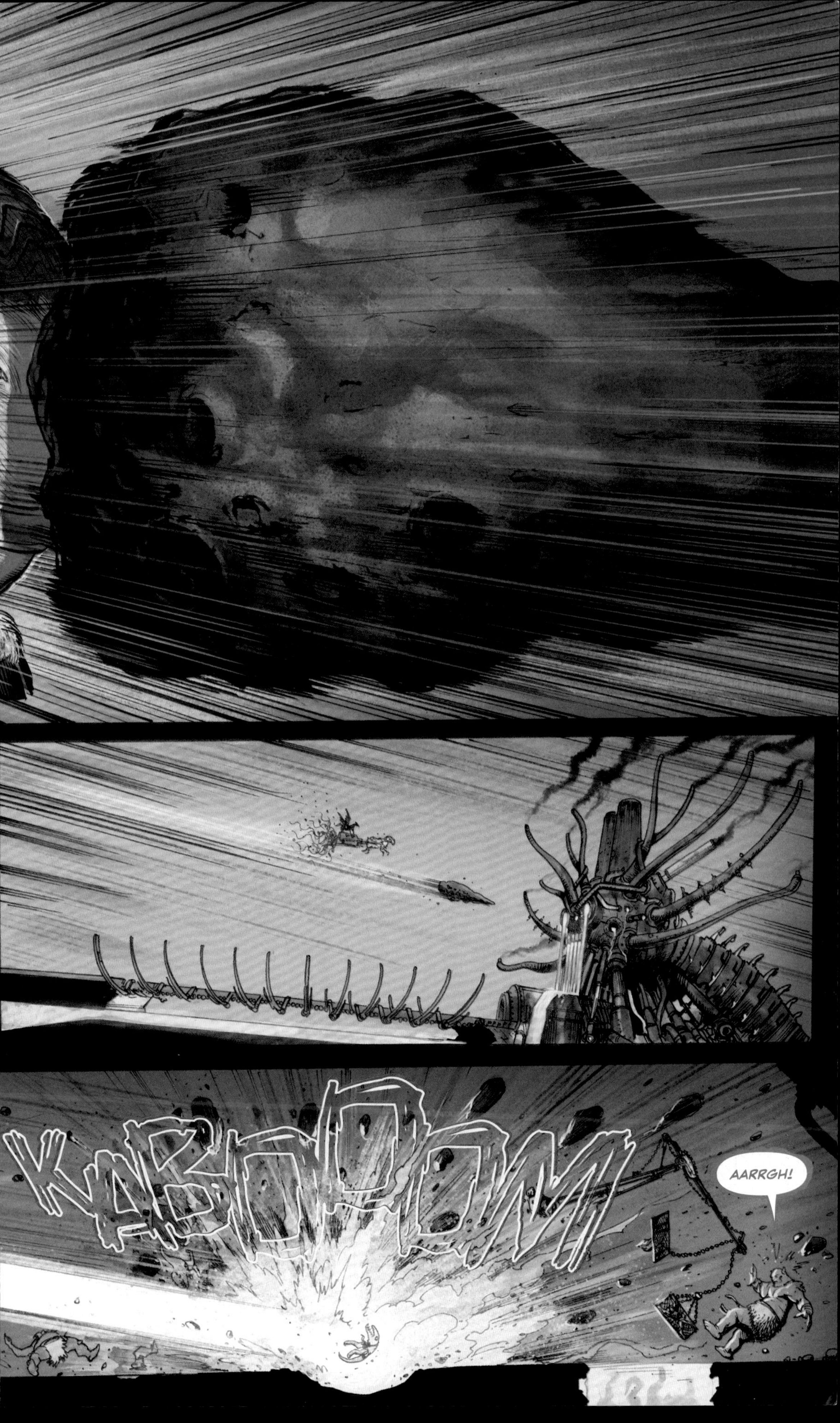
KABOOOM
AARRGH!

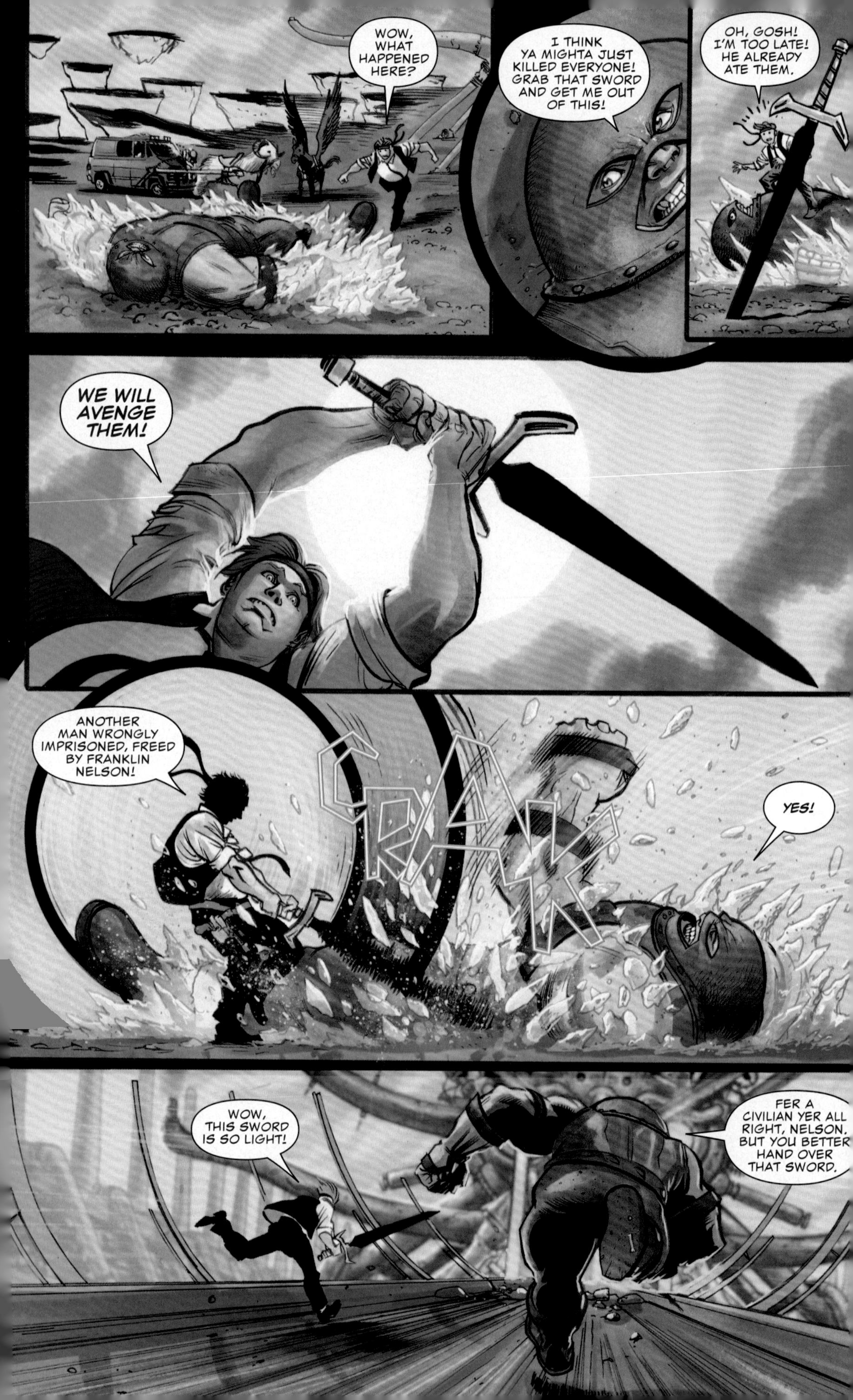
WOW, WHAT HAPPENED HERE?
I THINK YA MIGHTA JUST KILLED EVERYONE! GRAB THAT SWORD AND GET ME OUT OF THIS!
OH, GOSH! I'M TOO LATE! HE ALREADY ATE THEM.
WE WILL AVENGE THEM!
ANOTHER MAN WRONGLY IMPRISONED, FREED BY FRANKLIN NELSON!
CRAAK
YES!
WOW, THIS SWORD IS SO LIGHT!
FER A CIVILIAN YER ALL RIGHT, NELSON. BUT YOU BETTER HAND OVER THAT SWORD.

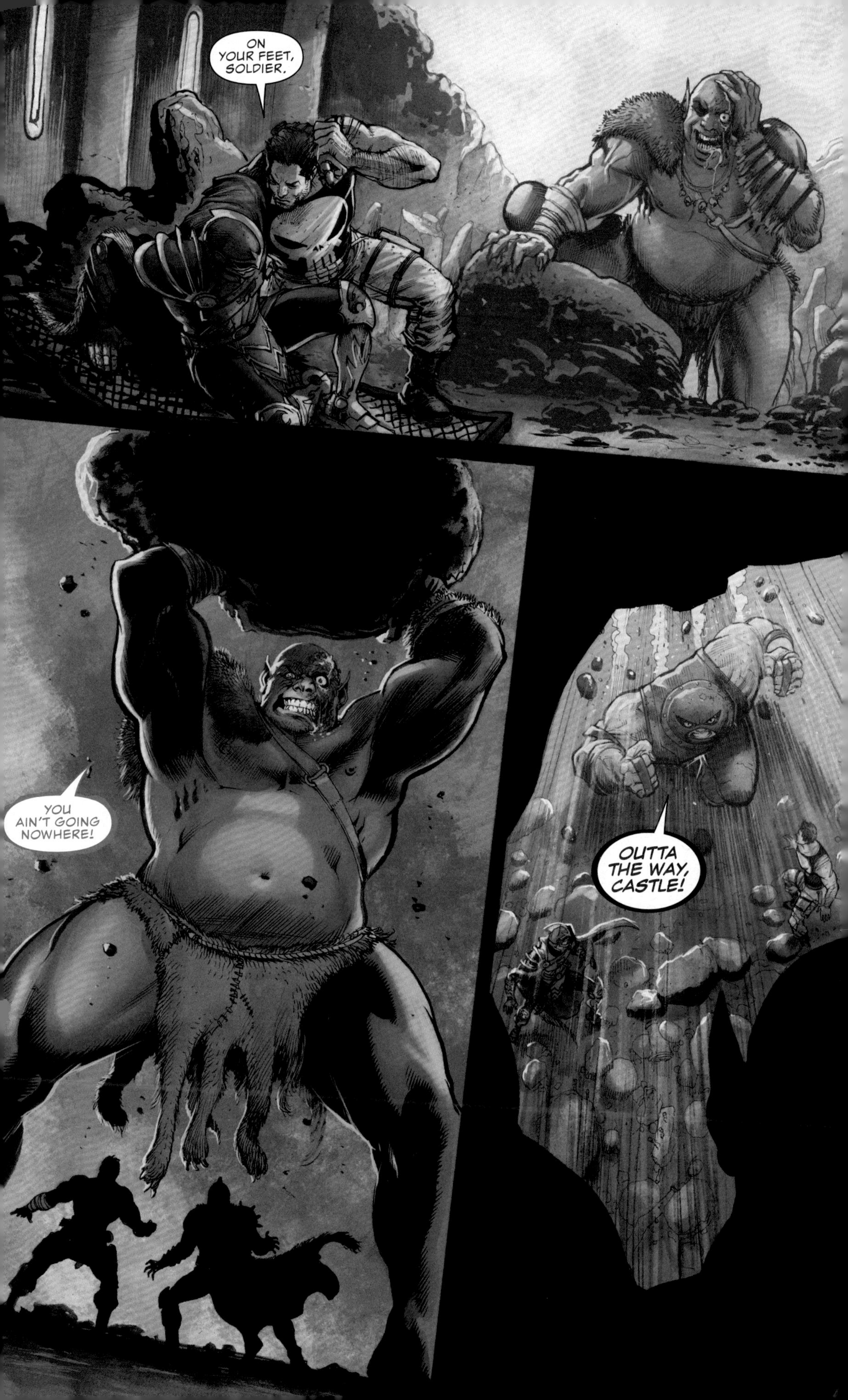
ON YOUR FEET, SOLDIER.
YOU AIN'T GOING NOWHERE!
OUTTA THE WAY, CASTLE!

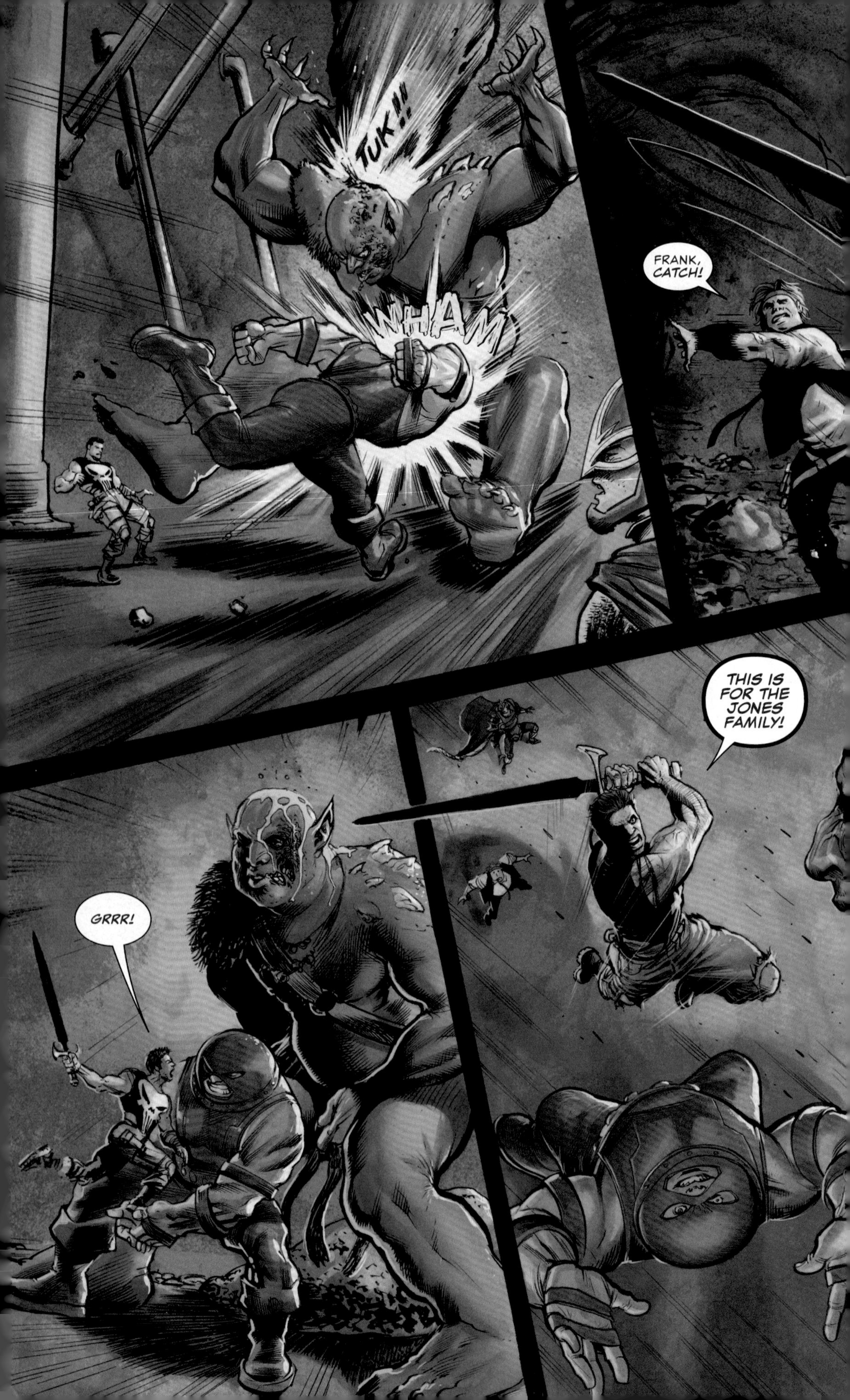
TUK!!
WHAM
FRANK, CATCH!
THIS IS FOR THE JONES FAMILY!
GRRR!

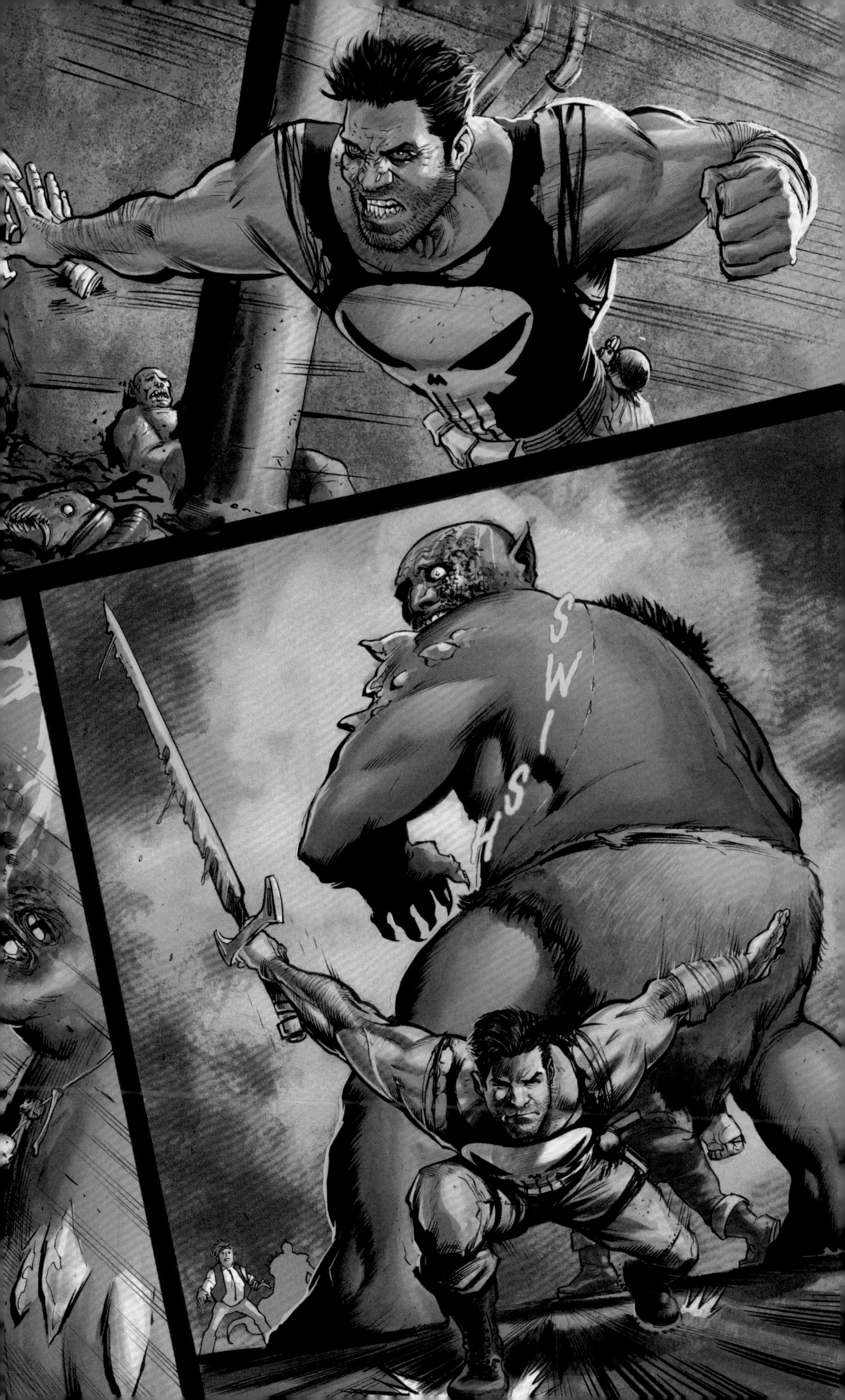
SWISH

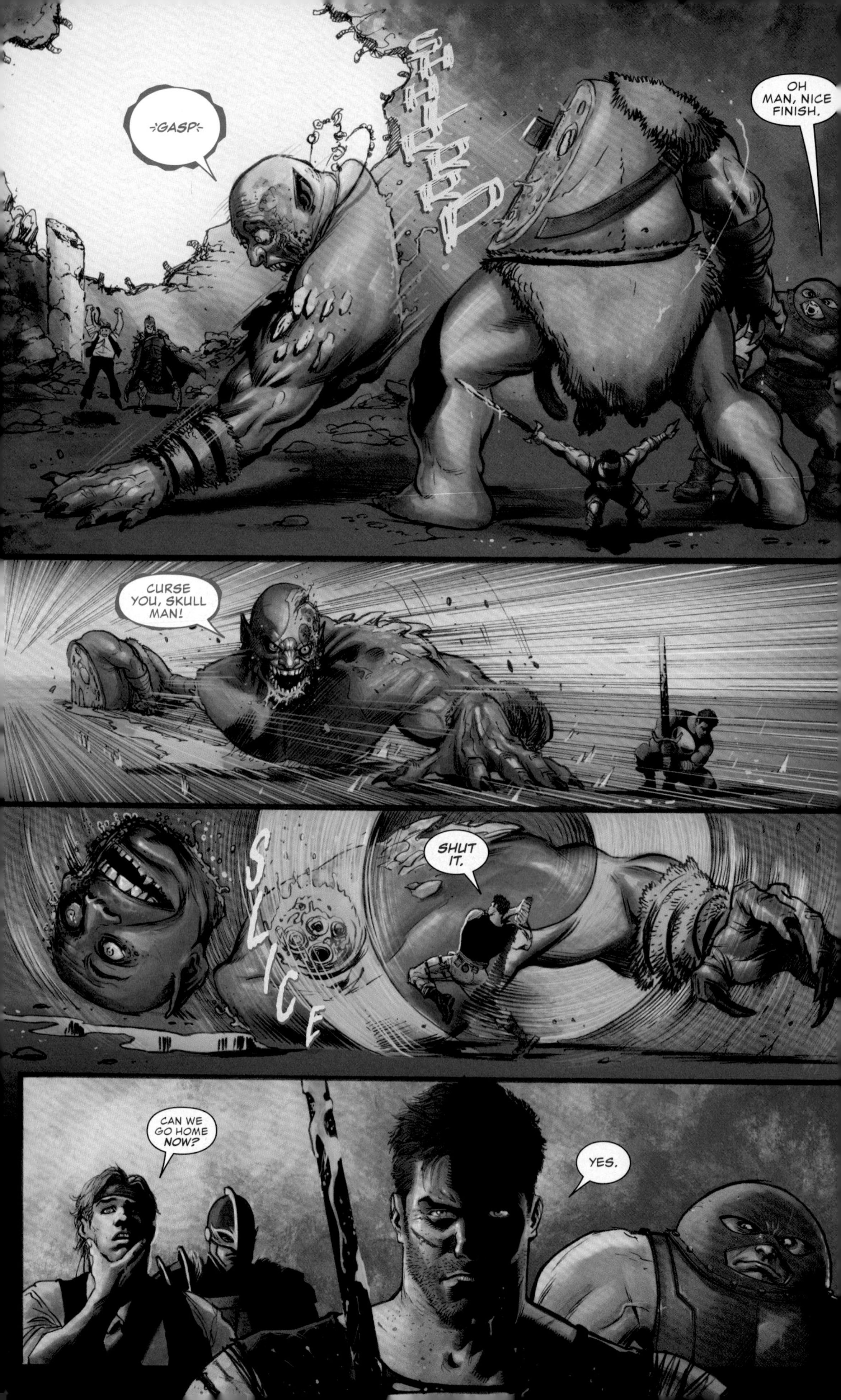

-GASP-
OH MAN, NICE FINISH.
CURSE YOU, SKULL MAN!
SLICE
SHUT IT.
CAN WE GO HOME NOW?
YES.

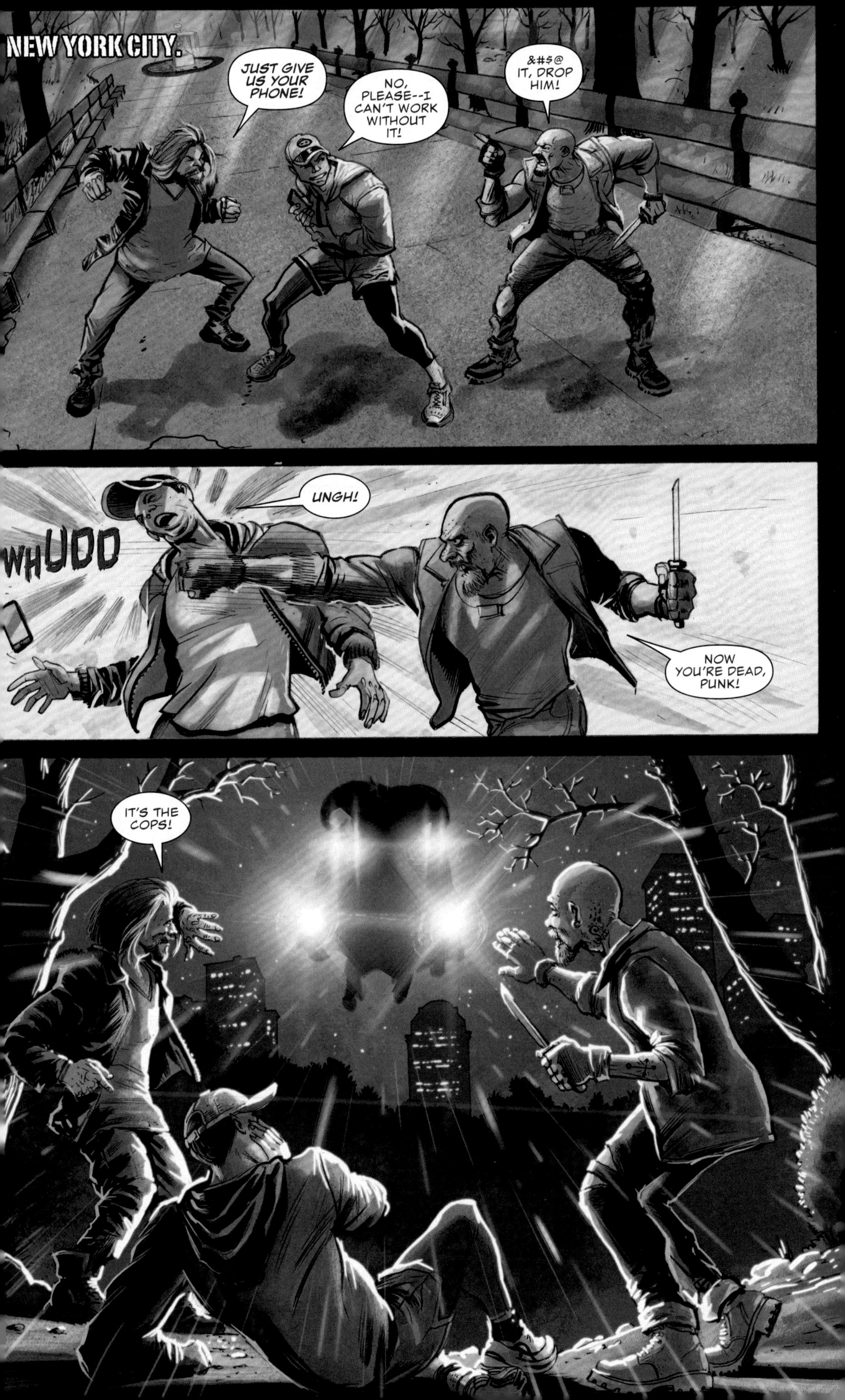
NEW YORK CITY.
JUST GIVE US YOUR PHONE!
NO, PLEASE--I CAN'T WORK WITHOUT IT!
&#$@ IT, DROP HIM!
WHUDD
UNGH!
NOW YOU'RE DEAD, PUNK!
IT'S THE COPS!

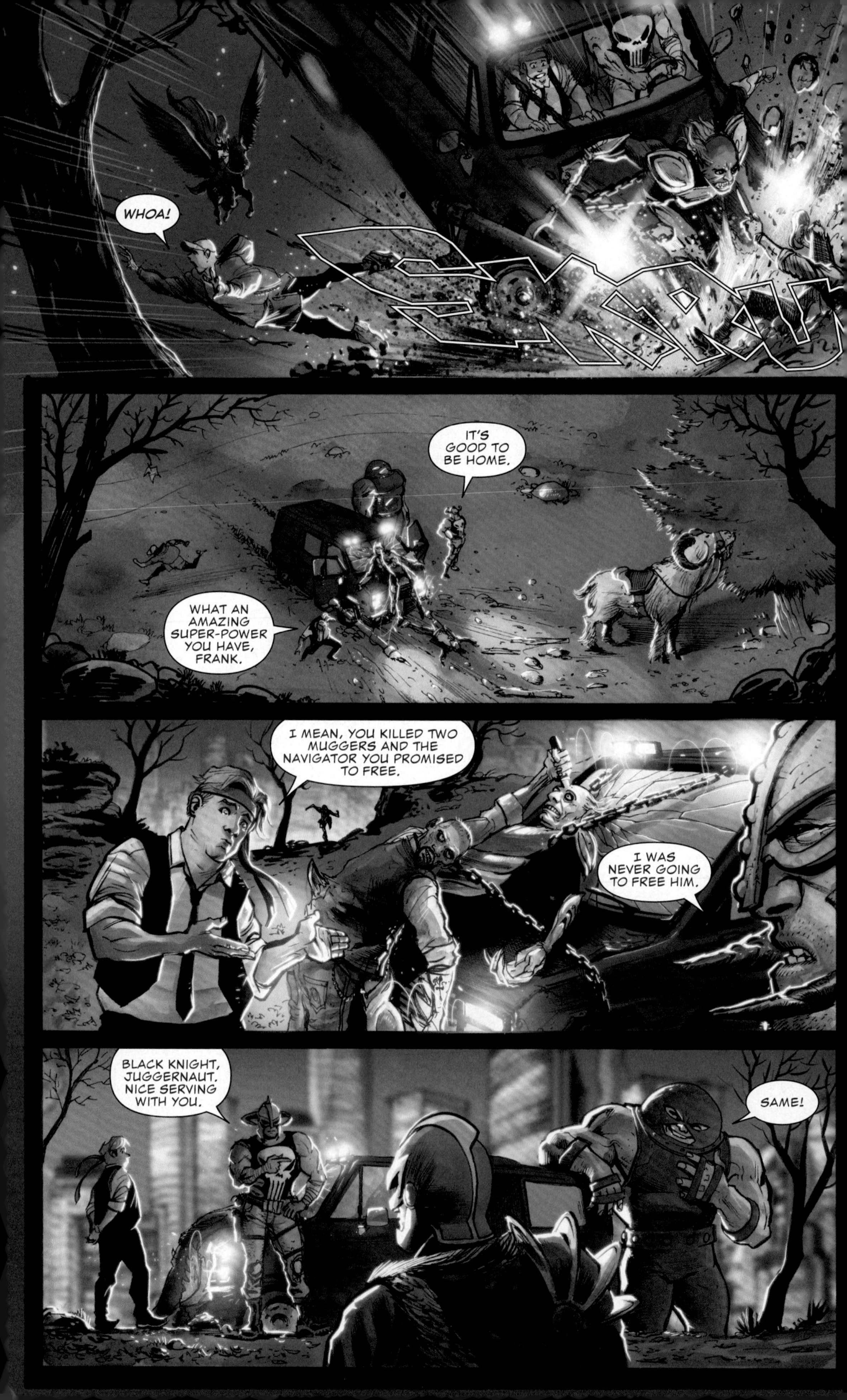
WHOA!
IT'S GOOD TO BE HOME.
WHAT AN AMAZING SUPER-POWER YOU HAVE, FRANK.
I MEAN, YOU KILLED TWO MUGGERS AND THE NAVIGATOR YOU PROMISED TO FREE.
I WAS NEVER GOING TO FREE HIM.
BLACK KNIGHT, JUGGERNAUT. NICE SERVING WITH YOU.
SAME!

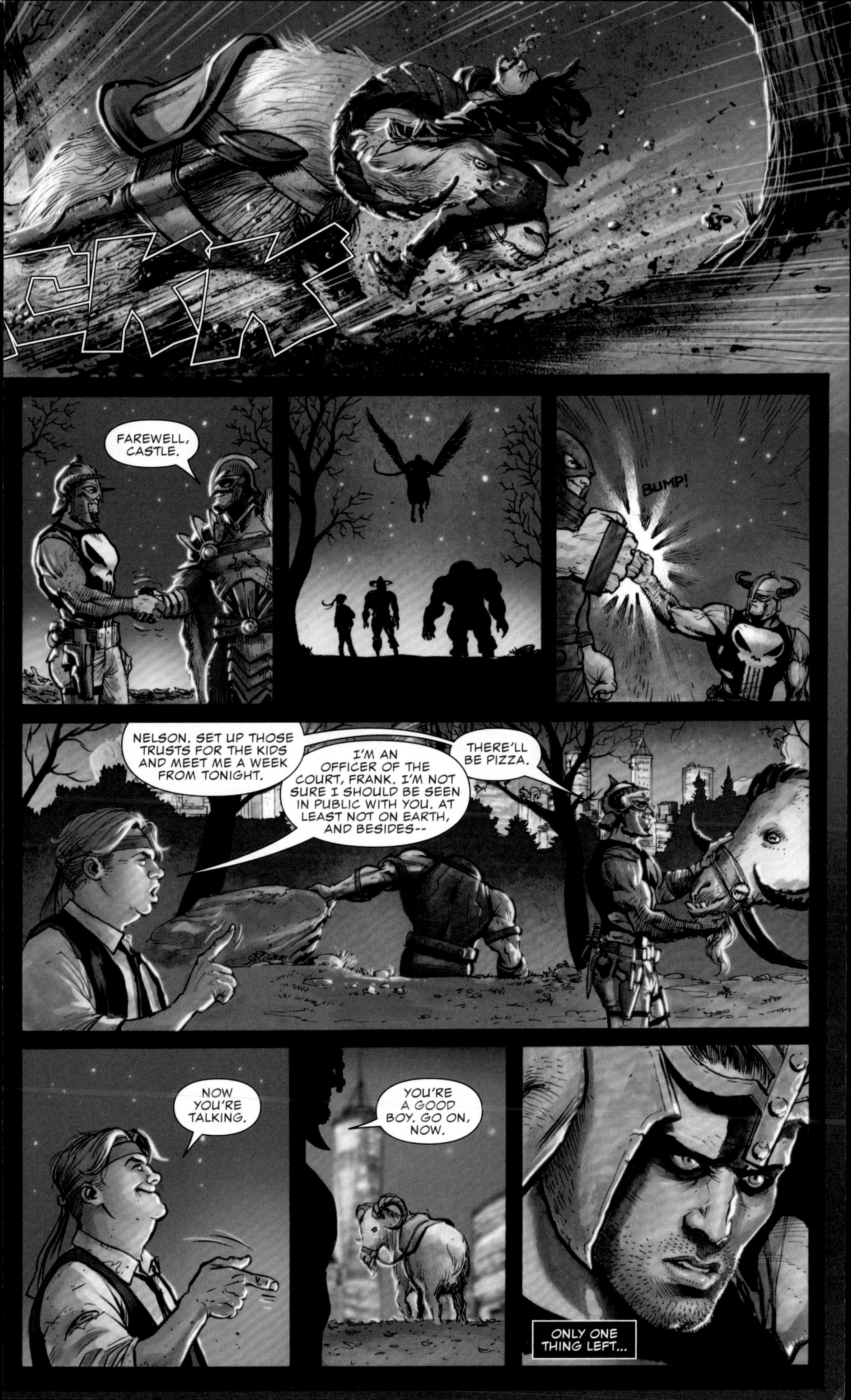
FAREWELL, CASTLE.
BUMP!
NELSON. SET UP THOSE TRUSTS FOR THE KIDS AND MEET ME A WEEK FROM TONIGHT.
I'M AN OFFICER OF THE COURT, FRANK. I'M NOT SURE I SHOULD BE SEEN IN PUBLIC WITH YOU. AT LEAST NOT ON EARTH, AND BESIDES--
THERE'LL BE PIZZA.
NOW YOU'RE TALKING.
YOU'RE A GOOD BOY. GO ON, NOW.
ONLY ONE THING LEFT...

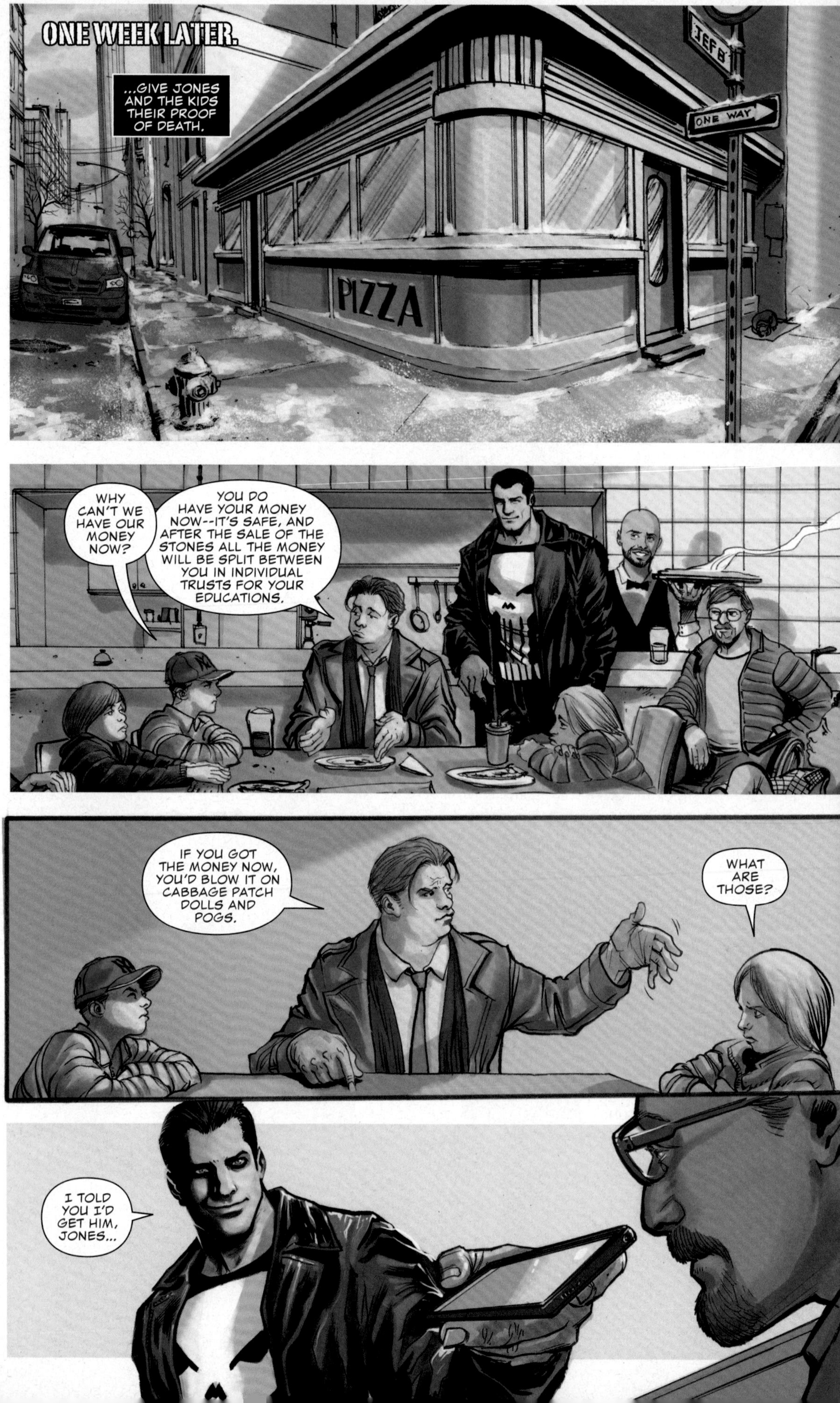
ONE WEEK LATER.
...GIVE JONES AND THE KIDS THEIR PROOF OF DEATH.
JEF B
ONE WAY
PIZZA
WHY CAN'T WE HAVE OUR MONEY NOW?
YOU DO HAVE YOUR MONEY NOW--IT'S SAFE, AND AFTER THE SALE OF THE STONES ALL THE MONEY WILL BE SPLIT BETWEEN YOU IN INDIVIDUAL TRUSTS FOR YOUR EDUCATIONS.
IF YOU GOT THE MONEY NOW, YOU'D BLOW IT ON CABBAGE PATCH DOLLS AND POGS.
WHAT ARE THOSE?
I TOLD YOU I'D GET HIM, JONES...

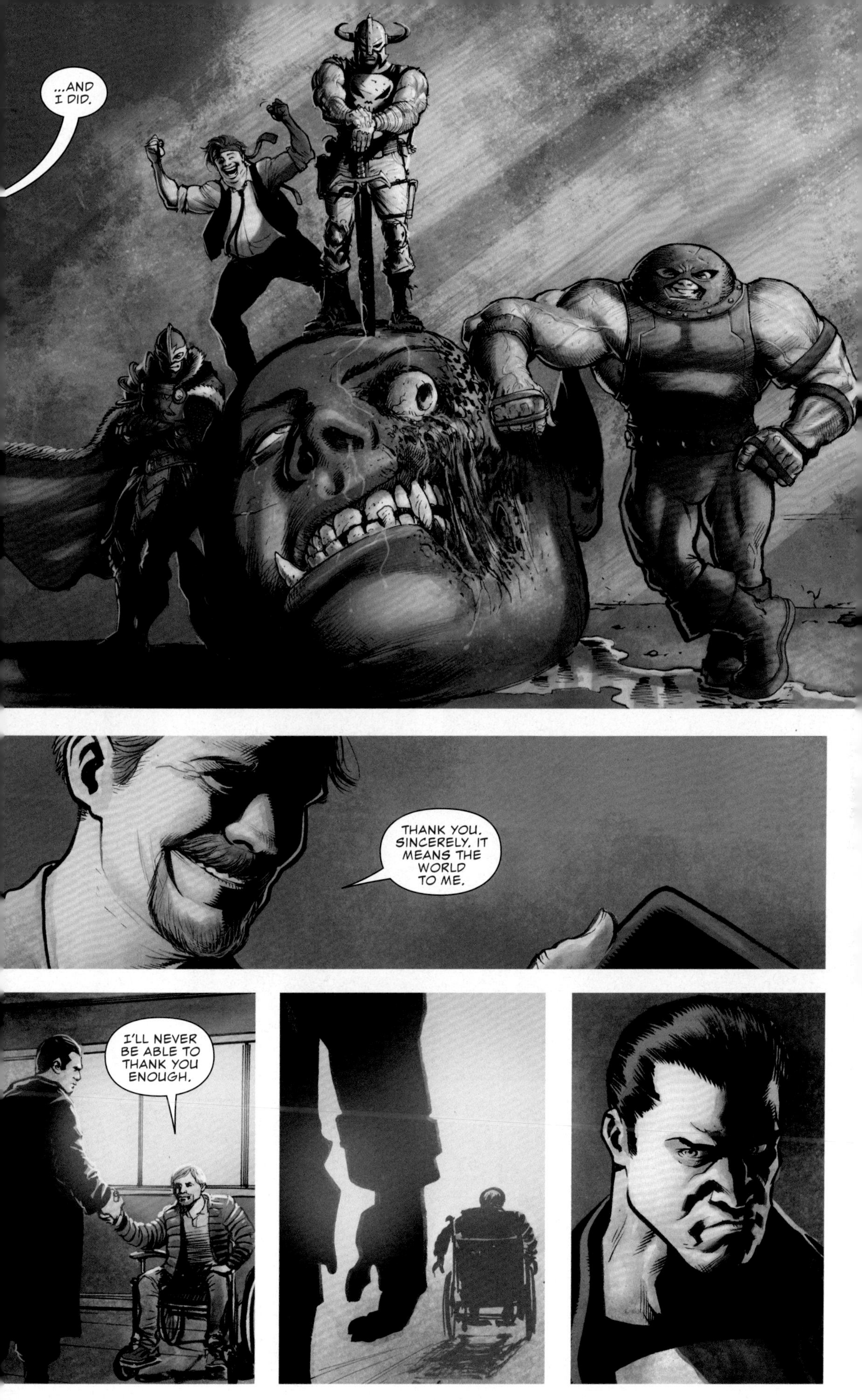
...AND I DID.
THANK YOU. SINCERELY. IT MEANS THE WORLD TO ME.
I'LL NEVER BE ABLE TO THANK YOU ENOUGH.

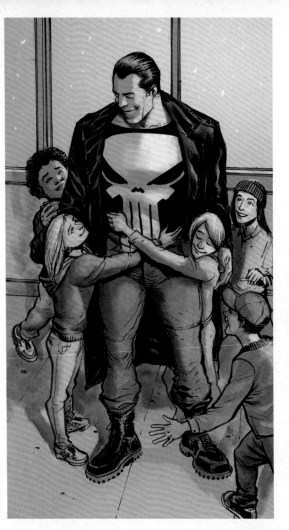

IF YOU EVER NEED AN ATTORNEY, DON'T HESITATE TO CALL.

YOU ACQUITTED YOURSELF WELL, COUNSELOR.

WELL, THANK YOU FOR KEEPING ME FROM BEING THAT GIANT'S SUPPER.

FRANK, YOU HAVE A LOT OF GOODWILL RIGHT NOW. YOU HELPED DEFEND THIS CITY, SAVED A LOT OF LIVES.

MAYBE YOU DON'T HAVE TO KEEP...BEING YOU?

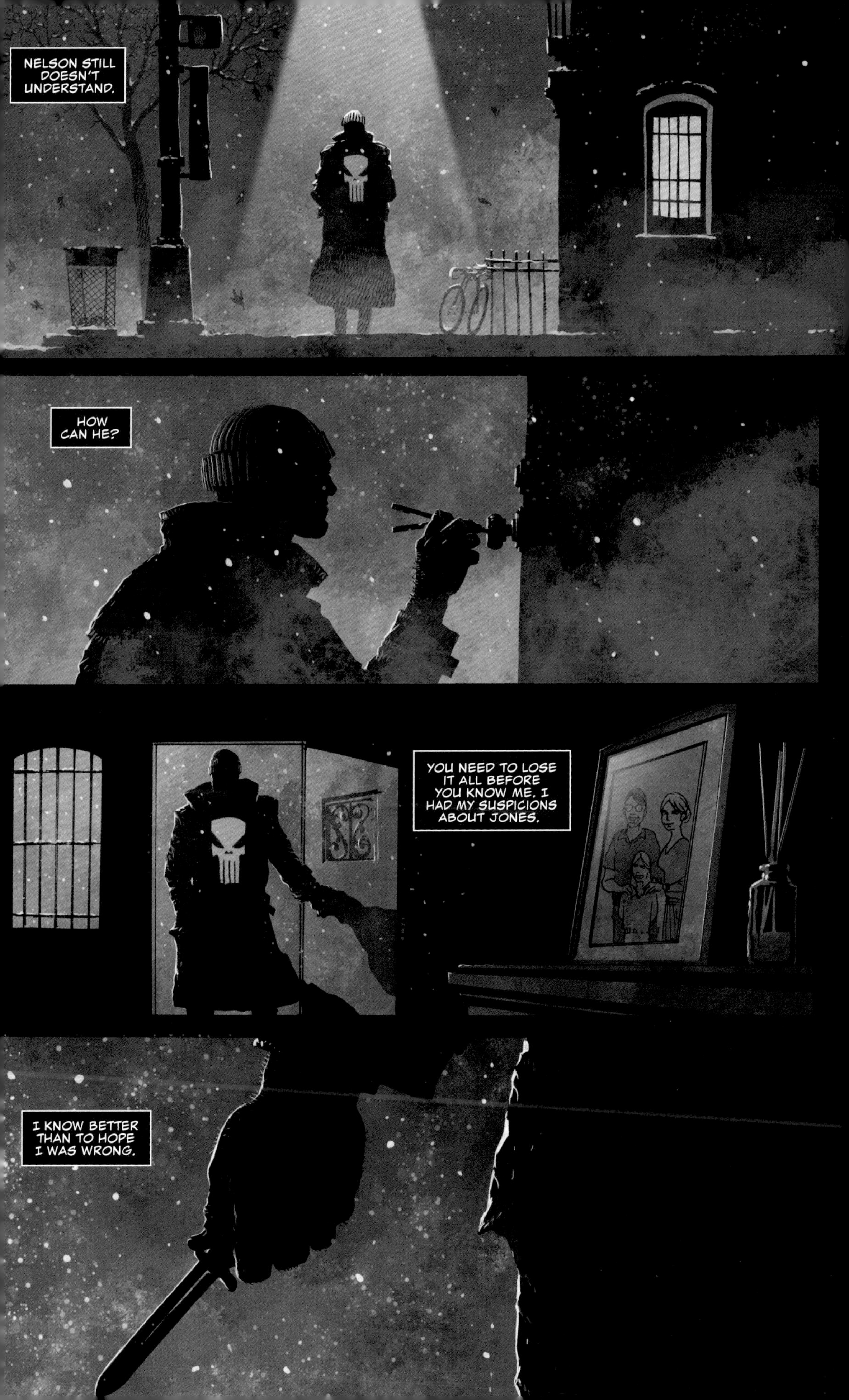

NELSON STILL DOESN'T UNDERSTAND.
HOW CAN HE?
YOU NEED TO LOSE IT ALL BEFORE YOU KNOW ME. I HAD MY SUSPICIONS ABOUT JONES.
I KNOW BETTER THAN TO HOPE I WAS WRONG.

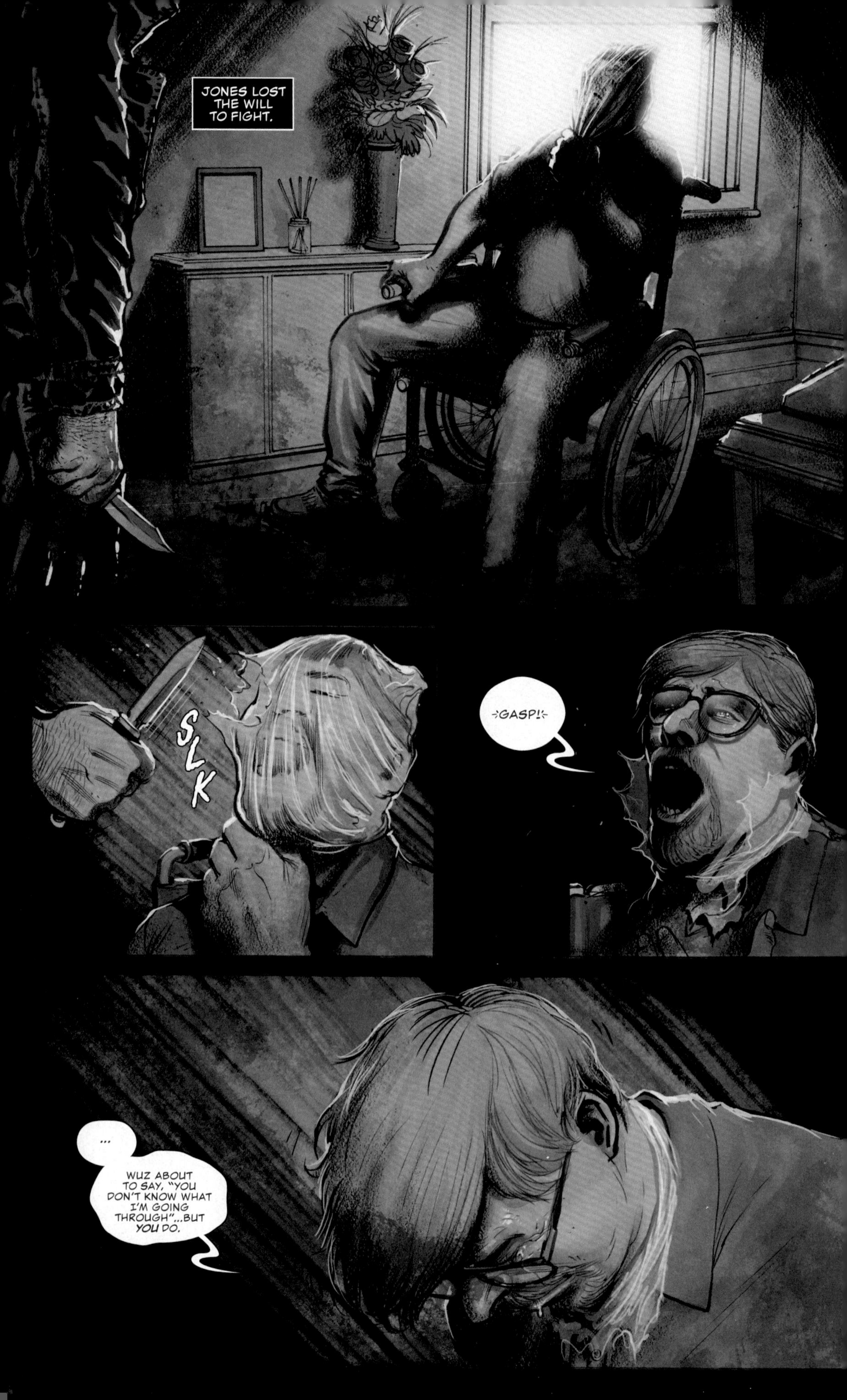
JONES LOST THE WILL TO FIGHT.
SLK
-GASP!-
...
WUZ ABOUT TO SAY, "YOU DON'T KNOW WHAT I'M GOING THROUGH"...BUT YOU DO.

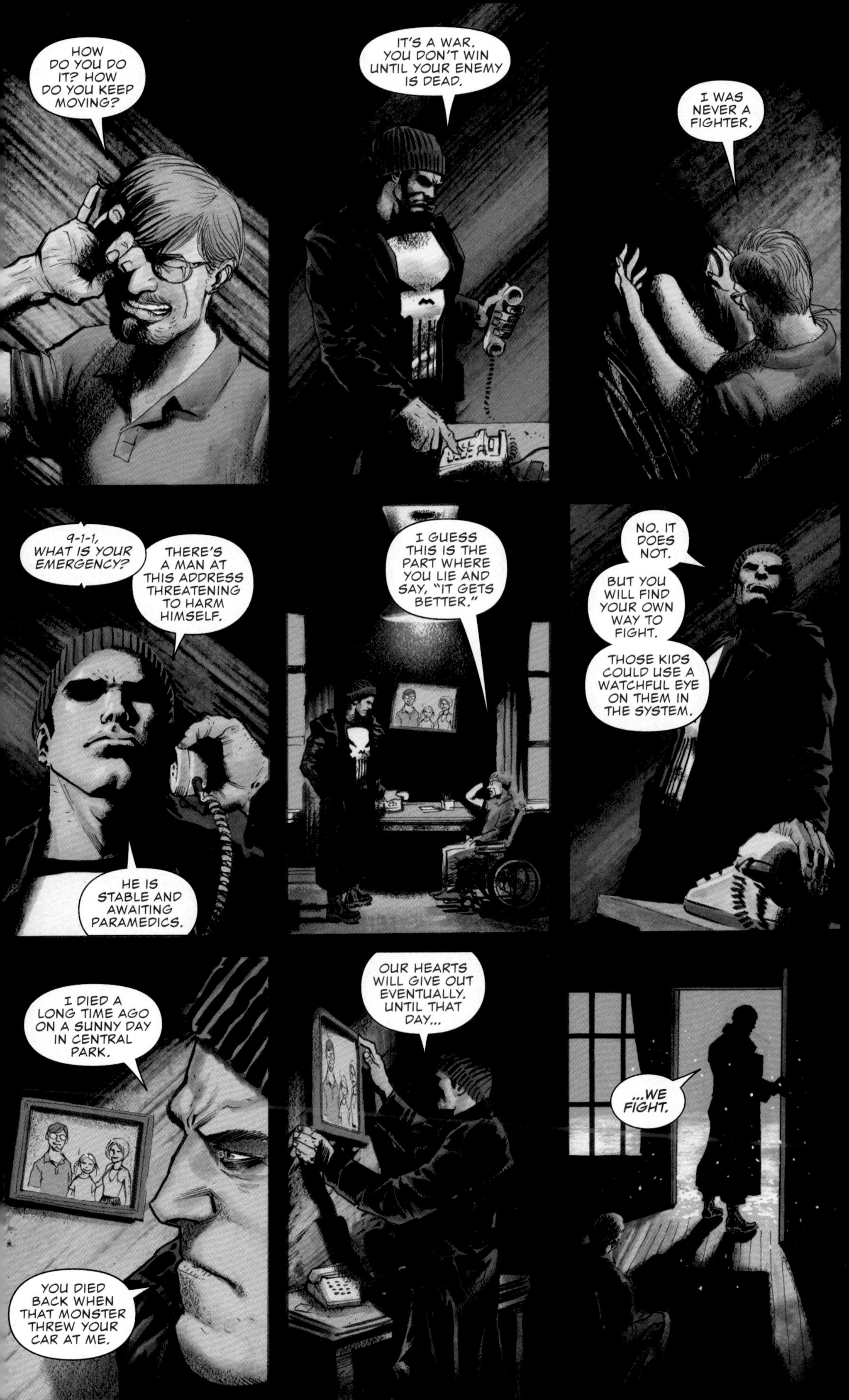
HOW DO YOU DO IT? HOW DO YOU KEEP MOVING?
IT'S A WAR. YOU DON'T WIN UNTIL YOUR ENEMY IS DEAD.
I WAS NEVER A FIGHTER.
9-1-1, WHAT IS YOUR EMERGENCY?
THERE'S A MAN AT THIS ADDRESS THREATENING TO HARM HIMSELF.
HE IS STABLE AND AWAITING PARAMEDICS.
I GUESS THIS IS THE PART WHERE YOU LIE AND SAY, "IT GETS BETTER."
NO. IT DOES NOT.
BUT YOU WILL FIND YOUR OWN WAY TO FIGHT.
THOSE KIDS COULD USE A WATCHFUL EYE ON THEM IN THE SYSTEM.
I DIED A LONG TIME AGO ON A SUNNY DAY IN CENTRAL PARK.
YOU DIED BACK WHEN THAT MONSTER THREW YOUR CAR AT ME.
OUR HEARTS WILL GIVE OUT EVENTUALLY. UNTIL THAT DAY...
...WE FIGHT.

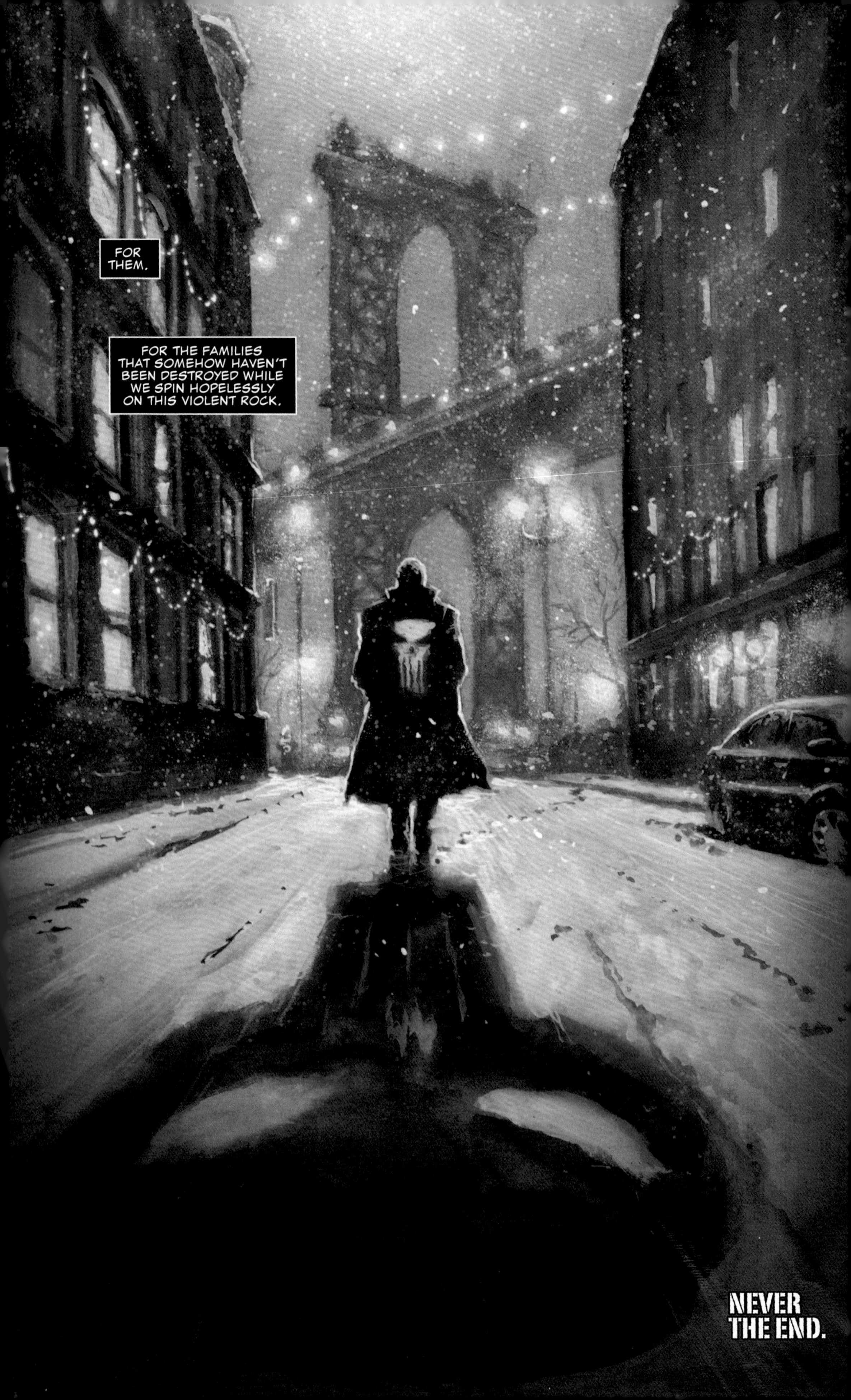
FOR THEM.
FOR THE FAMILIES THAT SOMEHOW HAVEN'T BEEN DESTROYED WHILE WE SPIN HOPELESSLY ON THIS VIOLENT ROCK.
NEVER THE END.

PUNISHER KILL KREW: OVER & OUT

All the Marvel writers and editors were excited when Jason Aaron walked us through what he and Russell Dauterman were cooking up for WAR OF THE REALMS.

The end of Jason's THOR was going to be a gift of chaos for the Marvel Universe, and one of the ideas that stuck was to recast the Punisher as a hunter of war criminals.

It'd take Frank into scenarios he wasn't always used to, but that's good for all of us from time to time. I wasn't sure about the mechanics of how any of it would work, but it wasn't my problem: I wasn't the PUNISHER writer... and then suddenly I was. I was very grateful for the chance to figure it all out. Simplicity and fun arrived when Frank "borrowed" Thor's goat and a chunk of the Black Bifrost.

Thanks to C.B., Jake, and Lindsey and of course to Juan, Tony, and Dean. Juan's got that great ability to shift tones from panel to panel, and he's the star of the show. Thanks for carrying this one, Juan. We can't wrap up without talking about the first image you saw on these books: Tony Moore's unreal covers. Detail that can only be described as "Darrowian" went into these five labors of love. They'll live forever. I only hope I see KILL KREW art on tattoos or on the sides of vans. Something tells me you may see those designs pop up down the road again...

I had the end in mind at the beginning, and we got to have our insane fun but managed to ground it all at the end in the tragedy that began the tale: the father whom Frank tries to help in, really, the only way that Frank can. But if you need a little help in your life, don't hesitate to contact the hotlines below.

Thanks for getting in the van with us.

Regards,
Gerry Duggan

If you are struggling with thoughts of suicide, or are worried about a friend or loved one, please reach out to a counselor or someone you trust; call your local helpline; or call the National Suicide Prevention Lifeline:
1-800-273-8255.

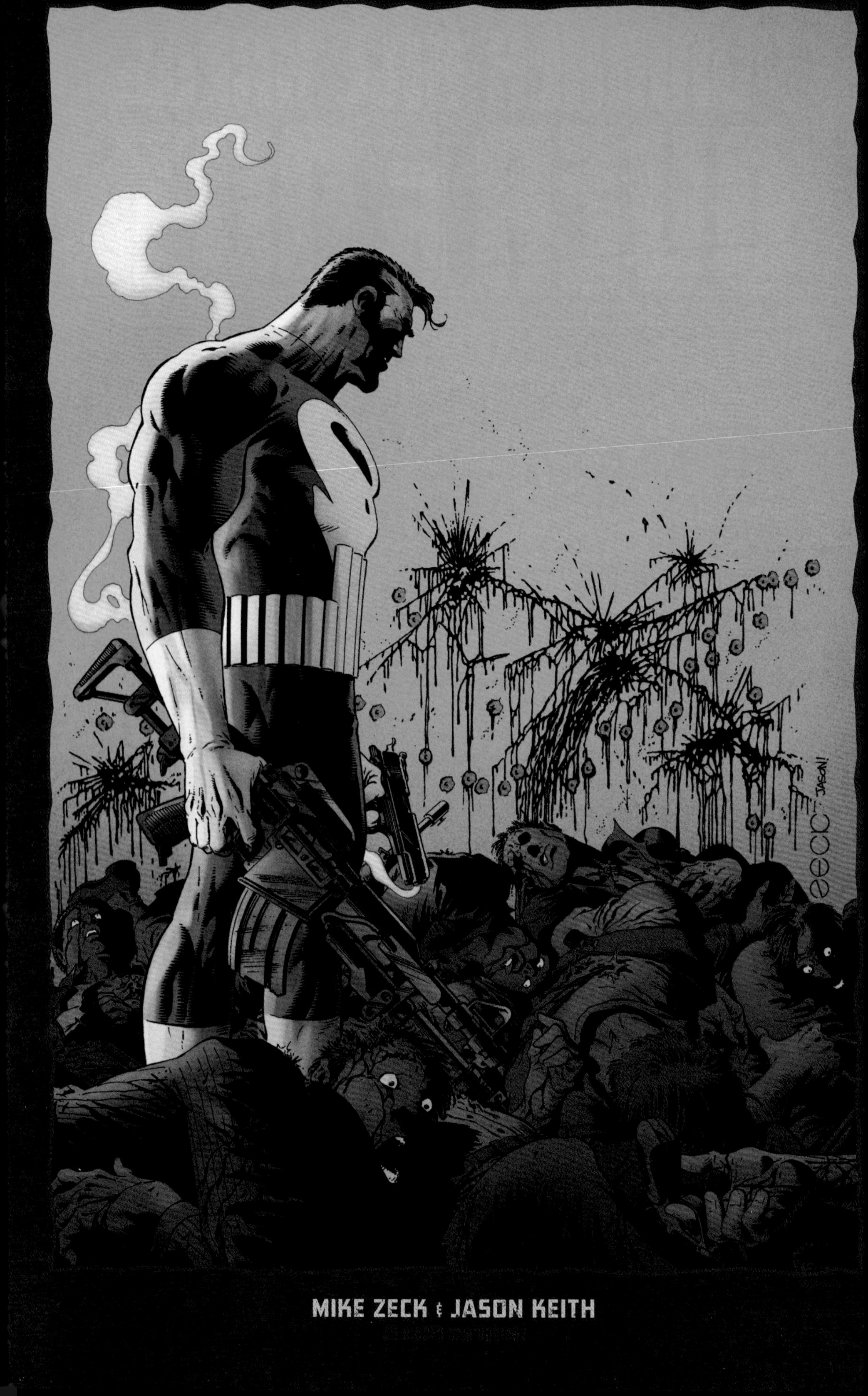

MIKE ZECK & JASON KEITH

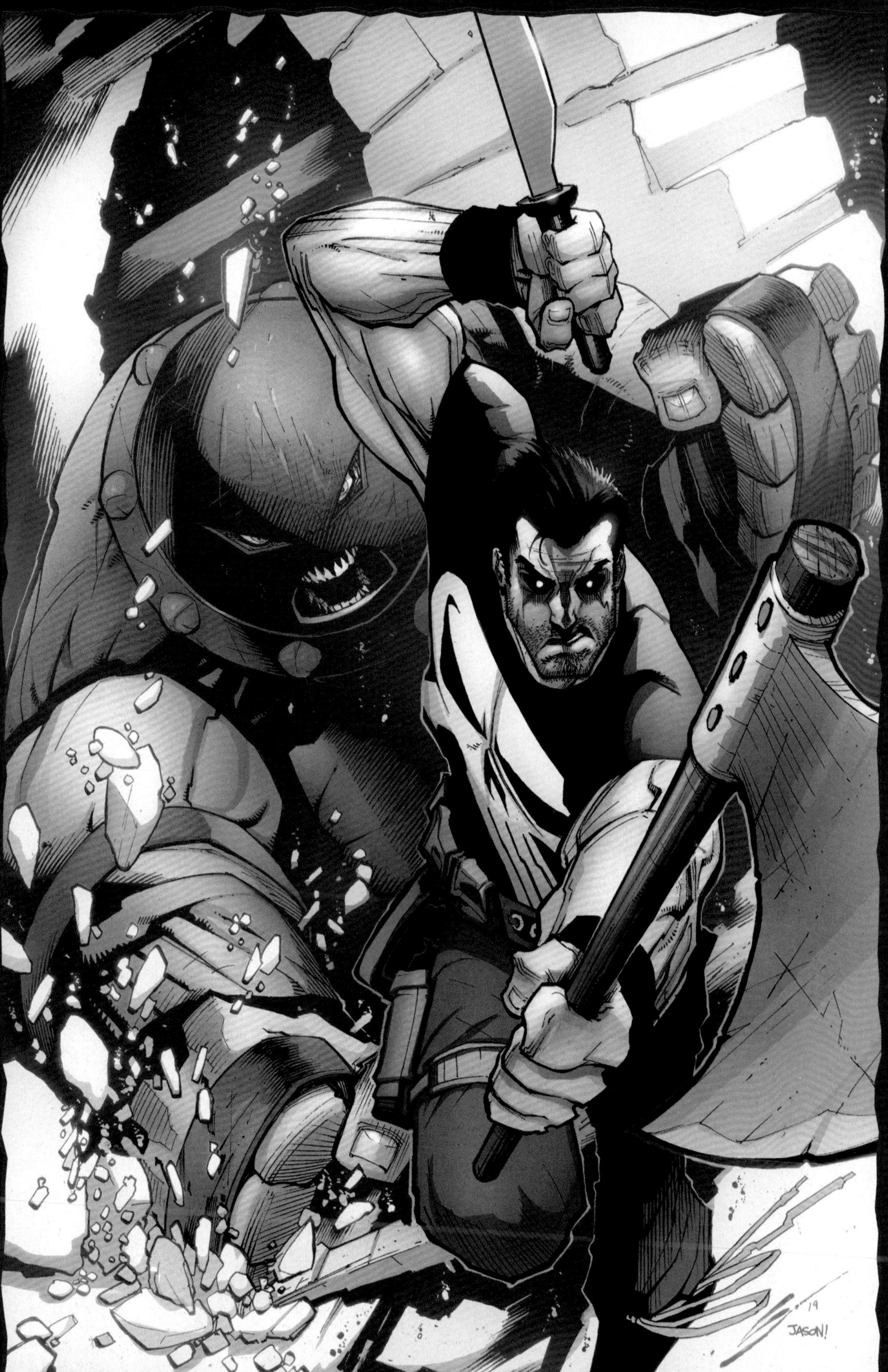
'19
JASON!

GERARDO SANDOVAL & JASON KEITH

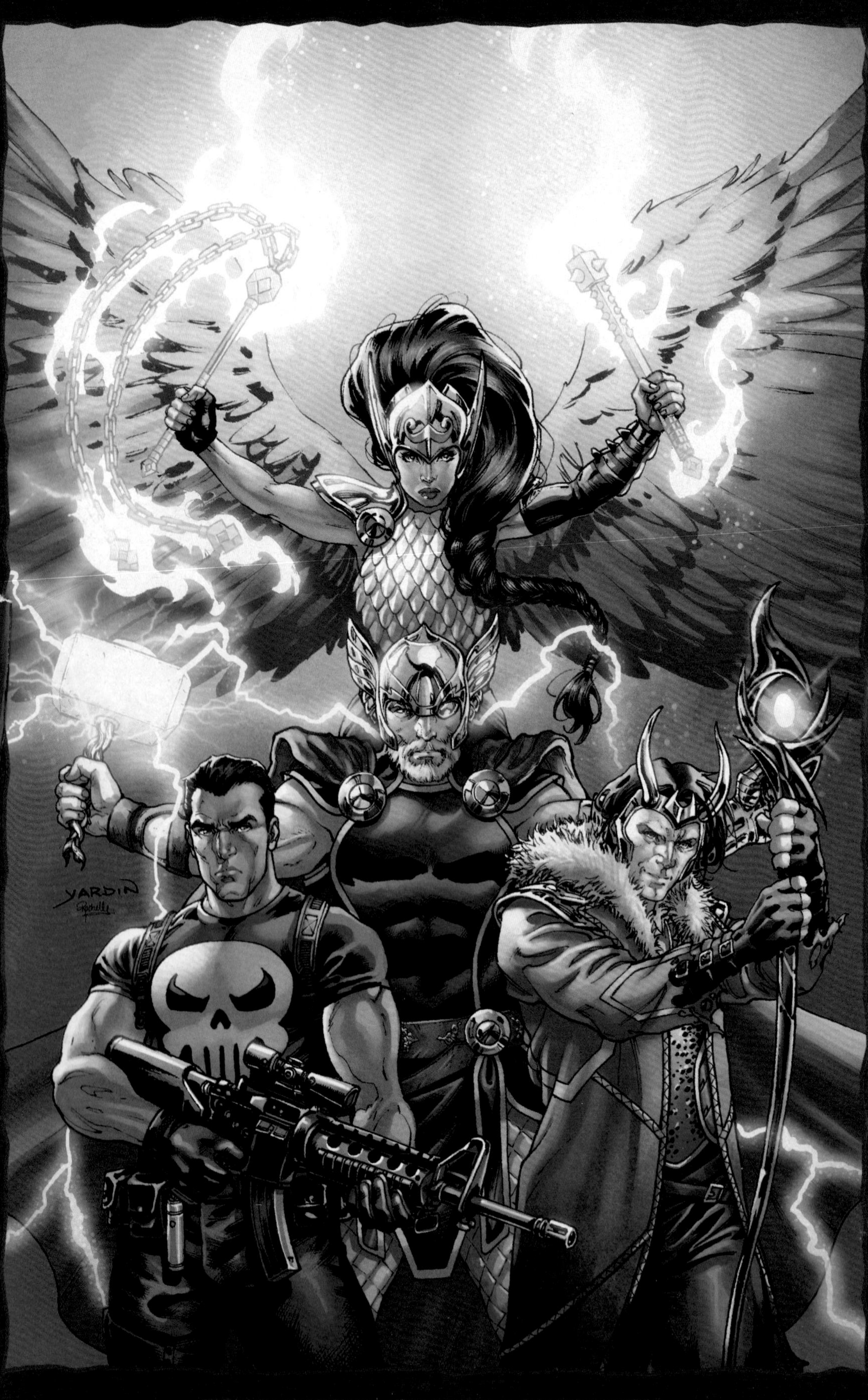
YARDIN

DAVID YARDIN & RACHELLE ROSENBERG